To my wife, Alice, the best friend I could have ever hoped to have

To our children, Teyjas and Shanthi, who remind me each day of how good it feels to love

To my mother, father, and Rashmi, who gave me everything and to whom I owe everything

Vivek H. Murthy, MD

Together

Loneliness, Health and What Happens
When We Find Connection

P
PROFILE BOOKS

wellcome
collection

This paperback edition first published in 2021

First published in Great Britain in 2020 by
Profile Books Ltd
29 Cloth Fair
London
EC1A 7JQ

www.profilebooks.com

Published in association with Wellcome Collection

**wellcome
collection**

183 Euston Road, London NW1 2BE

Wellcome Collection publishes extraordinary books that explore health, science, life, art and what it means to be human.

First published in the United States of America in 2020 by
HarperCollins Publishers

10 9 8 7 6 5 4 3 2

Printed and bound in Great Britain by CPI Group (UK) Ltd, Croydon, CR0 4YY

A CIP catalogue record for this book is available from the British Library.

ISBN 978 1 78816 278 4
eISBN 978 1 78283 563 9
Audio ISBN 978 1 78283 563 9

Contents

Foreword

This is a book about the importance of human connection, the hidden impact of loneliness on our health, and the social power of community. As a physician, I've long felt compelled to address these issues because of the physical and emotional toll of social disconnection that I've watched rising throughout society over the past few decades.

What I could not anticipate, however, was the unprecedented test that our global community would face just as the first edition of this work was going to press.

In early 2020, the Covid-19 pandemic turned physical human contact into a potentially mortal threat. The novel coronavirus arrived like an invisible stalker, and any of our fellow human beings could be its host. Almost overnight, it seemed, getting close enough to breathe on another person became synonymous with danger. The public health imperative was clear: to save lives, we'd need to radically increase the space between us. We'd have to "socially distance."

Social distancing demanded that parents like me and my wife Alice cancel our children's play dates and keep them home from school. It meant that nursing homes banned visits to the elderly, who were most at risk of severe illness from this virus. And engaged couples either had to postpone their long-planned wedding celebrations or figure out ways to include friends and family online. Most of the opportunities for socializing that we once took for granted—live theater, concerts, ball games, bars and pubs, movies and dining out with friends, office gatherings, and congregational worship—were put on hold indefinitely.

As I write this new foreword, more than ten months after the first Covid-19 cases were diagnosed, the coronavirus remains on the loose. The world is cycling through various stages of reopenings and lockdowns. In some countries, people are emerging, seeing friends and resuming normal life, while others are shutting down again. Wherever we live, however, one thing we've learned through this global event is just how much we miss being together when we're forced apart.

In the beginning, it seemed that this crisis must inevitably lead to emotional, as well as physical, isolation. If we could not meet, how could we connect? If we could not share the same space, how could we help each other? If we could not touch, how could we love? Even that term, social distancing, seemed to condemn us to loneliness.

And then there was the issue of trust. Fear of infection and panic over the potential economic fallout drove some to defy the official mandates, hoard emergency supplies, and regard one another with suspicion. Alongside the looming specter of a global financial recession rose an equally disturbing prospect of social recession—a fraying of communal bonds that would deepen in severity the longer we went without human interaction.

As the pandemic has continued, however, it's become ever clearer that we humans are more socially resilient than we could have imagined. We've also discovered that social distancing is a misnomer. To be sure, we must practice physical distancing to stop the spread of Covid-19, but each day has brought new examples of our collective ingenuity as we meet this crisis together.

In Italy, one of the first countries to be hit hard by the virus, neighbors isolated in their homes found shared comfort by singing from their windows in unison. In China, patients in quarantine units turned to square dancing to lift their spirits as they recuperated. Many of us have found creative workarounds, such as forming exclusive "pods" with extended family or close friends who have all tested negative for the virus. We may try to compensate for the loss of physical visits by calling or emailing loved ones more often. And all over the world, families, friends, and strangers have been performing acts of generosity—bringing groceries to the ill and elderly, calling to check on vulnerable neighbors, and sharing local updates on everything from grocery store hours to the best sources of protective face masks.

We are fortunate today that technology offers many of us ready opportunities to strengthen our connections remotely. The pandemic is inspiring creativity online as artists dance and sing together through videos from home. Families celebrate birthdays through FaceTime. Audiences enjoy live opera performances streamed over the internet, and students, from kindergartners to doctoral candidates, meet in classes online. As we learn to play, work, and collaborate virtually, we are helping each other fend off loneliness and reminding each other just how vital we are for our mutual well-being.

This new lifestyle is not without complications. Videoconferencing fatigue is rampant, which contributes to our general pandemic fatigue. Online learning can be difficult for children, parents, and teachers (as Alice and I have discovered with our kids). And as much as we are grateful to be able to connect via technology, we still miss seeing one another in real life. We humans are wired for direct contact with each other. We need to touch, smell, and be fully present in each other's company. Online connections are not and will never be a satisfactory replacement for the real thing. Yet the net result of all of these losses and workarounds is that many of us feel closer and more grateful for our friends and families than ever before. We yearn to get back together.

Our collective experience during the pandemic has only confirmed the many lessons I learned while writing this book. Four strategies in particular stand out as I reflect on life before, during, and (soon, I hope) after Covid-19. These core practices will not only help us weather the current crisis, but they will also strengthen our human connections for the rest of our lives.

1. *Spend time each day with those you love*—and not just the people in your immediate household. Devote at least fifteen minutes each day to connecting with those you most care about via phone or, better yet, videoconference, so you can hear their voices and see their faces.

2. *Focus on each other without distraction.* When you concentrate your attention, time seems to stretch, becoming more meaningful and delivering extra value. So stop multitasking, and give the other person the gift of your full presence. Make eye contact, if possible, and genuinely listen, concentrating on what they are truly saying, thinking, and feeling.

3. *Embrace solitude.* The first step toward building stronger connections with others is to build a stronger connection with oneself. Solitude helps us do that by allowing us to check in with our own feelings and thoughts, to explore our creativity, to connect with nature, and to recenter ourselves. Meditation, prayer, art, music, and time spent outdoors can all be sources of solitary comfort and joy.

4. *Help and be helped.* Service is a profound source of connection that reminds us of our value and purpose in life. Giving and receiving *both* strengthen our social bonds, so checking on a neighbor, seeking advice, even just offering a friendly wave to a stranger six feet away, all can make us stronger.

I once had a physician mentor who would pause and take a deep breath before he entered a patient's room, using those few seconds to remind himself how grateful he was for the chance to help someone heal. Today we all share this opportunity. Helping relationships are as essential as vaccines and ventilators for our collective recovery.

As painful as the pandemic has been, it's offered us a rare opportunity to step back and reassess our lives. Many of us have gained a new appreciation for the joy, support, and sustenance we derive from our relationships. The question now is whether we will build on that clarity and learn from this shared experience how to construct a truly people-centered world.

The choice is between social recession and social revival. If we slide back into our old ways of interacting, the physical separation this pandemic has imposed on us will deepen the loneliness that existed before Covid-19. But if we use this moment to recommit to our relationships, to prioritize them and put people first, then we can build a life that is more deeply connected, stronger and more vibrant and joyful than before this crisis began. And if we learn from this moment to be better together, we won't just endure. We will thrive.

November 2020

Preface

On December 15, 2014, I began my tenure as the Nineteenth Surgeon General of the United States. I expected that my focus as the "nation's doctor" would encompass issues like obesity, tobacco-related disease, mental health, and vaccine-preventable illness. That's what I'd told the US Senate at my confirmation hearings some ten months earlier, and there was plenty of data to support these as important focus areas. But the surgeon general's position, which oversees more than six thousand uniformed Commissioned Corps officers working throughout the federal government to protect, promote, and advance the health of the nation, comes with high expectations. For more than a century, the physicians holding this office have addressed national health crises ranging from yellow fever and influenza outbreaks to the aftermath of hurricanes and tornados to the terrorist attacks on 9/11. Over the past few decades, the nation's doctor also has become America's most trusted voice on public health issues such as smoking and HIV/AIDS. It mattered to me that the issues I selected as focus areas also mattered most to the people I served.

I hadn't grown up in the public eye or as a creature of politics. I was a child of medicine. Much of my youth was spent in my father and mother's medical office, where my father practiced medicine and my mother managed everything else. My sister and I spent many afternoons after school helping out with paperwork, filing charts, cleaning the office, and greeting patients as they came and went. It was there that I found my inspiration to go into medicine. I saw the way people arrived looking anxious and left more peaceful and reassured, with my parents as partners in their healing. Medicine for my parents was all about relationship, and they built those connections by listening. Insurance companies would protest their spending more than the approved fifteen minutes with their patients, but my parents understood that to truly listen, you have to meet people where they are, emotionally and physically, however long that takes.

That was the kind of medicine I strived to practice. That was the kind of leader I wanted to be. And so, as I began my tenure, I decided to listen before setting my agenda and laying out my plans. That meant taking time. And it meant showing up where Americans lived. "Let's go talk to people and see what they need," I told my new team.

We spent the next few months on a listening tour of America. We were welcomed into communities from Alabama to North Carolina, from California to Indiana. We sat down in small group meetings and large town halls, spending time with parents, teachers, pastors, small business owners, philanthropists, and community leaders.

Everywhere we went, we asked a simple question: *How can we help?* The answers in some cases confirmed what I suspected were major pain points: the opioid epidemic and rising rates of obesity, diabetes, and heart disease, to name a few. Other responses took me by surprise. Teachers in Washington State, for example, told me that children were vaping *during* class. Kids weren't allowed to chew gum or smoke in class, yet there were no rules prohibiting the use of e-cigarettes in school. It turned out, the schools were waiting for guidance from the local government, which in turn was waiting for the federal government.

These conversations played a central role in guiding the agenda I pursued during my time in office and beyond. They moved me to produce the first surgeon general's report on the addiction crisis and to launch a national campaign to address the opioid epidemic. And it was those teachers, along with parents, scientists, and policymakers, who inspired me to issue in 2016 the first federal report on e-cigarette use by youth.

But one recurring topic was different. It wasn't a frontline complaint. It wasn't even identified directly as a health ailment. Loneliness ran like a dark thread through many of the more obvious issues that people brought to my attention, like addiction, violence, anxiety, and depression. The teachers and school administrators and many parents I encountered, for example, voiced a growing concern that our children were becoming isolated—even, or perhaps especially, those who spent much of their time in front of their digital devices and on social media. Loneliness also was magnifying the pain for families whose loved ones were struggling with addiction to opioids.

One of the first times I recognized this connection was a chilly morning in Oklahoma City when I met a couple named Sam and Sheila, who had tragically lost their son Jason to an opioid overdose. We met at their local treatment facility more than a year after Jason's death. The pain that both carried was visible in their exhausted faces. Once they started talking about their son, it didn't take long for their eyes to well up. Their wounds were still raw. Losing Jason had been unimaginably painful. But what made it even worse was that, at their hour of greatest need, they found themselves without the people they'd counted on for years.

"When bad things happened to our family before," Sheila said, "our neighbors would show up to help or express their support. But when our son died, no one came by. They thought we might be embarrassed that he died of a disease they believed was shameful. We felt so alone."

Sam and Sheila were far from alone in their loneliness. In Phoenix, Anchorage, Baltimore, and many other cities, I listened to men and women who told me that the hardest part of addiction to alcohol and drugs was the profound loneliness they experienced when they felt like their family and friends had given up on them. This loneliness, in turn, made it harder for them to stay on the path of treatment and recovery. It's not easy handling a substance use disorder, they would tell me. "Everyone needs some support."

The people of Flint, Michigan, felt much the same way, though for different reasons. I went to Flint at the height of their water crisis and visited the home of a couple whose daughters had toxic levels of lead in their bodies from the city's contaminated water. It was bad enough that they felt they'd failed to protect their daughters, but as the weeks went by with no agreement on how to fix the city's water supply, they also felt forgotten by their government and their country. This was loneliness as abandonment; the feeling of being left behind, cast out, ignored by society.

In some cases, loneliness was driving health problems. In others, it was a consequence of the illness and hardships that people were experiencing. It wasn't always easy to tease out cause and effect, but clearly there was something about our disconnection from one another that was making people's lives worse than they had to be.

As much as I learned about how prevalent loneliness is, I also learned a great deal about the healing power of human connection. In Oklahoma, for example, I met a group of Native American teenagers who felt lost in their identity and forgotten by the outside world, so they developed the "I Am Indian" program to strengthen a sense of culture and belonging among their peers and reduce their risk of alcohol and drug addiction. I saw the power of connection in a support network formed by parents in New York whose children struggled with addiction. Having a community of fellow parents who truly understood what they were going through made it easier to cope when a child relapsed or when they blamed themselves for what was happening. In Birmingham, Alabama, where obesity and chronic disease were on the rise, I met a community of people who gathered to run, walk, and swim together. Even those who felt too ashamed and discouraged to exercise alone came out because their friends were participating. In Flint, too, human connection became part of the solution when community members organized to go door-to-door to educate neighbors about how to properly install filters and avoid the lead in their city's drinking water.

In these instances and so many others, I could see the vital role that social connections can play when individuals, families, and communities face difficult problems. While loneliness engenders despair and ever more isolation, togetherness raises optimism and creativity. When people feel they belong to one another, their lives are stronger, richer, and more joyful.

And yet, the values that dominate modern culture instead elevate the narrative of the rugged individualist and the pursuit of self-determination. They tell us that we alone shape our destiny. Could these values be contributing to the undertow of loneliness I was witnessing? In Baltimore, a couple expressed joy at having young children, but they also confided that so much of their time was devoted to child care that they felt cut off from their friends. In Los Angeles, a successful hospital executive reluctantly told me he had just spent his birthday alone at home because his intense work schedule had caused him to lose touch with his friends. People didn't easily volunteer these stories. Many were embarrassed to admit how alone they felt. This shame was particularly acute in professional cultures, like law and medicine, that promote self-reliance as a virtue.

Deeply committed doctors, nurses, and medical students I met in Boston, Nashville, and Miami said they felt emotionally isolated in their work, but they didn't tell anyone for fear of repercussions from colleagues and patients. Some even worried the medical licensing boards might question their fitness to practice medicine if they even remotely admitted having mental health concerns. Nevertheless, they knew that their loneliness was contributing to their burnout and emotional exhaustion. They just weren't sure what to do about it.

Others didn't even realize that loneliness was what they were feeling. But once one person in the room broke the ice by naming loneliness, I'd see hands go up with more stories to share. Men, women, children. Highly trained professionals. Tradespeople. Minimum-wage earners. No group, no matter how educated, wealthy, or accomplished, seemed to be exempt.

Many people described what they were feeling as a lack of belonging. They'd tried to do things about it. Many had joined social organizations and moved to new neighborhoods. They worked in open-office settings and went to happy hours. But the sense of being "at home" remained elusive. They missed the foundation of home that is genuine connection with other people.

To be at home is to be known. It is to be loved for who you are. It is to share a sense of common ground, common interests, pursuits, and values with others who truly care about you. In community after community, I met lonely people who felt homeless even though they had a roof over their heads.

Sitting in my hotel room late at night at the end of a packed day of town halls and community meetings, I would reflect on these stories with a mix of curiosity and concern. I was no stranger to loneliness myself. During my early years in grade school, when my parents dropped me off in front of my school each morning, I'd have this sinking feeling in the pit of my stomach. It was like first-day jitters, except that it repeated every day of the school year. I wasn't scared about exams or homework. I was worried about feeling alone. And I was too ashamed to tell my parents that I was lonely. Making that admission would have amounted to much more than saying I didn't have friends. It would feel like admitting I wasn't likable or worthy of being loved. The shame that accompanied loneliness intensified that familiar pain for years until I eventually found a group of friends in high school with whom I felt I truly belonged.

In spite of my personal bouts of loneliness, however, I'd never considered this issue as a potential public health priority. It certainly wasn't on the agenda I'd shared with the US Senate during my confirmation hearings less than a year earlier. But suddenly it loomed very large indeed.

The question was how to address it. Many of the people I was meeting assumed I had billions of dollars in discretionary spending and a staff of tens of thousands. I often had to tell them this was off by a few orders of magnitude. Despite this, my new position gave me a bully pulpit from which to raise public awareness about loneliness, to convene conversations with key stakeholders, and to make the case for shifts in everything from research and policy to infrastructure and individual lifestyles.

The more I studied the seesaw relationship between loneliness and togetherness, the more convinced I became of the great power of human connection. So many of the problems we face as a society—from addiction and violence to disengagement among workers and students to political polarization—are worsened by loneliness and disconnection. Building a more connected world holds the key to solving these and many more of the personal and societal problems confronting us today.

Social connection matters to an office worker who wishes to be seen and appreciated, or a CEO who wants to connect with employees. It matters to parents of young children who need more support from friends but wonder how to ask. Or to citizens who see a way to make their community better but wonder who'd care if they spoke up. And yes, social connectedness matters to a doctor who wants to help patients get better but doesn't know how to heal their loneliness—or the doctor's own.

To my surprise, the topic of emotional well-being, in general, and loneliness in particular, received the strongest response from the public of any issues I worked on as surgeon general. There were few issues that elicited as much enthusiastic interest from both very conservative and very liberal members of Congress, from young and old people, or from urban and rural residents alike. After my presentations to city mayors, medical societies, and business leaders from around the world, it was what everyone seemed to want to talk about. I think this is because so many people have known loneliness themselves or have seen it in the people around them. It's a universal condition that affects all of us directly or through the people we love.

The irony is that the antidote to loneliness, human connection, is also a universal condition. In fact, we are hardwired for connection—as we demonstrate every time we come together around a common purpose or crisis. Such was the collective action of the Parkland high school students in South Florida after the 2018 mass shooting at their school claimed seventeen lives. We also see this instinct in the outpouring of aid and assistance by volunteers that follows major hurricanes, tornados, and earthquakes around the globe.

One of the most dramatic demonstrations of community in the wake of tragedy occurred on September 11, 2001. When the twin towers of the World Trade Center fell that terrible morning in New York City, thousands of people in lower Manhattan fled south in search of escape from the growing inferno behind them. When they reached the Hudson River and realized they had no way to cross, panic mounted. Recognizing they had no way to rescue so many people in time, the US Coast Guard made an unprecedented decision. It issued a radio call asking civilian boats to help.

The response was swift. Scores of boats pierced the dense cloud of dust and debris and ferried their frightened, soot-covered passengers to safety. In nine hours, the 9/11 Boat Lift rescued nearly half a million people, becoming the largest boat rescue in the world's history—even larger than the Dunkirk evacuation of WWII.

Vincent Ardolino, the captain of the *Amberjack*, said his wife thought he was crazy for wanting to take his boat toward

Manhattan that morning after the call. But he knew that he had to go. "Never go through life saying you should have," he said later, reflecting on the decision.[1]

Our community instincts remain alive and well. When we share a common purpose, when we feel a common urgency, when we hear a call for help that we are able to answer, most of us will step up and come together.

My own desire to heed this call continued beyond my tenure as surgeon general. So did the persistent questions around loneliness that arose from the people and experts I'd met. What exactly has led to the fraying of relationships in communities and such high levels of loneliness? What other aspects of health and society are affected? How can we overcome the stigma of loneliness and accept that all of us are vulnerable? How can we create stronger, more enduring and compassionate connections in our own lives and communities, and a more unifying sense of common ground in our larger society? How do we shift the balance of our lives from being driven by fear to being fueled by love?

These are just a few of the questions that launched my journey to write this book. Many more unfolded as I absorbed the research that's shaping our understanding of the critical roles that both loneliness and connection play in every one of our lives. Beyond the facts and data are the people you will meet throughout the pages of this book—scientists, philosophers, doctors, cultural innovators, community activists, and people from all walks of life—whose stories continually remind us that, truly, we're better together.

The first section of the book is focused on the underpinnings of loneliness and social connection—the reasons why loneliness evolved in our highly social species and the ways in which different aspects of culture may help or hinder our efforts to bond with others and establish a sense of communal belonging. The second section addresses the process of connection that each of us individually must navigate in our own lives, beginning with our relationship with ourselves and moving outward through family and friends to ultimately build a more connected world for coming generations. My hope is that the stories you are about to read will deepen your awareness of your own place in our social universe and also inspire and encourage you to reach out to those around you with a renewed sense of the vital role we all play in one another's lives. As you'll see, when we strengthen our connection with one another, we are healthier, more resilient, more productive, more vibrantly creative, and more fulfilled.

In the writing of this book, I've come to realize that social connection stands out as a largely unrecognized and under-appreciated force for addressing many of the critical problems we're dealing with, both as individuals and as a society. Overcoming loneliness and building a more connected future is an urgent mission that we can and must tackle together.

Making Sense of Loneliness

CHAPTER 1

Under Our Noses

The whole conviction of my life now rests upon the belief that loneliness, far from being a rare and curious phenomenon, peculiar to myself and to a few other solitary men, is the central and inevitable fact of human existence.

—Thomas Wolfe, *God's Lonely Man*

My first day as a doctor began one bright June morning when I walked through the doors of Boston's Brigham and Women's Hospital. I was wearing a pressed white coat and my best shirt and tie. I smiled at the security guards and passing staff. For them, this was just another day at a busy urban hospital, but for me, it was a day I'd remember for the rest of my life.

My head was stuffed full of medical facts and trivia that I'd gathered from medical school. My pockets were overflowing with tools, including a stethoscope, ophthalmoscope, tuning fork, reflex hammer, *Pocket Medicine* handbook, three black ball-point pens, blank index cards for recording patient details, a list of phone numbers for key hospital services, and laminated cards filled with algorithms for everything from cardiac resuscitation to the treatment of diabetic ketoacidosis. Yet none of those cards and manuals mentioned the most common ailment I was about to encounter among my patients.

In the days ahead, as I went on bedside rounds with my team of medical residents and senior physicians, I focused my attention on getting the right diagnosis and prescribing the right medications, treatments, and tests. It was overwhelming at times, but as the months wore on, I got more and more comfortable managing common illnesses like diabetes and cancer and unusual ones that I had only read about in textbooks. As I slowly ascended the steep learning curve of medical training, I began to notice other aspects of the people I was caring for, including their social lives—or lack thereof.

Some patients always had a visitor in their room to keep them company in the unfamiliar hospital setting. If they took a turn for the worse or were nearing the end of life, they had an entourage of family and friends who traveled from near and far to be with them and to explain to the doctors and hospital staff how much their loved one meant to them. But other patients went days and even weeks with no visits, no phone calls, no one from the outside world asking how they were doing. Some of them died alone with nobody but me and my hospital colleagues to witness their last moments.

It wasn't just the physical presence or absence of friends and family that I noticed. It was the hunger for companionship that was evident in so many of the men and women who came through our hospital doors. While most patients were eager to get out of the hospital and resume their lives, a sizable minority turned to the medical staff for a long-missed friendly ear. They shared lengthy stories of their lives with anyone willing to bear witness to their existence. I often found myself torn between wanting to be there for those patients and knowing that I had many other patients who were waiting for me.

My focus as a physician was medical. The social issues, as wrenching as they were, seemed outside the domain of doctoring.

It would take a patient named James to teach me just how wrong I was about this.

I only met James once, on the afternoon he walked into our clinic for help with his diabetes and high blood pressure, but this middle-aged gentleman taught me a profound and indelible lesson about loneliness and connection that day.

James was stocky, with brown hair and red, rugged skin that bore the signature of many New England winters. His face was set in a grim look of frustration, which I assumed was related to the health problems I saw noted in his chart.

"It's good to meet you," I said. "Tell me how I can help."

James described the challenges of dealing with diabetes, high blood pressure, his weight, and the accompanying stress he often felt. He looked tired as he spoke. His gestures were listless. He seemed defeated by life.

Then, out of the blue, he delivered what seemed to me at the time a complete non sequitur. "Winning the lottery was one of the worst things that ever happened to me," he said.

"Really?" I'm sure my bewilderment showed in my voice. "Why?"

Given this invitation, James poured out his whole story. It turned out he was being quite literal: he actually had won the lottery. Prior to that, he told me, he'd been a baker. He was good at his craft, and his customers appreciated his talent. He enjoyed his work and was gratified that the food he prepared gave people happiness and pleasure. Although he was single, he had a community of people he liked. They worked alongside him at the bakery, so he never felt alone. When he won the lottery, all that changed.

Suddenly, he was "rich," so he thought he should upgrade his life. Taking his cue from the messages he'd absorbed from television and movies and advertising and other cultural media, he decided to enter the world of luxury and leisure. He assumed this would make him happier than slaving away in the kitchen. It was as if his new status compelled him to become a different person.

James quit his job and moved to an upscale neighborhood in an oceanside community. There, with all his needs met and a constant stream of money coming in, he was living the proverbial dream. Yet despite his new trappings, this dream felt like a nightmare. Instead of being fulfilled, he was sick and miserable. Previously good-natured, humorous, and outgoing, James grew increasingly withdrawn, isolated, and angry. He put on weight and eventually was diagnosed with the diabetes and high blood pressure that brought him in to see me. Instead of spending time with his bakery colleagues and regular customers, he now visited doctors and otherwise sat alone at home.

Too late, James realized that it had been a terrible mistake to do what he thought a lottery winner ought to do, instead of heeding his own heart. "I traded in my friends and a job I loved and moved to a neighborhood where people keep to themselves in their giant houses. It's lonely."

James's experience was an example of how what we seem to value most in modern society—status, wealth, achievement, and fame—doesn't guarantee happiness. With more money, we can purchase more privacy, we can live on secluded estates, we can even travel exclusively on our own boat or plane. While all of these privileges have their appeal, there can be a hidden human cost. If we're not vigilant, such success can lead to a life that feels increasingly lonely as the distance between the individual and other people grows.

If James could find a way to break out of his gilded cage and strengthen his human connections, I suspected his health would improve dramatically. He'd likely become more active, engaged, happier, and more *himself*. After all, he'd had community and connection before he won the lottery. But that would mean bucking the prevailing assumptions about success and redefining his own ambitions in social, rather than financial terms. He seemed to understand this, but the process of change was daunting, especially now that his health was in jeopardy. How could I, as his doctor, help him?

In our one session together, I did my best to serve James. I listened carefully and asked questions. I recommended adjustments to the doses of his diabetes and blood pressure medication to bring his readings into a healthier range. And I offered to refer him to our hospital social worker, who might be able to help him make some community connections. Beyond that, though, I honestly had no idea how to address the loneliness that seemed to be driving his medical problems. It saddens me even now to think about it, but as a fledgling doctor, I learned far more from James on this subject than I was able to offer him.

My medical education did not prepare me to recognize the impact of social connection on health, and it certainly didn't give me tools to help my patients who were struggling with loneliness. Instead, my training had been focused almost entirely on the physical body. When we did discuss emotions, it was primarily in the context of managing a psychiatric illness like depression or building a trusting doctor-patient relationship so that patients would feel comfortable to participate in the healing process.

This was simply not enough when meeting patients like the young woman I took care of who had a bacterial infection on her heart valve related to her intravenous drug use. I could counsel her on the dangers of future intravenous drug use and the precautions she needed to take going forward. I knew how to discuss the complexities of treatment pathways, antibiotic courses, and the timing of follow-up imaging studies. I could empathize with the stress and emotional toll of being seriously ill, and I could listen to her and her family as they shared their worries. All of this was very important, but it failed to address the critical need for healthier connections in her life. Her relationships or lack thereof were an important factor in both causing addiction in the first place and determining whether or not she would return to drugs again. I was never trained to assess or address loneliness, and now when confronted with it, I didn't know where to start.

One Isn't Always the Loneliest Number

What is loneliness, anyway? This seemingly simple question becomes unexpectedly complex upon closer examination.

Many people think of loneliness as *isolation*, but the difference between these two terms is substantial. Loneliness is the subjective feeling that you're lacking the social connections you need. It can feel like being stranded, abandoned, or cut off from the people with whom you belong—even if you're surrounded by other people. What's missing when you're lonely is the feeling of closeness, trust, and the affection of genuine friends, loved ones, and community.

Researchers[1][2][3] have identified three "dimensions" of loneliness to reflect the particular type of relationships that are missing. *Intimate*, or emotional, loneliness is the longing for a close confidante or intimate partner—someone with whom you share a deep mutual bond of affection and trust. *Relational*, or social, loneliness is the yearning for quality friendships and social companionship and support. *Collective* loneliness is the hunger for a network or community of people who share your sense of purpose and interests. These three dimensions together reflect the full range of high-quality social connections that humans need in order to thrive. The lack of relationships in any of these dimensions can make us lonely, which helps to explain why we may have a supportive marriage yet still feel lonely for friends and community.

Because everyone's level of need for social connection is different, it's impossible to say how many friends are required to prevent loneliness. The level varies not only throughout life, but also by personality. People who are more extroverted tend to crave human contact and social activity, feeling energized by networking with strangers. Those who are more introverted need more time by themselves and feel drained by too much interaction, preferring to socialize in smaller groups or one on one. Both introverts and extroverts can experience loneliness, however, and both need strong relationships in order to feel a secure sense of belonging. What often matters is not the quantity or frequency of social contact but the quality of our connections and how we feel about them.

Unlike the feeling of loneliness, which is subjective, isolation describes the objective physical state of being alone and out of touch with other people. Isolation is considered a risk factor for loneliness simply because you're more likely to feel lonely if you rarely interact with others. But physically being alone doesn't necessarily translate into the emotional experience of loneliness. Many of us spend long stretches by ourselves when we're so involved in our work or creative pursuits that we don't feel at all lonely. On the other hand, we can feel lonely and *emotionally* alone even when we're surrounded by other people. What defines loneliness is our internal comfort level.

This is what makes loneliness distinct from *solitude*. When we feel lonely, we're unhappy and long to escape this emotional pain. Solitude, by contrast, is a state of peaceful aloneness or voluntary isolation. It is an opportunity for self-reflection and a chance to connect with ourselves without distraction or disturbance. It enhances our personal growth, creativity, and emotional well-being, allowing us to reflect, restore, and replenish. For millennia, monks and ascetics from various spiritual traditions have sought out solitude as an opportunity for introspection and to renew their connection with the divine. Unlike loneliness, solitude is not burdened with shame. Rather, it can be a sacred state.

Solitude also can feel a bit daunting, even scary, since it allows both positive and negative thoughts and emotions to surface. The space where we confront our demons is not always a space we enter willingly. But it's in the grappling that we work through issues, gain clarity about our feelings, and build comfort with ourselves. Developing comfort with solitude, then, is an essential part of strengthening our connection to ourselves and by extension enabling our connection with others. Solitude, paradoxically, protects against loneliness.

The Loneliness Question

According to a 2018 report by the Henry J. Kaiser Family Foundation, 22 percent of all adults in the US say they often or always feel lonely or socially isolated.[4] That's well over fifty-five million people—far more than the number of adult cigarette smokers and nearly double the number of people who have diabetes. A 2018 AARP study using the rigorously validated UCLA loneliness scale found that one in three American adults over the age of forty-five are lonely.[5] And in a 2018 national survey by the US health insurer Cigna, one-fifth of respondents said they rarely or never feel close to people.[6]

Studies in other countries echo these findings. Among middle-aged and elderly Canadians, nearly one-fifth of men and around a quarter of women said they feel lonely once a week or more.[7] One-quarter of Australian adults reported being lonely as well.[8] More than two hundred thousand seniors in the United Kingdom "meet up with or speak on the phone with their children, family and friends less often than once a week";[9] 13 percent of Italian adults report having no one to ask for help;[10] and in Japan, over 1 million adults meet the official government definition of social recluses, or *hikikomori*.[11] [12]

What prevents all these people from simply joining a club, making new friends, or reconnecting with family and old friends? In a word, loneliness itself.

When we already feel lonely and then see others having fun together, enjoying the company of those around them, there's a natural tendency to withdraw instead of approaching the group. We fear being labeled and judged as social outcasts. (To understand this worry, just spend some time in a grade school cafeteria or playground.) So we hide our true feelings even from those who may try to connect with us. Shame and fear thus conspire to turn loneliness into a self-perpetuating condition, triggering self-doubt, which in turn lowers self-esteem and discourages us from reaching out for help. Over time, this vicious cycle may convince us we don't matter to anyone and that we're unworthy of love, driving us ever inward and away from the very relationships we need most.

This emotional spiral also contributes to the stigma that surrounds loneliness. Because people tend to hide and deny their loneliness, others who might help—including friends, family, and doctors—shy away from probing what seems like a sensitive emotional issue. Then the risk of self-destructive behaviors increases. Many people use drugs, alcohol, food, and sex to numb the emotional pain of loneliness. In this way, the combination of loneliness and stigma creates a cascade of consequences that affect not only our personal health and productivity, but also the health of society.

As intractable as the cycle of loneliness may seem, however, it can be interrupted. By learning to recognize and address the signals early, we can intervene to forge connections when loneliness strikes, instead of allowing it to become a constant in our daily lives. A first step is to acknowledge the vital need that all humans have for social connection.

Quite simply, human relationship is as essential to our well-being as food and water. Just as hunger and thirst are our body's ways of telling us we need to eat and drink, loneliness is the natural signal that reminds us when we need to connect with other people. There's no cause for shame in that. Yet hunger and thirst feel much more acceptable to acknowledge and talk about than loneliness. To combat this silencing effect, then, we need to more deeply appreciate the relationship between loneliness, social connection, and physical and emotional health. In so doing, we can lift the burden of shame, blame, and criticism that fuels the stigma around loneliness.

We've seen this approach work with conditions like depression. For a long time, depression has been so stigmatized that most people would suffer in silence rather than admit they felt depressed. Now, professional athletes like twenty-three-time Olympic gold medalist Michael Phelps[13] and cultural figures like

Lady Gaga,[14] Dwayne "The Rock" Johnson,[15] and J. K. Rowling[16] have opened up about their depression. Schools and workplaces have begun to recognize how widespread the problem is, and many now are setting up programs to get people help. We are seeing a similar evolution in how we think about addiction. While there still is much work to be done to ensure that people with depression and substance use disorders do not feel shamed or discriminated against because of their illness, a great deal of progress has been made. There's every reason to believe that the stigma around loneliness also will decline if and when we're willing to speak openly about our experiences and understand loneliness for what it is: a near-universal human condition.

A Matter of Life or Death

Dr. Julianne Holt-Lunstad learned the power of social connection firsthand growing up in Saint Paul, Minnesota. The fourth of six children, she came from a clan that prided itself on hard work and sticking together. Her father's four siblings all had large families of their own, which meant there were many cousins, aunts, and uncles, and everyone spent a whole week together every year. This tradition was encouraged by her grandparents, staunch believers in the importance of family.

"Growing up, we always had family around, and my family were often my closest friends," Julianne told me. The power of these social connections was destined to inform her career path. After college in Utah, where she developed a fascination for the biological processes of mental health, Julianne pursued a PhD in health and social psychology focusing on the impact of our relationships on everything from our behavior to our cellular function.

By the time she'd joined the faculty at Brigham Young University, there was good data supporting the connection between relationships and health, but Julianne still found that many inside and outside academia were skeptical about her whole area of inquiry. They thought it was fluff. Julianne wanted to change their minds. So she and her collaborators spent more than a year painstakingly analyzing 148 studies with over three hundred thousand participants from around the world.[17]

The team pored through study details and wrote countless lines of computer code for the analytics software—all in an effort to answer one simple but profound question: Do social relationships reduce our risk of dying early?

Finally, in the summer of 2009, Julianne had her answer. As the long-awaited analysis was pulled up on her computer, she stared in disbelief. "This is going to be huge," she said to herself. And she had good reason to think so.

Julianne's study showed that people with strong social relationships are 50 percent less likely to die prematurely than people with weak social relationships. Even more striking, she found that the impact of lacking social connection on reducing life span is equal to the risk of smoking fifteen cigarettes a day, and it's *greater* than the risk associated with obesity, excess alcohol consumption, and lack of exercise. Simply put, Julianne had found that weak social connections can be a significant danger to our health.

On the surface, this might seem hard to believe. What if the real issue driving more heart disease and early deaths was obesity or poverty, and people with these conditions just happened to be lonely? In statistical terms, what if loneliness was just a confounder and not the culprit? Julianne had been concerned about this, too. So she'd designed her study to also analyze a broad range of risk factors among participants, including age, sex, initial health status, and cause of death, that would help clarify what was responsible for the health effects she was seeing. The protective effect of social connection remained consistent across these variables, as did the contribution of loneliness to premature death.

Public reaction to Julianne's study was swift. Newspaper reporters began writing articles about her curious findings. Television and radio producers invited her to their studios to speak with their audiences about this previously neglected condition that might be as dangerous as smoking. Organizations in the UK and Australia reached out for her counsel as they worked on plans to address loneliness in their countries.

Five years later, Julianne published another massive analysis of data confirming the higher risk of early death among the lonely.[18] By that point, a growing number of research papers were reporting that loneliness was associated with a greater risk of coronary heart disease, high blood pressure, stroke, dementia, depression, and anxiety. Studies were also suggesting that lonely people were more likely to have lower-quality sleep, more immune system dysfunction, more impulsive behavior, and impaired judgment.[19]

Calls from mainstream media and organizations around the world quickened, all asking the same question: Why is loneliness so dangerous to our health?

The Missing Link

By this time, many physicians were noticing loneliness among their patients. In a 2013 poll, 75 percent of general practitioner physicians in the United Kingdom reported that they saw between one and five patients each day whose visit was *primarily* driven by loneliness.[20]

One of these doctors was Dr. Helen Stokes-Lampard, a primary care physician in Lichfield, about twenty miles from Birmingham, England. Helen is as enthusiastic and excited about caring for her patients as if she were just out of medical school. When we met in her office, she greeted me warmly and set about making me tea as we spoke. There was no pretense with Helen. She's compassionate, brilliant, and down-to-earth.

But Helen is not only a practicing physician, she's also the chair of the Royal College of General Practitioners, one of the largest medical associations in the UK, representing over fifty-three thousand British family physicians. When she assumed her position as head of the Royal College, she took the surprising step of giving her inaugural speech on her patients' struggles with loneliness. More than three decades earlier, a series of studies had found an association between loneliness and the rate at which people utilized British medical services, yet the medical profession had made little effort to address loneliness. Helen, who wanted to make loneliness a high priority for the Royal College, was determined that this time would be different.

She focused her speech on a patient named Enid, who'd fallen into a deep spell of loneliness after losing her husband late in life. Helen could have simply prescribed antidepressants and moved on to the next patient. Instead, she did something increasingly difficult to do in modern medicine's highly regulated checkbox culture: she listened closely to Enid and allowed the patient's needs to guide the session.

As Helen put it in her speech:

I didn't follow the rules. I chatted to her, I listened. I did what all good GPs [general practitioners] do—I saw the world through Enid's eyes for our precious few minutes together. I prioritised what Enid wanted over [the] guidelines . . . sometimes I offered advice about a new class, group, or a charity that I thought might suit her, might benefit her health and well-being.

In the end, Enid connected with a local primary school that is linking mature women with young mums who are a long way from their own families. [It] was exactly what Enid needed. A couple of hours, twice a week where she has purpose, is needed and appreciated. Where she can use a lifetime of experiences to help others.

Enid isn't making GP appointments as regularly anymore—she is not taking up space in a hospital bed for a hip replacement she didn't really need. She's not taking antidepressants, and actually, she's not taking much medication at all . . . I noticed that Enid has started to wear makeup again. She's had her hair done properly for the first time since Brian died. Social isolation and loneliness are akin to a chronic long-term condition in terms of the impact they have on our patients' health and well-being . . . they must be addressed if we are to be patient-centred in our approach.

Talking about loneliness to the leading medical organization in the country was unconventional. "But the reaction was overwhelming," Helen told me. "Everyone in the audience could think of patients who struggled with loneliness."

What these doctors were beginning to grapple with was the link between social and emotional health that often shows up in the physical health of medical patients. If neglected, loneliness can have long-term health implications, yet it is not a state that can be fixed with a pill or a procedure. It is a human condition that reminds us of our need for the love, compassion, and companionship of fellow human beings.

Helen's approach to helping Enid followed a practice known as *social prescribing*. Clinicians recommend—or "prescribe"—resources and activities in the community that can help patients forge healthy social connections. This practice reflects a recognition that loneliness affects our health, and we have a universal need to connect with one another.

Dr. Sachin Jain, too, has come to this conclusion, and like Helen, he's been working on ways to focus on social connection at scale among his patients in the United States. Sachin is CEO of CareMore, a health care delivery system that primarily serves the elderly and poor. In 2017, Sachin and his team launched the Togetherness Program to identify and assist patients who are lonely. Within a short time, they'd enrolled six hundred patients in the program, which included home visits, weekly phone calls, and connection to existing social programs in the community. One of CareMore's participants was a woman in her late fifties named Virta.

When I first met Virta in 2019, at the CareMore Care Center in Downey, California, I could tell it had taken a lot of effort for her to come see me. Struggling with the debilitating effects of diabetes, she spent much of her day confined to a wheelchair. Neuropathy caused excruciating pain in her legs and feet. Yet Virta seemed optimistic for the future. She told me I was meeting her at a major turning point in her life.

Originally from Memphis, Virta's parents had moved the family to Long Beach, California, when she was just a baby. After high school, Virta worked many odd jobs before landing a position as a security guard at the Port of Long Beach. She enjoyed the work and kept the job for fifteen years.

Although I'd only just met her, I could tell that Virta had had a big personality in her youth and a highly social lifestyle to match it. "When I was healthy," she told me, "you couldn't catch me." But she also lived on a diet of fast food and sugary sodas, and eventually, she developed diabetes and resulting complications, which made it difficult for her to walk and left her with chronic pain. Soon, she could no longer work, and she found herself housebound. That changed everything.

"I got so lonely," she told me. "I was too sick to go out and too sick to have people over." Although she shared an apartment with her adult daughter, they rarely interacted, and when they did, they fought. Other family members didn't show any interest in talking with her, either. Unable to sustain the relationships that nourished her, Virta began to lose hope.

She vividly remembers the day she got a postcard in the mail touting the services available at CareMore's Togetherness Program. These included counseling, an exercise program, social engagement opportunities, and health care services. The center even provided transportation. "I read the letter and I started crying," she said. "I felt like it was talking to me."

Virta signed up for the services, and a few days later she got a call from one of CareMore's Togetherness Program "Phone

Pals." He said his name was Armando, and that he was calling to check on her and see how she was doing.

"He just listened to me," she said. She found Armando's voice soothing. He promised to call again the next week, and he followed through. Sometimes he'd tell her about his children's busy schedules, his daughter's soccer game the day before. Virta soon began looking forward to Armando's calls.

But without being able to work and with bills piling up, Virta couldn't pay rent. She eventually lost her home and was forced to live out of her car in the parking lot of a city park. It was a scary place at night. Her legs were causing her pain, and her health was declining.

CareMore had assigned Virta a social work intern named Ruby, who desperately wanted to help, but rents in Southern California were impossibly high for people on low incomes. Then one day Ruby spotted an in-law unit on Craigslist for $700 a month, utilities included, a steal in the rental market. "I wanted to take a shower first," Virta recalled, "but Ruby said, 'No, no, just go!'"

The homeowners, Sonya and Earnest, were waiting for Virta when she arrived. Ruby had already told them about her situation and her ill health, and the couple was eager to make it work. All they needed to find out was if Virta would hit it off with their dog, a pit bull named Protector. With huge jaws and a massive chest, the dog leapt up and licked Virta's face. "When Sonya called later to say I got the place, I cried."

Sonya and Earnest welcomed Virta like family, and their friendship helped her open up and start connecting with other people again. Armando continued to call every week, and he often asked her what she was doing to take care of herself. He encouraged her to try to get out of the house.

Sometimes Virta worried that she was taking too much of Armando's time. Afraid of letting him down, she tried to show him she could do better. "Armando would call, and I'd say, 'I got cleaned up,' or 'I put makeup on today.'" She started losing weight.

It was the human connection that made the difference. Even though theirs was a phone relationship, Virta found it easy to be open and vulnerable with Armando because he listened without judgment and seemed to genuinely care about her well-being. When Virta finally got the opportunity to meet Armando in person at the Togetherness Program's holiday party, she was surprised to learn that he was not middle-aged, as she'd pictured him, but in his early thirties. "Young man, *you're* Armando?" Virta asked, unable to contain her surprise. "You're such an old soul on the phone."

When I spoke with Virta, she was still getting weekly calls from Armando and proudly told me she'd lost thirty-nine pounds. "Without Mr. Armando calling, I wouldn't have made it."

Virta is grateful to have a place to live that's quiet and safe and close to her new friends. She still has more work to do on her health, and she still finds herself feeling very alone at times, particularly at night. But she's determined to keep working to re-build her health and start living a fuller life. And she intends to reach out to share the power of connection that's changed her life.

"There are so many lonely people out there," she said. "I want to help somebody else."

Virta's right. There are so many lonely people, and among those who are struggling with illness, the health care system too often compounds their sense of isolation. Particularly in hospitals, patients may feel that they're reduced to their illness—a problem to be diagnosed and treated rather than a person with hopes, yearnings, dreads, and a terrifyingly immediate need for solace. The pain of this experience also can extend to patients' loved ones.

Mychele spent most of the last year of her husband's life at Ronald Reagan UCLA Medical Center. Her husband, Vincent, had myelodysplastic syndrome, or MDS, a disease where your bone marrow stops making the healthy blood cells you need to survive. He'd endured chemotherapy, constant blood transfusions, and a stem cell transplant from his brother. But by Christmas Day,

2017, Vincent was in the intensive care unit (ICU). Nothing seemed to be helping him. Mychele had never felt so alone.

When we spoke two years later, Mychele recalled her husband as "the most loving, hugest man you ever met. He was six foot one, a big Samoan man who loved everyone." Vincent had been an active duty member of the US Navy when he was diagnosed. But by that Christmas, he'd already been in the ICU for over a month. His face was half-hidden behind the ventilator tube in his mouth, and he was surrounded by machines keeping him alive. He was a shadow of the man Mychele had married.

Mychele knew things were bad, and she was terrified of losing him. The medical staff paid attention to what was of immediate concern, but it felt impersonal to Mychele. With little to guide her as Vincent's fiercest defender and decision-maker in his incapacity, she was scared and frustrated and didn't know where to turn.

And that is how things might have stayed had it not been for Dr. Thanh Neville, a pulmonary and critical care doctor who is known for her laser-like focus on making sure patients' wishes are honored. Thanh is self-deprecating, hardworking, and fiercely protective of her patients. She had recently started a program modeled on the work of a Canadian physician Dr. Deborah Cook. The 3 Wishes Project granted wishes to patients who were dying in the ICU. Their goal was to shift the experience from what can be an impersonal and alienating experience into something that honors the dying and their loved ones.

Mychele remembers how skeptical she was when she first met Thanh and her team that Christmas Day. "I was such a Negative Nancy given the situation we were in. She talked to me about the program, and I looked her in the eye and said, 'I want the truth and I want it now. Is he dying?' She took my hand and said, 'I will be honest with you. Your medical team told me, as they have shared with you, that they don't believe he will survive this hospital stay. We are here to honor him in his remaining time and to help you prepare.'" Vincent was indeed dying, and there was nothing the medical team could do to change that. "At first, I was angry. I was rude. 'You don't know me. How much is this going to cost me?' It took a minute to believe that she was there only because she cared." But that was the whole point of 3 Wishes.

When Mychele realized this, her guard came down. "I said to Thanh with tears in my eyes and a whole family of frogs in my throat, 'I'm afraid to be alone.' She embraced me and said, 'We won't let you be alone.' Her colleague took my hand with tears in her eyes and said, 'We're going to be here with you the whole way.'"

Mychele paused. "Honestly, when I realized I didn't have to go through this alone, there was a sense of acceptance and gratitude that I'm not going to have to watch the machines get turned off alone."

The team made good on their promise for the remaining three days of Vincent's life. He requested to be moved to the cancer floor, where he knew the nurses so well he had nicknames for many of them. He wanted his wife to be around the people who had journeyed with them through the last year. And even though the cancer unit wasn't equipped for patients on ventilators, Thanh's team was able to get approval for an exception and honor Vincent's wish.

"Without me even asking," Mychele recalled, "they brought in fresh flowers. I'm Hawaiian, and my husband is Polynesian, so flowers are important to us. They brought in as many Polynesian flowers as they could. That small detail meant so much."

And when the time came to let Vincent go, Thanh's team was there for them. "Till today," Mychele said, "I'm dumbfounded that anyone would even care to stand with me for the half hour it took for me to decide that it was time to pull out my husband's tube. It made such a difference to have someone sit with me as we were removing my husband's life support even though it wasn't the doctor's duty."

For Thanh, the basic premise and power of the program is simple: "The goal of 3 Wishes is to stop asking what's the matter with the patient and start asking what *matters* to them."

In less than two years, the program has helped over two hundred patients and their families. They have performed two weddings, set up a final date night complete with a tablecloth over the bedside table and a Netflix movie, arranged for a local arts school to perform a patient's favorite musical live in her bedroom, decorated a woman's room with photos of Hawaii because that was her favorite vacation spot, and created numerous keepsakes for bereaved families, including hand molds—castings of couples holding hands for the last time.

Part of the program is sending a sympathy card a few weeks later signed by ICU doctors, nurses, and other members of the care team. Thanh is always surprised at the response: "I'm shocked at how much it means to people. So many families during interviews say the card shows that 'we haven't been forgotten, that we mean something.' One person wrote us a letter that said, 'A few weeks after I lost my mom, I thought I lost everything, but your card showed me that people still care.'"

Medicine and technology may fail us at times, but human connection grounded in love and compassion always heals. Perhaps the sense of loneliness and disconnection that comes with death can't entirely be prevented, but it can be eased. Helping patients and their families feel known, helping them feel seen and loved, is perhaps the most powerful medicine we have.

How much, I wondered, is a program like 3 Wishes worth? It's not easy to put a price on fulfillment, peace, and connection for patients and their families during one of life's most stressful moments. Which makes it all the more striking that the average cost of Thanh's 3 Wishes program has been just $30 per patient. Not $30,000. Just $30. When you consider the additional impact on the doctors, nurses, and staff involved in the care of each of the patients, this represents a staggering return on investment. Mychele, for example, now aspires to start a program to support caregivers in the hospital. One of the reasons that family members are afraid to leave the bedside is fear of missing the doctor's brief visit, so one of the things Mychele wants to do is give caregivers a break by sitting with the patient and calling family members if the doctor shows up. These are the kinds of priceless gifts that connect us as human beings, that help reassure us and remind us we're not alone.

These and many other stories I've encountered over the years leave no doubt in my mind that loneliness can wreak havoc on our physical and emotional lives, yet the very same stories persuade me just as compellingly that social connection is the bigger subject here. We all have a deep and abiding need to be seen for who we are—as fully dimensional, complex, and vulnerable human beings. We all need to know that we matter and that we are loved. These are the deep-seated needs that secure relationships satisfy, and when they are met, we tend to live healthier, more productive and more rewarding lives. When they go unmet, we suffer.

When we're in the throes of such suffering, it's difficult to imagine that this misery is part of some evolutionary design. Yet it's clear that loneliness serves a vital function by warning us when something essential for our survival—social connection—is lacking. The scientists who first recognized this vital function thought that perhaps, if we could learn to respond to loneliness (like we do to hunger and thirst), instead of surrendering to it, we might be able to reduce both its duration and negative effects and actually improve the overall quality of our lives. The first step was to study the tandem evolution of social connection and loneliness.

CHAPTER 2

The Evolution of Loneliness

With every true friendship, we build more firmly the foundations on which the peace of the whole world rests.

—Mahatma Gandhi

If we have no peace, it is because we have forgotten that we belong to each other.

—Mother Teresa

One warm fall afternoon in 2017, while visiting my parents in Miami, I joined Iowa Public Radio by phone to speak with callers about loneliness. I was pacing outside on the driveway as I listened and talked, and my feet were bare, an old habit from childhood, when I would run through this very yard feeling the earth between my toes. The combination of my bare feet, my childhood home, and the discussion topic unexpectedly brought back memories of the times I had struggled with loneliness during elementary and middle school. When we moved to our neighborhood, we were the only immigrants and we didn't have anyone who shared, much less understood, our culture or traditions. It was what we expected, but it took me a long time to feel that I belonged here.

The radio station had reached out to me in response to a *Harvard Business Review* article about loneliness that I'd written a few months earlier. Truth be told, the response to the piece surprised me. I hadn't expected many business journal readers to be interested in the topic of social connection, yet week after week, messages poured in from all corners of the globe. Some came from reporters who wanted to know why a former surgeon general was talking about loneliness instead of traditional topics like smoking or obesity, but many more were from people who'd experienced loneliness and felt a sense of relief when they realized they weren't alone in their feelings.

The first listener to call into the radio show was Maureen. "I want to talk about my daughter [who is] just back from college," she said, her voice quivering as she struggled to hold back tears. Maureen's daughter loved being around friends but she confided to her mom that the relationships she had felt one-sided. "She said to me last night, 'No one ever asks about me. Mom, I'm lonely.' I didn't know what to do." Maureen began crying softly. I could feel my heart breaking for her. Maureen had sent her daughter to college thinking she would be part of a community. Yet, as much as she was connected to people online and surrounded by them on campus, she still hadn't found the genuine, fulfilling relationships she craved.

A few minutes later, Rod, a middle-aged man, called in saying that he'd felt profoundly lonely since his best friend died from cancer ten years earlier. He hadn't spoken about this much and wasn't quite sure what to do. He wondered if there were things that could ease the pain of his loneliness. "It's hard to find another good male buddy," he said.

Rachel, who drove trucks for a living, joined the conversation next. She worked long, solitary hours on the road and found that friendships and romantic relationships were few and far between. "I feel lonely a lot," she said, "and I basically want to know, is there something wrong with me?"

Her question made me stop pacing, even as the hot asphalt started to burn the soles of my feet. How many times over the course of my life had I asked myself the same question: *What is wrong with me?* As a child I thought not only that I was bad at making friends but that there was something inside that made me unlikable. I imagined that everyone in my school except me had someone—or many people—to confide in, that I was the only outcast. This was the very same anxiety that the caller was expressing, which suggested an important question. Could it be that this kind of self-doubt was not a reflection of actual flaws but, rather, a misperception resulting from loneliness itself?

As the radio interview concluded I reflected on my own periods of loneliness. When you're chronically lonely—as a child or an adult—it seeps deeply into your state of mind. It colors how you think about nearly everything, especially your own character. You imagine that you're a misfit. You worry that you'll feel lonely even when you're with people. And most destructive of all, you question your self-worth, thinking that there might be something truly wrong with you that's causing this pain.

But I could see how a long-haul trucker, a grieving friend, and a college student away from home for the first time could feel lonely. I could see why I'd felt socially insecure trying to fit in to a suburban American school. What was much more difficult to grasp was how someone like me now—an adult surrounded by people, with a history of close friendships, fulfilling work, and a loving family—could struggle as I still did from time to time with these same feelings of social disconnection and loneliness. And for that matter, why do any of us feel lonely?

Dr. Loneliness

The late Dr. John Cacioppo was the first to liken loneliness to hunger and thirst, identifying it as a necessary warning signal with biochemical and genetic roots. His work was regarded as so central to the field that many called him "Dr. Loneliness."

I first met John at the US Department of Health and Human Services in Washington, DC, in 2017. My team had invited him to share his work with us as part of our initiative on emotional health and well-being. Tall, slim, and bearing a full head of salt-and-pepper hair, John had an intense, focused expression when he was speaking that would periodically give way to a warm, disarming smile.

John's decision to focus specifically on loneliness began with a harrowing car accident when he was in college. When driving one day, he accidentally struck a horse, totaling his car and injuring himself so severely he nearly died. During those moments when he thought his life was ending, his thoughts flew to the people he loved. Not to his work or reputation, but to the people he loved.

The experience caused him to reexamine his life and his academic focus with fresh eyes. What mattered most in life was love and human connection. This realization was at once obvious and profound. It led him to change the direction of his studies and research to focus on the biological underpinnings of human relationships and on the tension between social connection and loneliness.

John went on to graduate school at Ohio State, where he became fascinated by the brain's connection with social behavior and the idea that mental states can have dramatic impact on the body. Skeptics—including his graduate school professors—did not see the biology of psychological factors as serious science. Social factors weren't relevant to the nervous system, he was told. But John was sure there was a connection. He forged forward and eventually teamed up with an old friend and fellow researcher from grad school, Dr. Gary Berntson. Together, they founded the field of "social neuroscience," which focuses on understanding the interaction between biological systems and social processes.

Cacioppo's work on loneliness gained traction when he landed at the University of Chicago in 1999. He built a major research program at the University of Chicago, led its social psychology department, and founded the Center for Cognitive and Social Neuroscience. The work he did there transformed the modern-day understanding of loneliness. He helped delineate the effects that loneliness and connection have on our biological processes, and the scientific rigor with which he pursued his research made the case for loneliness as a hard science deserving of more study and attention.

When looking at loneliness through the lens of history and biology, John and his team found that the human need for social connection is more than a simple feeling or convenience—it's a biological and social imperative rooted in thousands of years of human evolution. And loneliness, he maintained, has evolved as a warning signal to satisfy that need.

"Loneliness is like an iceberg," John said in a 2016 interview with the *Guardian*. "We are conscious of the surface, but there is a great deal more that is phylogenetically so deep that we cannot see it."[1]

The Evolutionary Trail

Cacioppo's evolutionary theory of loneliness was rooted in the observation that humans have survived as a species not because we have physical advantages like size, strength, or speed, but because of our ability to connect in social groups. We exchange ideas. We coordinate goals. We share information and emotions. "Our strength is our ability to communicate and work together," he said.[2]

In 2011, a team of anthropologists at the University of Oxford published evidence that reached back some fifty-two million years in support of Cacioppo's theory.[3] The very first monkeys and apes, they found, connected not in pairs, as some scientists had previously thought, but in groups of both sexes. The study's lead author, Dr. Susanne Shultz, theorized that this happened as formerly nocturnal primates began to hunt during the day, when they were more visible to predators. The value of connection was easy to see: there was strength in numbers.

Psychologist Dr. Bill von Hippel, who wrote *The Social Leap*,[4] told me that groups became especially valuable to our hominid ancestors about three million years ago, when the body of the Australopithecus adapted in ways that enabled them to throw. "Now they had the most important innovation in military history," Bill said. "The ability to kill at a distance." Back then, even if fifty hunters tried to club a lion at close range, the casualty rate would have been high, but throwing enabled them to hurl stones from a position of relative safety. "Once we can kill at a distance, everything changes. Now we all have incentive to work together as a group. We can survive if we coordinate and throw all at once."

As humans developed, evolutionary pressure selected for more cooperation because of the advantages it conferred. Cooperation made it possible to plan for the future. Division of labor became feasible. In groups, our hominid ancestors could take turns keeping watch for wolves or sabretooths, and if they were attacked, they could organize to fight back, increasing their chances of overpowering the tiger and saving one another. They could pool the food they hunted and gathered, making it less likely that any individual would starve from day to day. As an early human, you soon learned that your odds of being attacked or of starving would increase dramatically if you became separated from your people.

But that wasn't the only reason to stick together. Connecting in groups also provided the numbers and security for individuals to mate, which enabled the tribe to multiply and endure. Cooperation further helped safeguard the tribe's survival through extended families of trusted adults who shared the responsibility of parenting. It made for efficiency when the work of teaching and protecting the tribe's children was a communal rather than a private enterprise. So, it wasn't only the individual whose survival depended on social connection, but our entire species.

Beyond basic survival, though, connection increased the rate of human innovation and empowered the tribe's creativity. "We're the only animal on the planet," Bill told me, "that goes out of its way to share the contents of our minds with others, even when there's no immediate gain." We do this because it helps get us on the same page and allows us to understand one another better, which has longer-term advantages for cooperation and efficacy.

Working together, early humans solved technological problems that would have stumped them individually, and by sharing their discoveries, they spread and improved on them. Just imagine the excitement when the very first group of hominids debated the uses of fire or figured out how to raft across a vast river.

Emotional knowledge was valuable, as well. Is that hunter generous with his kill? Does that mother treat her children kindly? Is this chief reliable? Can we count on one another for mutual aid? "We evolved to seek emotional consensus," Bill said. And stories evolved to record and cultivate such consensus, "so others can share our emotional reaction."

It's worth noting here that our ancestors' default setting was togetherness. Anthropologists estimate that hunter-gatherers spent about one-third of their time working, one-third socializing and playing with their kids, and one-third sleeping. They had plenty of time to swap stories because they were rarely apart— and they liked it that way.

"We also evolved to find the experience of being alone aversive," Bill said. "That's when loneliness likely became an issue." And here, too, stories helped.

Even in the absence of others, stories make individuals feel connected and promote a sense of belonging. This helps to explain the enormous role that storytelling plays in securing human values, purpose, and identity, and in bonding us emotionally. Ever since the first cave drawing, we've been encoding our experiences in stories through words, pictures, music, and rituals to be passed down generation to generation. These tales help us understand who we are. They give meaning to our struggles, and comfort us when we are suffering or afraid. They bring us together.

All this means that our social evolution is deeply intertwined with our physical evolution. And this whole process is still baked into our collective psyche today, Bill told me. "If I'm not sharing knowledge and emotions, then I feel lonely."

The reason for that, according to John Cacioppo, is that loneliness "serves as a signal to attend to and take care of the social connections that define us as a species."[5] We know we *are* attending to those connections when we feel "at home" with a closely knit group or family. We're wired to associate belonging with the sharing of stories, feelings, memories, and concerns. That's why our bodies relax and our spirits lift when we connect in genuine friendship and love. Strong personal relationships not only add joy and meaning to our lives, but they have positive effects on our health, mood, and performance. They buffer stress and make it more likely that we'll have the help and support we need to weather life's inevitable challenges, be they illness, job change, the loss of a loved one, or other major life transitions. The stronger our connections with each other, the richer our culture and the stronger society become.

Wired for Connection

I now had a better understanding of our evolutionary need for connection and loneliness, but the next question before me was *how* this wiring works. For help with this, I turned to Dr. Steve Cole, a genomics researcher at the University of California, Los Angeles. What might explain biologically why social connection enhances our health?

Apart from practical reasons such as increased safety and consistent food supply, Steve told me, the benefits from connection include and result from decreases in the body's stress response.

Prosocial behavior, like helping others, leaves people feeling less anxious and threatened and more secure. Moreover, he said, this low-stress state of connection is our default state. We're biologically primed not just to feel better together but to feel *normal* together.

This mechanism is supported by responses in the body that are mediated by an array of hormones and neurotransmitters, including oxytocin, dopamine, and endorphins. Oxytocin, which means "quick birth" in Greek, is perhaps best known for its role in pregnancy, labor, lactation, and mother-child bonding. It has also been found to promote bonding within your group by reducing fear and stress while making you more defensive against those who are not part of your group. Put another way, it may make strong bonds stronger and weak bonds weaker.[6] Endorphins are naturally occurring opioids that reduce our perception of pain and contribute to a feeling of euphoria and pleasure. Endorphins can be released when we experience pain or when we exercise (as in the "runner's high"), but they are also released when we physically touch and when we move in synchrony with others. This explains why dancing and love make such excellent partners. Additionally, dopamine, a key player in the brain's reward systems, is a powerful motivator for connection, surging in response to isolation and driving us to seek companionship.[7]

We might not guess that we're thinking about social connection all the time, but it actually occupies more time than we are aware. Another UCLA neuroscientist, Dr. Matthew Lieberman, has spent the past two decades using functional magnetic resonance imaging, or fMRI, to watch the brain's activity when people are talking, hugging, solving math problems—or just sitting alone. What he's found is that humans rely on two separate networks to process social and nonsocial thinking. He likens the back-and-forth activity between these networks to a "neural seesaw." When we're doing our taxes or chemistry homework or engineering a bridge, our *non*social pathways are active. When we're meeting a friend for lunch or helping our kids with their homework, the action shifts to the social network.

But what happens, he wondered, when we're just kicking back and doing nothing? What's our default network? The answer astonished him.

"Whenever we finish doing some kind of non-social thinking," he told *Scientific American*,[8] "the network for social thinking comes back on like a reflex—almost instantly." In other words: "Evolution has placed a bet that the best thing for our brain to do in any spare moment is to get ready to see the world socially. . . . We are built to be social creatures."

This means that we're constantly preparing for our next meeting, love affair, confrontation. Even if we don't realize it—even if we think of ourselves as profoundly introverted or task-oriented—we spend most of our time thinking about other people. To a large extent, Lieberman says, that's because our relationships with other people define us.

He explains this point by indicating a region right between our eyes called the medial prefrontal cortex. This area lights up with activity when we're thinking about ourselves and making personal decisions, such as what we're going to wear or what we think of our appearance, or when we're identifying a personal preference, such as our favorite color or hobby. This activity, which neuroscientists describe as "self-processing," is also involved in remembering past experiences or feelings. It shapes our identity and would seem to be completely self-centered. But there's a catch, according to Lieberman.

If self-processing were purely inner directed, the medial prefrontal cortex should shut down when we turn our attention to others. But just the opposite happens. When we're engaged with others, activity in this supposedly self-centered region accelerates. In other words, we're defining ourselves even as we socialize.

Lieberman takes this a step further. He says that our identities absorb the influence of others, like social sponges. Not everyone is equally susceptible to suggestion, of course, but we all are to some degree—whether we realize it or not. And the more interested we are in someone who's trying to impress or persuade us, the more likely we are to adopt this person's belief. Lieberman likens this process to a Trojan horse: "letting in the beliefs of others, under the cover of darkness and without us realizing it."[9]

So we evolved to have brains that are wired to seek connection, to focus our thoughts on other people, and to define ourselves by the people around us. This all sounded to me like a mixed blessing. It would be great if the person we were "sponging" up was someone we admired and trusted, but what if the influencer was a con artist or enemy? And what would stop us from becoming "oversaturated" by too many people? While we definitely need other people in our lives to help us thrive, our capacity for connection can't be limitless. Evolution must have provided some sort of mechanism to prevent our social circuitry from becoming overloaded.

Of course, it did.

Friend or Foe?

John Cacioppo described this dilemma in an interview in the *Atlantic* in 2017.[10] Early humans, he said, "were not uniformly positive toward each other. We exploit each other, we punish each other, we threaten each other, we coerce." This posed an existential risk. "If I make an error and detect a person as a foe who turns out to be a friend, that's okay, I don't make the friend as fast, but I survive. But if I mistakenly detect someone as a friend when they're a foe, that can cost me my life."

Not only did humans need neural networks to push them toward connection, then, but they also needed mechanisms to help them decide who *not* to befriend. As Cacioppo suggested, the mechanisms that evolved hinge on trust—specifically, on the ability to quickly differentiate those who are trustworthy from those who aren't. It's a skill that humans begin to develop midway through the first year of life.

At the very beginning of life, infant researchers have found, the social sponge of the human brain is attentive to everyone and anyone. Newborns come into the world without preference. They are drawn to faces, and for the first month or two, almost any face will do.[11] They'll pay as much attention to a monkey's face as to their own father's.[12] Moreover, infants have an astonishing ability to tell individual faces apart—even those of individual monkeys. They also can distinguish between faces of any race. For example, in their first months, white babies can tell one Asian face from another or one African face from another. In the beginning, it's as if all the faces on the planet belonged to their own trusted family.

By the age of three months, however, research has found that babies start to favor faces of their family's race and ethnicity. A process that researchers call *perceptual narrowing* begins to blur faces that are different from those within the infant's small, trusted circle. As a result, babies start to view members of other races as indistinguishable from one another, even as they become more closely attuned to the nuances and subtle signals from the people who are closest and most familiar to them—the people the child most depends on.[13]

Given the complexity of close human interactions, this narrowing serves a practical function. For babies to develop a strong connection with their caregivers, they need to learn how to read their cues, including body language, tone of voice, patterns of speech, facial expression, and eye movements. They must figure out how to assess their mother's emotional reactions, their brother's trustworthiness, their father's moods. They also have to find ways to respond to the cues that bring their family members closer and strengthen the child's sense of protection and trust. This early education forms the basis for attachment, relationship, and love, and it requires a lot of brainpower. Perceptual narrowing helps to focus that power.

It's worth mentioning that not even the most sophisticated artificial intelligence today can match these intricate signaling systems, much less the profound human connections they generate as they circuit through the brain. This is one reason why the social network of technology is—and likely always will be—an inferior substitute for face-to-face interpersonal communication.

But what about all those unfamiliar faces that the infant now tunes out? The faces of unfamiliar races and ethnicities gradually blur. Studies of babies exposed predominantly to one race have found that by nine months of age, Caucasian babies can't tell the difference between one Middle Eastern face and another,[14] and to Chinese babies, all white faces look alike.[15] Now, when we are exposed to other races and ethnicities, we become better at differentiating among those faces, but we can never recapture the universal ability to read faces that we possess at birth. From our earliest experiences, our attention focuses on those who are most important to us.

A similar pruning process occurs linguistically. Humans are born with the potential to adopt any language on earth, but with time, they lose facility with all but the languages they hear in their tribe—the languages they must master in order to communicate with the people they trust to keep them safe. This is why it becomes increasingly difficult for most people to learn foreign languages as we age.

In our ancestors' tribal world, this perceptual narrowing served the critical purpose of securing a sense of belonging and protecting a clan's members against befriending possible enemies. But what happened if they strayed from their tribe or got stranded alone, perhaps among the very outsiders they'd now learned to distrust? This, Cacioppo said, was when the hypervigilance that underlies loneliness would kick in.

At the first sign of isolation, whether alone or among strangers, the stranded individual's sympathetic nervous system would go on alert, triggering fear and immediate preparation to fight or flee the situation. Central to this stress response is a surge in hormones known as catecholamines, such as epinephrine. These course through the body, causing the pupils and airways to dilate and increasing heart rate and blood flow to the muscles, heart, and brain. The hypothalamic-pituitary-adrenal (HPA) axis is also activated. Starting from the hypothalamus in the brain, signals cascade to the pituitary gland, then the adrenal glands, triggering the release of mineralocorticoids and cortisol, which in turn raise our blood pressure and increase blood sugar levels so we have energy readily available. In this sense, our bodies read isolation, and often even the threat of isolation, as an emergency.

With the senses on heightened alert it was possible for our stranded ancestors to detect the slightest noise or smell or shift of light that might signal a predator. The lungs were able to take in more air. The muscles were able to generate more power and speed. The heart was able to get more blood and oxygen to vital organs. And the immune system was activated in case of injury and infection. In this state, the whole body was engaged in self-preservation, narrowing attention to immediate signals, ignoring more leisurely thoughts, such as desire or wonder or reflection, and keeping sleep shallow and fragmented, lest a predator attack in the night.

Such hypervigilance could be lifesaving in moments of acute danger, but it placed a lot of stress on the body. Nor was it sustainable for long periods. However, that time-limiting feature alone helped motivate the stranded to quickly rejoin their tribes.

Over millennia, this hypervigilance in response to isolation became embedded in our nervous system to produce the anxiety we associate with loneliness. When we feel lonely, our bodies still react as if we were lost on the tundra surrounded by wild animals and members of alien tribes. When loneliness persists, the same stress hormones that surged to provide short-term protection instead begin to produce long-term destruction as they increase cardiovascular stress and inflammation throughout the body. This, in turn, damages tissues and blood vessels and increases the risk of heart disease and other chronic illnesses. Studies have also found that loneliness leads to changes in gene expression in white blood cells, which in turn results in increased inflammation and reduced defenses against viruses.[16]

John Cacioppo helped us understand an additional way loneliness causes mental and physical exhaustion: it takes a toll on the quality of sleep. When we're profoundly lonely, we tend to sleep lightly and rouse often, just as our ancestors did to prevent being overtaken by wolves or enemies. Cacioppo's team—including his frequent collaborator University of Chicago psychologist Dr. Louise Hawkley—found that lonely people come out of deep sleep many times throughout the night, and though they may think they've slept through, these microawakenings undermine the quality of their sleep, leaving them fatigued and irritable.[17]

While our body's global stress response to loneliness is designed to increase our chances of survival, it can do just the opposite when it lasts too long or when it comes on suddenly and severely. One example of an extreme stress reaction is takotsubo syndrome, also called "broken heart syndrome."

First described in Japan in 1990, takotsubo syndrome was named after a pot-shaped octopus trap, or *takotsubo*, when it was noticed that the most powerful pumping chamber of the heart took on this unusual shape during episodes of extreme stress—such as in response to overwhelming grief.

While most of us have experienced the pain of heartbreak at some point in life, the loneliness of losing someone we love generally subsides over time, especially if we have strong emotional support. In rare instances, however, the shock of being left behind—abandoned—can literally break the survivor's heart.

I learned about the biological power of heartbreak during high school when my maternal grandfather unexpectedly died of a heart attack. We were extremely close, and his death was the first major loss I experienced. I was devastated. So was his younger brother Vasana, who had grown up with my grandfather under very difficult circumstances. Their mother had died when they were young, and their father remarried a woman who severely neglected and mistreated the two boys. The brothers often went hungry and frequently didn't have proper clothing or a bed to sleep in at night. For years, they took care of each other when it seemed that no one else would. They remained as close as twins throughout their life, and when my grandfather died, the loss was simply too much for my great-uncle. He came to pay his respects soon after hearing the news of his brother's passing. Standing there with the body of the man who had been his companion his entire life, Vasana was overcome with grief.

"Leaving me, you have gone," he said, tears streaming down his face. He then clutched his chest and collapsed. A short while later, he was pronounced dead.

I thought of Vasana a decade later when I was in residency training and began seeing patients with the onset of sudden cardiac failure in the setting of emotional distress. I learned that what I was seeing were emerging cases of takotsubo syndrome. Because the shock of loss is most intense when the death is recent, the risk of experiencing takotsubo is greatest immediately following the death of a loved one.

What makes the heart react to loss this way? Technically, the shock of grief floods the body with an outpouring of epinephrine and other stress hormones, causing the heart to dilate and lose some of its pumping function. As blood stagnates, it backs up in the lungs, causing difficulty breathing, and eventually leads to swelling throughout the body. The chest pain and shortness of breath that can accompany takotsubo syndrome can feel identical to a heart attack. So, although it's generally survivable if the patient receives supportive medical care, it's often misdiagnosed.

But why does loss trigger this outpouring of hormones? Put simply, this distress signal is a biochemical echo of the stress state our distant forebears experienced when they were cut off from the tribe and had to face the threatening uncertainties of the wilderness alone. It's like an intensely concentrated dose of loneliness.

The Paradox of Loneliness

If loneliness is so bad for our health, it would make sense that we would do everything in our power to connect with other people at the first sign of social isolation. Often, that's just what does happen. When the biological process works as designed, the anxiety we feel in the first flush of loneliness will motivate us to find "our people." We'll go home to Mom. Or hug our spouse. We'll help a neighbor or call an old friend. If we're able to find and connect with people we trust, and if they're responsive and genuinely understanding, the loneliness will subside and our stress state will recede. This is how most of us get through situational loneliness, such as the lost feeling that can descend when we move to a new town or start a new school or job.

But it's not always easy to find or make those connections. When we become chronically lonely, most of us are inclined to withdraw, whether we mean to or not. John Cacioppo determined that our threat perception changes when we're lonely, so we push people away and see risk and threat in benign social opportunities. John's widow, Dr. Stephanie Cacioppo, a neuroscientist who was his close collaborator and has taken on the role of continuing and expanding his work on loneliness at the University of Chicago, found that lonely brains detect social threats twice as fast as non-lonely brains.[18] This may seem like a paradoxical response to a mechanism that evolution designed to *prevent* isolation, but from an evolutionary standpoint it makes sense.

When our ancestors were separated from the safety of the group, they needed to react defensively even to marginal threats, since they might well turn out to be lethal. But in modern life that same hypervigilance causes us to misread harmless or even welcoming people and situations as threats. Fleeing into self-preservation mode, we'll avoid people and distrust even those who reach out to help us. With prolonged loneliness, we'll decline invitations and stop answering the phone.

Hypervigilance also creates an intense preoccupation with our own needs and security, which can appear to others as self-involvement. These two elements—the threat perception shift and the increased focus on self—are key parts of the hypervigilance story that make it difficult to engage with others when we're lonely.

Then the reactions begin. Those who'd like to help start turning away, leaving us feeling even more alone. Before long we're trapped in a vicious cycle of suspicion, jealousy, and resentment. Loneliness thus fuels more loneliness until the fracture leads to severe alienation. Clearly, the solution is more complicated than telling someone who's lonely to go to a party or "just be with people."

"What's disturbing about this," Steve Cole observed, "is that we have created a culture of living which is different from our historical default state. I think we are relaxed and at ease by default and are bonding oriented in our resting state. But few of us feel this way. It's less common for us to be sitting around our fire talking with neighbors. Instead, we are racing around trying to get work done all the time. So, I think our current state is different from what our physiology is engineered to support."

Loneliness doubles down on the negative feelings a sometimes threatening world can evoke. The increasing diversity and mobility of modern society sharpens this disconnect even more. When among strangers with our stress hormones spiking, we may be more susceptible to cultural bias, racial stereotyping, and discriminatory practices. We'll misinterpret social cues and see social threats where none exist. Small irritations can lead to exaggerated reactions. A misplaced pen or accidental spill may drive us into a rage or make us feel like the world is collapsing. A person merging into your lane may be taken as a personal offense. Loneliness can make it especially hard to establish friendships when moving to a new neighborhood or starting a new job or school where everyone seems to belong to a different and inaccessible "tribe."

So why can't we just train our bodies to react differently when we feel isolated? When John and Stephanie Cacioppo examined this question, they noticed that, in fact, not everyone is equally susceptible to loneliness. While some people feel as if they've been lonely since the day they were born, others experience loneliness only fleetingly and rarely. For some, loneliness is profoundly painful, while others experience it only as mild distress. John observed that, in evolutionary terms, this variability is useful, since it means that some members of a community will be "so pained by disconnection that they are willing to defend their village," while "others are willing to go out and explore but hopefully still have enough of a connection to come back and share what they found."[19]

But this led to more questions. Are these variations caused by choice and conditioning? Because life trains certain people to be more distrustful than others? Or could they be genetic?

When Cacioppo and his colleagues conducted the first genome-wide association study of loneliness, published in 2016 in *Neuropsychopharmacology*,[20] they confirmed that genes do play a role in chronic loneliness, though not nearly as much as experience and circumstance do. After studying data from more than ten thousand people aged fifty or older, they concluded that the tendency to feel lonely over a lifetime, rather than just occasionally due to circumstance, is between 14 and 27 percent heritable based on an analysis of common gene variants. Other studies, including twin studies, looking at the total heritability of loneliness have pegged that number as high as 55 percent.[21] But it's important to note that loneliness is not a discrete condition but an emotional response. "What's being inherited is not loneliness," Cacioppo said, "it's the painfulness of the disconnection."[22]

What he meant is that the overall experience of loneliness is a complex product of our genes, past experiences, current circumstances, the culture in which we live, and our personalities. Which of these factors *causes* us to feel lonely on any given day is nearly impossible to say.

The challenge of responding to loneliness becomes even more complicated when you consider that loneliness overlaps with and is often inherited with anxiety disorders or depression. The co-existence of all these conditions can be confounding, since they may feel similar at times. All have a negative impact on mood and can cause social withdrawal. They also can feed off each other, as depression and anxiety make it harder to connect with other people, and this can deepen the pain of loneliness.

True Pain

London-based Michelle Lloyd knows all about the bundling of depression and social anxiety with loneliness. She's struggled with all three for most of her life. Now in her thirties, Michelle is a human relations manager who blogs about mental health. One reason she blogs is to help others understand the social responses of people with these three conditions. It's not easy, she's found, to explain how the experience of loneliness differs from that of depression or social anxiety, and how the three overlap.

"I think it's a really difficult distinction to make," Michelle said. "Being lonely can lead to mental health issues. And also, mental health issues make you more susceptible to loneliness. It's very hard to understand yourself when you're dealing with depression and anxiety, let alone to let someone else in to try and understand it. When I struggle with my mental health, I can push people away, for fear of judgment or just not wanting to be honest about it. That has led to losing friends, which then sort of perpetuated that feeling of loneliness."

This sounded like a brutal cycle. I wondered when she first began to struggle.

"I think my loneliness was probably first from quite a young age. I felt slightly different from the other children. So I spent a lot more time on my own than my other friends did. My parents got divorced. That made me feel very, very lonely, because I didn't feel like I could talk to anybody."

And the depression?

"The second year of university was when my depression and anxiety really took hold. I was spending long periods of time just sort of locked away in my room, not really socializing with people, and not telling anybody the reason why, either, so keeping it hidden from family and friends, and everybody."

After graduation, Michelle was living in Manchester. "I was working and I had just come out of a relationship. I felt very alone and very helpless. I just didn't want to be around anymore. I never wanted to kill myself. I just wanted to stop feeling, to stop having to deal with life really."

Finally, she consulted a doctor who prescribed antidepressants, which she's taken ever since. "But you know," she said, "a lot of people just want somebody to talk to. I have had counseling, but I think what they always lacked for me is that kind of personal element. And then you think, like, how could anybody want to be my friend? Why would anybody want to get to know me?" That kicks up the loneliness.

"When it comes to loneliness, the more you feel alone, the more you assume that everybody hates you, so the less you try and reach out to people. It is a vicious circle."

And how does social anxiety dovetail with all this?

Michelle told me she tends to be unnerved by large groups of people. "Like any more than say three or four people I do get quite anxious. I often have been out at an event with friends, and I just have to leave because I've felt so uncomfortable and had panic attacks. You just, you have to get out. And it's hard when you're in situations where you can't see an escape. So I will make sure I plan a way to get home or a way of getting out.

"If I'm in a situation where I feel anxious, then I would much rather be on my own. I think that sometimes it can come across as being quite rude or really aloof. It's my way of coping. And I have been a lot more open with my friends about it. It's helpful that they say, 'If you can just come for an hour or whatever' or 'Don't feel like you have to stay all night.'"

The irony is that Michelle loves being around other people, but it's the quality of connection that really matters to her. The friends she cherishes are those who know and understand the ways she struggles with depression and anxiety, who neither dismiss her struggles nor stigmatize them.

"There was a select group of people that I was honest with that did understand. And I think there's something to be said for making yourself a little bit vulnerable sometimes, because when you make yourself open to those connections, they can happen. But if you shy away from being yourself and reaching out to people, then you do perpetuate loneliness."

At the same time, withdrawal could be a signal that her depression is worsening. "I tend to realize it a little bit too late," she admitted. "I am very close to my family, and if I don't answer their phone calls, then I'm possibly on the verge of having a very low mood. If I'm starting to avoid people that I like, then I know that I'm probably in a bit of a cycle. I still manage to go to work. But it's literally go to work, come straight home, and get over the day."

I wondered what other strategies she'd developed to manage her depression and anxiety without letting loneliness creep up on her.

The answer, she admitted, is socializing, but only with her closest friends. "I will reach out to somebody, text message, email, just saying, 'You know, I have been having a bit of a bad weekend, do you fancy meeting for coffee this week or something?' I do try my hardest, even though every part of me is saying, no, I don't want to see anybody. I do try to be a bit more honest with people as well. When somebody understands what you are going through, and they feel it, too, there's a bond there. It's not about just having a friend for the sake of having a friend. You have to have something that brings you together with that person, there's got to be a kind of a connection. And that has to be a natural thing. It can't be forced."

It's almost as if she has to suppress the internal systems of depression and anxiety to accomplish all this—but she makes the effort because she knows that these relationships have the power to heal.

"It's really draining," she acknowledged, "because you do have to override that fear inside you. But I found when I have gone a little bit outside of my comfort zone in that respect, it has paid off. The last few years, I've realized how many people have similar issues. They are not weird or strange for feeling that way. It's actually a really common thing. It's just something that we don't talk about."

While Michelle's story helped highlight the difference between the felt experiences of depression, social anxiety, and loneliness, the question still remained: Why are these three so closely aligned and so often clustered together? It's known that loneliness is a strong risk factor for depression, but do the two merely overlap in some unlucky people, or are they actively linked?

I posed these questions to New York psychologist Dr. Guy Winch, the author of *Emotional First Aid*.

"I see them more as distinct clinical entities," he told me. "Somebody can feel lonely, but still feel very interested in the things they do to keep themselves occupied or in their hobbies, or in their work. Someone who's depressed, they're not going to show a lot of vitality, or interest or passion about anything. It's much more global and much more systemic."

"Why do they so closely resemble each other?" I asked.

"Someone who's been chronically depressed for a long time can end up being lonely just because they're not cultivating their relationships," he said. "Somebody who's lonely can become depressed when their isolation becomes profound. And it can be profound for people very quickly."

To illustrate, Guy described a client who came for therapy thinking he was depressed, but in fact he was feeling disconnected from his spouse. When the man was able to reengage with his spouse, the depression lifted. "It really was about the loneliness, not about the depression."

In cases like this, Guy said, "I will work with them intensively on connecting, either with their spouse in a way that they haven't been connecting or maybe connecting with an old friend in a way that's substantial."

On the other hand, Guy told me, he often sees people who are very depressed, yet also very connected. "They have spouses who love them, and until they were depressed, they were very clear about that connection. Now that they're depressed, they feel shut off and removed from them, but once the depression lifts, they'll feel more connected again."

As for social anxiety, personal history plays as important a role as genetics. One underlying assumption about loneliness is that relationships help. But not all relationships are desirable or help us feel connected. Steve Cole explains, "Human beings are great assets to other human beings, but they can also be great threats."

John Cacioppo put it this way: "You're motivated to connect. But promiscuous connection with others can lead to death. A neural mechanism kicks in to make you a little skeptical or dubious about connecting."[23] And if you've been wounded deeply and frequently in prior relationships, that neural mechanism can become agonizingly powerful.

Let's say you were raised in an abusive or emotionally indifferent household. You may find it hard to trust strangers. And this can make you extremely anxious in new social interactions because you're understandably afraid of being hurt again.

Cole, who studies the effects of loneliness at the molecular level, says that repeated or extended experiences of threat will actually change the brain. People who carry emotional scars develop a "kind of neurobiological sensitivity to threat and rejection." This sensitivity mirrors the instincts of people who are born with social anxiety—and exacerbates them in people un-lucky enough to have both a genetic propensity toward social anxiety and a painful social history. Whether conscious of it or not, they're always on guard in social situations, assessing the trustworthiness of people around them, trying to distinguish potential friends from foes.

"If I'm the kind of person who's had a rough upbringing," Cole says, "when I go into new social settings, I am not going to come up to the first person I see and be immediately friendly to them."

Instead, the first response is caution and wariness, which may appear to others like reserve, standoffishness, or even arrogance. People who are naturally friendly may take offense and back away, and before you know it, the fear of social threat becomes a self-fulfilling prophecy of rejection.

It's important to note, Cole says, that not everyone who has this sensitivity to threat and rejection feels equally lonely. This is where personality comes in. Some people are naturally intro-verted. Like Michelle, they're comfortable with a social circle of a few trusted friends and with one-on-one or small group inter-actions as opposed to large group events. They're often content on their own and don't mind observing rather than interacting with strangers. Loneliness only occurs when you want to connect and be accepted, but can't, in this case because life has trained you to be afraid of being exploited or hurt by other people. That, Cole says, creates the "classic paradox of loneliness in a room full of people."

When I began my rotations in the hospital as a third-year medical student, I was struck by the distinctions we typically made between emotional pain and physical pain. When we encountered physical pain in our patients, we would rush to determine the origin of the pain, asking questions, performing exams, and obtaining laboratory and imaging studies. And we would be aggressive about monitoring and treating the pain. When we discovered someone was experiencing emotional pain, we reacted with concern and compassion, but there was an underlying assumption that this was less of a concern and less consequential than physical pain. What few of us understood at the time was that, within the brain, there's less difference between the two than we think.

The sensory fibers that register emotional and physical pain overlap in the brain. This proximity means that loneliness, loss, or disappointment can produce symptoms similar to those caused by physical blows or wounds.[24] If you feel shunned, researchers have found, you're likely to flinch the same way you would if slapped. If the shunning and slapping occur during an fMRI, the same region of the brain (the dorsal anterior cingulate cortex) will light up in both events.[25]

Neuroscientist Dr. Naomi Eisenberger and psychologist Dr. Nathan DeWall put this effect to the test with the help of the painkiller Tylenol. They conducted a pair of experiments that divided subjects into two groups, one of which was instructed to take Tylenol every day for three weeks while the other took a placebo.[26] In the first experiment, those who took Tylenol reported fewer days when they felt social pain over those three weeks. In a second experiment, subjects were asked to play an online video game called *Cyberball* with two avatars that the subjects believed to be human players. During the game, the avatars "snubbed" the human by playing ball only with each other. Eisenberger and Matthew Lieberman had previously demonstrated that when people were rejected in *Cyberball*, their brains showed increased activity in the dorsal anterior cingulate cortex and the anterior insula, two parts of the brain that typically light up when one experiences physical pain.[27] In this experiment, however, the subjects who had taken Tylenol had significantly *less* activity in these regions than people who had taken a placebo.

These studies and others like them have confirmed something most people suspected: rejection hurts. But they also showed that emotional and physical pain are both *processed* by the brain in very similar ways.

The overlap between physical and emotional pain in the brain sheds light on why people may reach for more powerful and dangerous substances—like opioid painkillers and alcohol— when they experience emotional pain from loneliness. With the opioid epidemic, in particular, we have increasingly appreciated the role emotional pain plays in driving use and overuse. Opioid deaths have been labeled deaths of despair for good reason.

While we recognize loneliness and other sources of emotional pain as risk factors for misuse and addiction, we don't make the connection often enough. I have found the opposite also to be true: social connection is an essential part of the addiction recovery process.

In caring for patients over the years and during my time as surgeon general, I met thousands of people who struggled with addiction to opioids, alcohol, and other substances, and when I reflect on those who made it through that dark tunnel and emerged in recovery, nearly all of them described a trusted relationship or a trusted group of close family or friends who had made their recovery possible. While loneliness has the potential to kill, connection has even more potential to heal.

All of this research would seem to confirm that our drive to connect is one of our most important survival instincts. It's in our relationships that we find the emotional sustenance and power we need in order to thrive. So strong is this instinct that when we move away from connection it induces genuine pain. And pain's role in our survival serves to remind us to pay attention to its source so we can address it.

Reflecting back on that Iowa truck driver's distraught fear that something was "wrong" with her, I wish I could reassure her again. What she was feeling was so normal, so natural, and so necessary. Her emotions were simply warning her that her life was out of balance, that she needed to tend to her social needs.

Loneliness was signaling, not accusing her. It was trying to help by reminding her just how vitally she needed to reconnect.

Evolution aside, we need social connection just as much today as we ever did—perhaps even more—as the world's increasing complexity makes it easy to feel lost and forgotten. I may not have to join a hunting party to ensure that my family has food, but I still need people with whom to share a meal. I may not have to take turns with my neighbors keeping watch for predators, but my wife and I still feel more secure with the knowledge that we and our neighbors are looking out for one another. Loneliness is a built-in reminder that we are stronger together, not just as clans and tribes or family and friends, but also as caring communities that form the foundation of a healthy culture.

CHAPTER 3

Cultures of Connection

Let there be no purpose in friendship save the deepening of the spirit.

—Kahlil Gibran, *The Prophet*

Call it a clan, call it a network, call it a tribe, call it a family. Whatever you call it, whoever you are, you need one. You need one because you are human.

—Jane Howard, *Families*

I f the need for connection and the signal of loneliness are wired into our bodies and minds, that means they must also have played a significant role in the evolution of human society and cultures around the world. Yet the value placed on social connection varies dramatically from continent to continent and among different cultural traditions. That in turn affects how and whether individuals experience loneliness.

I was reminded of this on a recent trip to the airport, when my wife, Alice, and I struck up a conversation about family with our Uber driver, a young man originally from Addis Ababa, Ethiopia. He said what he missed most about Addis was that people around you there took care of you, and you did the same. He added, "You can just leave your kids with your neighbor and go away for four or five days and they will take care of them. It's what we do. We cook for each other, we take care of each other's kids, and we spend time together."

As working parents raising our two small children far from our extended families, Alice and I were quite taken by this last remark and wanted to know more.

He then told us that his own wife and children were still in Addis. I asked if he felt lonely without them. "Of course, I miss them," he remarked, "but I met other Ethiopian families in the DC area, and we have built a smaller version of what we had in Ethiopia. We have each other so we're not lonely."

Alice and I looked at each other. The world he was describing felt so different from the one we lived in. When it comes to our day-to-day life, we resort to modern stopgap solutions just like many of our friends. We hire a nanny to help us balance work and child care. We use reputable online sites to find babysitters when we travel for work with the kids. We think about how to attach tracking devices to our children for security and peace of mind when they go around town with various caregivers, and we have spent countless hours in the middle of the night between diaper changes searching for parenting advice on everything from wipes and strollers to how to get your toddler to eat vegetables (we still haven't figured out the last one).

Because we haven't grown up taking care of children in an extended family and don't have family living with us, we are trying to figure out parenting largely on our own. Yet despite all the innovation, technology, and resources that promise to make modern life easier, I found myself thinking I'd rather have the strong community that this man was describing. Family close by and neighbors who were like family. I'd take the traditional solution over the modern-world solution of community-for-hire any day.

This encounter reminded me fondly of another Ethiopian family I'd met during my first year as a medical resident. I received a page one Saturday afternoon to evaluate a patient with advanced liver failure due to hepatitis C, acquired through a blood transfusion many years earlier. Checking her chart on my way to the hospital's main patient tower, I read that Mrs. Bekele was in the final stages of her illness. At this point, no treatment could cure her, and she had come to terms with that. She'd been admitted for comfort care, meaning that she was being maintained on a morphine drip and other medicines to relieve symptoms such as nausea and pain.

I entered Mrs. Bekele's pod, where hers was one of twenty beds. There was the usual hustle and bustle on the floor, with patients arriving, being discharged, and being wheeled off for tests, but as I approached Mrs. Bekele's room, the noise softened, and I sensed the stillness inside. Thinking she must be asleep, I knocked and inched her door open.

Ten people were gathered quietly around her bed. Some were dressed in traditional Ethiopian garb. Others wore jeans and fleeces. As I later learned, these were sons and daughters, nieces, nephews, and grandchildren who had traveled from great distances to pay their respects to their family matriarch, who lay on the bed wearing a bright traditional Ethiopian dress.

With a nod, Mrs. Bekele acknowledged my presence. I detected no hint of distress on her face. Her arms rested at her sides, and despite the physical evidence of her disease—her enlarged belly, yellowed eyes, and emaciated arms and legs—she looked regal and at peace.

I introduced myself and asked some questions about her symptoms. The pain was similar in quality and location to the pain with which she had been admitted. There didn't appear to be fever or worsening tenderness—no indication of an infection or blood clot. Her blood pressure, heart rate, and respiratory rate were normal, and her oxygen levels remained stable. I told Mrs. Bekele I thought there was nothing new to be concerned about and that we could gently increase her morphine drip for comfort if she would like. She said she would.

Ordinarily, I would have moved on quickly to my other duties, as my pager was continuing to buzz with additional requests, but the network of human connection around Mrs. Bekele was so rare among my patients that I felt compelled to learn more, so I spent a few additional minutes talking with her family about their background.

Like our Uber driver, they said that traditional Ethiopian culture stressed mutual support and friendship, in good times and bad. They'd all grown up being there for one another, whether they were a few houses away or separated by oceans and continents. Hardship and triumph were to be experienced together. That's why so many of them had come to see Mrs. Bekele not only at her time of death but often during the preceding years of her illness.

This extended family's strong sense of connection was palpable. They shared with me their admiration and love for a woman who had been part of their lives from the very beginning. They were sad, too. But the predominant feeling in the room was one of peace and gratitude for the wonderful relationship they enjoyed with Mrs. Bekele. While I could adjust her pain medications, the most important medicine she needed—love and connection— were right there at her bedside.

Looking back I realize these Ethiopian traditions are not so different from traditional Indian practices. My parents described equally close-knit community networks when they told me about growing up in India. And when I used to stay at my great-grandmother's house in Bangalore as a child, spontaneous drop-in visits from friends and extended family were daily occurrences. Most of the visitors lived nearby and, whether or not we were related to them, my sister and I were encouraged to call everyone "uncle" and "aunty." This made it seem as if we were all part of one enormous family. Later, as an honorary uncle myself, I discovered that this practice has a reciprocal bonding effect; whenever a child calls me uncle today, I feel both more connected to and more responsible for that child.

Also like Mrs. Bekele's family, my relatives often fall silent for long pauses during group conversations. Even as a child, I noticed that they didn't feel an urgency to fill each moment with talk. What mattered was simply being together.

In the US, my parents tried to replicate the sense of a large communal network by welcoming friends and relatives to stay with us, though it was never quite the same. Although they found a wonderful community of families from India, everyone was geographically dispersed, which made day-to-day interaction and support impractical. And while we had good neighbors on our street, there were lines of formality you didn't cross.

Growing up, I was aware that the world of my parents' childhood was different from mine. Traditional households in India (and in the Indian American community in South Florida) seemed messy and complicated, with everyone always around and deeply immersed in one another's business. No one seemed bothered about privacy. That had its share of drawbacks, to be sure, but we also enjoyed, even counted on being intertwined with one another. The nuclear families I saw around me in Miami seemed, in many ways, the exact opposite, with privacy and independence placed in high regard.

This was echoed in the programs I saw on television. Westerns featuring cowboys and wagon train pioneers, and TV families like the Keatons of *Family Ties* or the Drummond family of *Diff'rent Strokes*, emphasized the individual and nuclear family as self-sufficient units. Aunts and uncles, neighbors and grandparents had more distant roles. It was as if the American nuclear family was as self-made as classic American heroes like Davy Crockett and Andrew Carnegie—heroes who embodied the triumph of the individual and demonstrated the courage to take risks and go it alone. The shift from extended to nuclear family networks had swept across the industrialized world in tandem with the shift toward speed, efficiency, and competition as the dominant terms of progress.

As much as I accepted these norms while growing up, after becoming a doctor and confronting widespread loneliness among my patients, I began to suspect we'd lost something more valuable than we realized in this transition to modern culture. On the rare occasions when large extended families like Mrs. Bekele's appeared in the hospital, their presence was almost always a net benefit, as they brought with them compassion, hope, support—and love. Seeing the variety of traditions around family and friendship that were represented in the patients I encountered over the years, I couldn't help but wonder, why do some cultures seem more connected than others?

From Oneliness to Loneliness

Though humans have experienced the physical symptoms of social isolation since the time of our first ancestors, "loneliness" as a term didn't enter the English language until the late sixteenth century. When Shakespeare likened his hero in *Coriolanus* to a "lonely dragon"[1] who goes alone and is feared, cut off from kin and friends, and talked about more than he's truly seen or known, he was describing a different state than "oneliness," as being alone was more commonly called in Western Europe at the time.

"Oneliness" didn't carry any negative connotations. Like "solitude," it meant that one had the time and space to reflect. Far from an emotionally unpleasant state, oneliness was viewed as an opportunity to feel closer to God. And God connected everyone. As John Donne wrote in 1624, "No man is an island entire of itself . . . any man's death diminishes me because I am involved in mankind."[2] Christianity, like the other major religious traditions, emphasized connective qualities such as care, humility, and empathy because they helped bond congregants to one another and to God. When everyone organized their lives around God, and the church provided not just community but also security, there was relatively little risk of parishioners voluntarily leaving the fold. But after Shakespeare, other writers began to take on social isolation as a moral hazard. In 1667, John Milton went so far as to link loneliness to Satan in *Paradise Lost*.[3]

When Milton described Satan taking "lonely steps" out of hell to reach the Garden of Eden and disrupt Adam and Eve's innocent bliss, he wasn't commenting on Satan's feelings. Rather, he was casting a moral shroud around loneliness. Satan, alone and exposed, is engaged in an "uncouth errand" between heaven and hell. If he weren't so lonely, he'd presumably appear in a more favorable light in the eyes of God.

Scholars such as British historian Dr. Fay Bound Alberti suggest that concerns over loneliness arose in Milton's time because of cultural shifts away from a congregational society toward more individualism. According to Alberti, "Since God was always nearby, a person was never truly alone"—at least, this was the assumption before the 1600s—so there was no need to warn anyone against isolation. But the trends that paved the way for the Industrial Revolution changed that. "The growth of the consumer economy, the declining influence of religion, and the popularity of evolutionary biology all served to emphasize that the individual was what mattered—not traditional, paternalistic visions of a society in which everyone had a place."[4]

Alberti further described that by the time Charles Darwin made "survival of the fittest" a household phrase, the population shift away from villages to the cities was underway throughout the Western world, and the pursuit of individual wealth was becoming its own kind of religion. Europeans then spread that culture as they colonized lands around the world. Instead of being educated in village schoolhouses, many children were packed off to boarding school, some as young as five.

One reason people in this era felt lonely was that they were caught between the new societal expectations of independence and the emotional pull of their old interdependent way of life. They must have felt a bit like my parents did, seesawing between the cultures of India and America.

The Social Terms of Culture

Psychologist Dr. Ami Rokach[5] has studied loneliness for decades in various cultures and countries—a career-long fascination first sparked during a business trip to Ottawa in 1981. His conference there was concluding when he realized that he'd mistakenly booked his flight home for a day later, meaning that he was stuck in Ottawa, a city where he knew no one. Standing in his high-floor hotel room after all his colleagues had left and looking through the window at the busy street below, he had an unexpected insight. "I suddenly had a perfect sense of how loneliness feels. I could see the world around me, but I was not part of it."

One thing he's learned from his studies is that culture and traditions affect the quality of loneliness and connectedness by shaping our social expectations. Loneliness, Ami told me, occurs when our social experience fails to meet our social expectations. We tend to feel lonely when something goes "wrong" and we don't make friends the way we "should," or marry the person we "should," or interact with our neighbors and colleagues as we "should." All these "shoulds" quietly seep into us as we grow up. They include the expectations for love, friendship, and community that are modeled by our family, schools, workplaces, neighborhoods, and the larger culture that surrounds us. We also absorb these norms through the messages transmitted by television, movies, and our social media feeds. And when our own social life doesn't mirror the cultural norms around us, we tend to feel lonely.

Ami's insight became clearer when I applied it to my own daily experience. When I walk into a coffee shop and sit down to work at a table by myself, I rarely feel lonely, since half the people in the shop are on their own, too. But if I go to a restaurant that is filled with big, boisterous families, and I am the only person who asks for a table for one, it feels different, somehow less socially acceptable and more awkward.

On a broader basis, it means that you're more likely to feel lonely if you're single and everyone you know is getting married than you'd be if all your friends were still single, too. Now, imagine that your culture didn't permit marriage at your age—or, conversely, that you were expected to be married by now, but you didn't want to. Loneliness involves a fine balance between social norms and individual needs and desires, and this balance can shift dramatically from culture to culture.

Ami pointed to Southern Europe, where family and community ties tend to be strong and relatively few people live alone, in contrast to Northern Europe, where this is less true.[6] Given that social expectations of having family and community support are much higher in Italy and Greece than they are in Sweden, where solitude is more accepted as a normal and familiar way of life,[7] what happens in Italy if your spouse dies and your family moves away or fails to show up when you need them? The more you count on them, the lonelier you're likely to feel if you find yourself without them. That phenomenon was first described by researchers as a "loneliness threshold" in which people with different cultural values and expectations need different levels of social connection. Thus, in Southern Europe, seniors who are socially isolated generally feel lonelier than do their counterparts in the north, where family isn't as frequently expected to be the primary support network.[8]

I think many of us feel pushed by modern society to be more independent, even as, deep down, we crave the interconnectedness that our ancestors depended on. There are certainly many families and communities in North America where the traditional centers of connection remain strong, but the cultural balance is trending in the opposite direction. What, then, does it look like today when a community goes all in on collectivism? I found one answer in the ethnoreligious colonies of the Hutterites.

The forebears of this Anabaptist Christian sect landed in North America in the late nineteenth century after enduring centuries of persecution in Europe. Their philosophy can be summed up by Acts 2:44 of the New Testament: "And all that believed were together, and had all things common."[9] This idea is taken seriously: private property is not permitted, and all income goes to the colony manager who then provides housing, food, and basic home goods to the rest of the colony.

Though often compared to other rural religious communities like the Amish and Mennonites, the Hutterites differ in that they embrace the use of modern farming technology.[10] Nearly five hundred colonies of Hutterites exist today in parts of Montana, the Dakotas, and Western Canada, each home to about 150 members.[11] The colonies are kept small so that everyone is accounted for and has meaningful work to do.

The Hutterites believe in self-surrender and a focus on serving one another. Within the colony, everyone is taken care of from cradle to grave. Elderly members are looked after and respected, and new mothers get help from family and community members. When a woman has a baby, a young girl between eleven and fifteen (or sometimes a young boy if no girls are available) becomes her "Sorgala,"[12] or apprentice, to help take care of the baby and any older children. The girl learns what it takes to be a parent, and the mother and her Sorgala develop a deep attachment.

Each Hutterite colony has a community kitchen where everyone takes meals together, men and women seated on opposite sides of the room. After the first bell goes off at seven a.m., the community gathers there for breakfast (children eat in an earlier shift). As the women clear up and begin preparations for the noon meal, the men take off for their respective jobs and children go to school. Everyone gathers again in the community kitchen at midday before a nap, then they finish off the day's work until evening prayer service. The day closes out with communal dinner after church and then singing, which is considered the ultimate form of entertainment for Hutterites.

Linda Maendel is a Hutterite who spent much of her life in a white wooden house she shared with her parents. Until recently, her aunt Anna lived there, too.

Linda's aunt was a beloved member of the community, and after she died, a stream of people visited to pray together and tell stories about Anna. But the neighbors didn't just stop by to talk. They took over the funeral arrangements. They did chores for the family and arranged to cover their jobs so they'd have time to grieve.

"We never had to feel overwhelmed or as if we were carrying this sorrow alone," Linda told me. "We had a whole community around for support. We were showered with encouraging songs, prayers, visits, while we were taking care of our aunt, after she passed away, and during the days leading up to the funeral and after."

In the Hutterite community, *everyone* receives this type of support. No one is left alone. With one exception: those who choose not to conform with Hutterite traditions.

As in many traditional societies, conformity is fundamental to Hutterite life. Though some may work outside the colony, individual career choices are by and large not allowed. Women and men accept traditional roles. Homosexuality is not condoned. Every Hutterite must accept the sect's faith and submit to the spiritual authority of the community head minister. Hutterites who can't or won't adhere to these conditions face excruciating disapproval, which often compels them to leave.

This is what happened to Mary-Ann Kirkby's family in 1969 after her father had a falling-out with the head minister of their Hutterite colony near Portage la Prairie, Manitoba. The family, with seven children, ended up moving not only to a town in Winnipeg but also into the modern world. In her book *I Am*

Hutterite, Mary-Ann recalled that period as "the loneliest summer of our lives."[13]

To be ejected from an intensely connected society creates a uniquely painful kind of collective loneliness. "We were so at odds," Mary-Ann told me. She and her sisters still wore their old-fashioned dresses and braids. "We stuck out like sore thumbs. Ringlets and hot pants ruled the playground. And we were so out of touch with the humor or with popular culture, and who was Walt Disney? When we heard the kids talk, we just couldn't figure anything out." In every way she felt different and lost in this new culture. "Books became my friends," she said, because books allowed her to find communities that she could understand.

Mary-Ann says it took her about ten years to feel comfortable in the "outside English world." She still considers herself a Hutterite and misses the deep commitment that Hutterites give to one another. For that reason, she's tried to stay in touch. "When we go back to a Hutterite colony today, there are no phones in the living room and every generation is there—young people, babies, middle kids, they are incurably curious. The living room is packed with women and men of all ages."

Like the gatherings I remember from my great-grandmother's house in India, all this closeness encourages sharing. "And sharing creates connection," Mary-Ann said, "because sharing our stories, reminiscing about our lives, and laughing at our own foolishness is deeply bonding." She recalled what Dr. Brené Brown, noted author and expert on shame and vulnerability, said: "People are hard to hate close up."

I first learned about the Hutterites from John Cacioppo. Recall that Cacioppo and Hawkley had shown that loneliness increases the frequency of microawakenings, those near awakenings that disturb the quality and restfulness of sleep.[14] This relationship between loneliness and microawakenings was demonstrated in the Hutterite community as well by a team of researchers led by

Lianne Kurina and Carole Ober, who also found the Hutterites have significantly lower rates of loneliness than other communities.[15] Cacioppo told me that the frequency of microawakenings in the Hutterite community was the lowest of any community he had studied.

As deeply connected as the Hutterite community is, their model as a whole is not a realistic choice for most of us. Their requirement of conformity and their restrictions on roles and privacy are incompatible with personal expectations of liberty and independence. The Hutterite stance on gender roles, sexual orientation, assigned jobs, and the requirement to contribute all your income to the community would likely rub many people the wrong way. Nevertheless, there are lessons the Hutterites can teach us about building a more connected culture.

Mary-Ann Kirkby has been following these lessons for decades now, as she lives apart from her colony of origin with her non-Hutterite husband and son. When she hosts a gathering, for example, she remembers how her childhood neighbors would ensure that time spent together was high quality. With this in mind, she tries to make meaning in every conversation. "I start with a question that we all discuss. Last time it was, 'What did your parents teach you about marriage?' Gathering together and taking the time for that is important. No phones. Just look into each other's eyes."

She also reaches out to strangers to bring them closer and help them feel connected. She told me about encountering a woman of Indian descent at her gym who seemed to be new and alone. Mary-Ann approached her because she thought perhaps she could use a friend. These small kindnesses reflect the Hutterite belief that each person is the responsibility of the community. Put another way, we take care of each other, even when we are strangers.

Many traditional societies around the world are grounded in shared history, intertwined lineage, local values, interwoven stories, and religious beliefs. As with the Hutterites, belonging is central to such cultures—so much so in South Africa that there's a special phrase in Zulu—"*Umuntu ngumuntu ngabantu*," which means "I am because you are, and you are because we are." This ideal is distilled in the term "*ubuntu*," meaning to live through others. In contrast to individualist cultures, *ubuntu* stresses one's connection to the group first, and harmony foremost.[16]

Researchers use the term "collectivist" to describe societies that structurally emphasize the group over the individual, in contrast to individualistic societies which do the opposite.[17] A third group of cultures are "in transition" from being collectivist to individualistic. Ami Rokach has found that the elderly in transitional cultures often are at particular risk of loneliness because they're accustomed to strong social support and may not know how to cope when their communities disperse. While the elderly in a country, like Norway, with individualistic traditions, may be used to living by themselves, Rokach says, the elderly who are left alone in Japan or Israel often view their aloneness as abnormal, which makes it both difficult to admit and depressing. They're also more likely to take social isolation personally, as if being alone means "I'm not worth visiting."

As easy as it may be to romanticize traditional and other collective cultures, however, it would be a mistake to think of them as an automatic antidote to loneliness. Many allow so little room for individual development and expression that a different strand of loneliness, akin to alienation, emerges if you stray outside the norms or resist the pressure to conform. When belonging is strictly conditional, even minor infractions can provoke painful repercussions. Rebels and violators of the code may be shunned or exiled. Or worse.

Honor killings of individuals accused of bringing shame on their families are an extreme example, but sadly, thousands of such killings still occur each year in South Asia, North Africa, and the Middle East. Long-simmering feuds between neighbors also can lead to group violence, splintering cultures, and war, as we've seen so tragically in Turkey, India, Rwanda, and the former Yugoslavia, not to mention the Middle East.

The roots of traditional societies are tribal, granting all the benefits of close connection to members who adhere to the community's prescribed creed and code of behavior, while opposing, and often demonizing, anyone who doesn't embrace the tribe's ideologies and rules. Like ancient tribes, traditional societies tend to be suspicious of outside influence, diversity, and change—not all of which are under an individual's control. So, as comforting as it may be to have the support of kindred friends and neighbors you've known your whole life, it also can be painfully lonely, even lethal, if your skin color, sexual orientation, or ethnicity differs from everyone else's—or if you're drawn to a prohibited vocation, religion, or lifestyle. In our own country, this is the experience of today's kids who are growing up in tightly knit extremist communities but come to question their families' values.

Derek Black was one of those kids. His father was a leader in the white nationalist movement, a former Grand Wizard of the Ku Klux Klan, and founder of the first and largest white power website, called Stormfront. Derek's godfather was David Duke, another former Grand Wizard of the KKK. Derek grew up feeling securely loved and protected. He was homeschooled by his extended family, and because they were all he knew, he never even thought to question their assumption of white supremacy until he left their tight-knit fold for college in the world "outside."

"There was a sense of meaning and purpose," he recalled when we spoke in 2019. "We felt like we were doing the right thing."

To illustrate the closeness, he told me about a cross-country road trip he took as a teenager. "I was able to stay with various people in our community whom I had never met before. It's this network of people who are connected together—and it's super fulfilling."

The problem, Derek told me, was that this closeness was based, in part, on anger and hatred toward people who were not part of the group, especially Jews and minorities. It was hard for him to empathize with outsiders because his culture emphasized their differences from him rather than their shared values or experiences, and it also painted them in a negative light.

This dilemma became profound in 2010 when Derek began his freshman year at New College of Florida. "College was the first time I saw a community that was not the one I grew up with, that I felt like I could identify with—a community that I came to care about." One of the callers to a radio show Derek cohosted with his dad had called New College "a hotbed of multiculturalism." His father acted as if Derek was on a covert intelligence-gathering mission in the enemy's liberal arts camp. But Derek was naturally inquisitive. Suddenly, he was surrounded by people of different faiths, political beliefs, and gender identities. "I wanted to understand more about what their complaints and problems were."

His hopes of doing so quietly suddenly came to an end one day when another student discovered who he was and "outed" him as a white nationalist on the college message board. He was widely condemned by much of the campus community. But not by everyone. A few fellow students reached out to connect and have thoughtful conversations with him. Their willingness to listen and share with respect and compassion gradually changed Derek's beliefs and helped him realize how destructive his original values had been. He came to reject the dogma of his family's culture, and though he tried to maintain his connection with them, they could not accept what they viewed as a betrayal of their core values. His relationship with his immediate family grew strained, and most in the white nationalist culture spurned him.

Though the break happened several years ago, it's still painful, Derek told me, and it's caused him to think long and hard about the positive and potentially negative impacts of community.

"Real meaning and purpose in community," Derek reflected, "comes from having a common cause, rooted in a common belief." Whether these beliefs are based in religion, politics, or the arts or sports, they reflect a particular vision of an ideal world. But when the beliefs that serve as a basis for connection are based on hatred and fear, they distill a poison that slowly corrodes the integrity of the community and, ultimately, the well-being of its people. This is true not just for extremists like white nationalists but also for the many less visible groups whose defining tie is rejection and hatred of others whom they view as "different."

While members of such communities may feel a sense of connection to each other, their suspicion of people unlike them makes affiliation strictly conditional, and that limits their bonds to the broader world. With this shrinkage goes trust, awareness, and understanding of others, which can intensify the sense of threat and loneliness for those, like Derek, who venture out. And few can remain entirely segregated, even by choice. In a society as diverse as ours today, we're bound to cross paths with people of varied backgrounds. To establish a sense of belonging in this society, we need to be able to recognize and appreciate our shared humanity across these variations.

This requires empathy that's unbounded by narrow strictures. We need to be free to imagine what another person is experiencing—even if that person comes from a different racial, ethnic, religious, or national heritage. We need to be willing to recognize and cultivate common interests and goals together.

This doesn't mean that we should completely ignore our differences and disagreements. But our commonalities have the potential to unify us and help us overcome the loneliness and anxiety that brew when we're in conflict. As Derek discovered, a community that reserves empathy only for its own like-minded members is destined to be alienated from the larger society. More often than not, its members are left angry, frightened, and increasingly vulnerable to loneliness as the world changes and grows around them. Connection, not hatred, is the glue that makes us feel we *all* truly belong.

A Third Bowl of Culture

I find it helpful to think of culture as the bowl in which relationships form. Depending on its size and shape, this bowl is bound to change our experience both of togetherness and of loneliness.

So, picture individualized culture as a very wide bowl of modest depth where people from all different backgrounds wander around, occasionally striking up friendships and finding kindred spirits but also spending lots of time apart. The shape of the bowl means that we're rarely forced together. There's plenty of room for everyone to choose their own path, but whether we find companions to join and help us on our path depends in part on how industrious, lucky, and determined we are in reaching out to strangers. While the culture offers so much room for exploration, variety, and change, it takes considerable effort to create common ground. Loneliness in this wide bowl can feel like aimless drifting.

The bowl of a more traditional collectivist culture, on the other hand, is narrow and deep. Common ground is literal and established at birth. People in this bowl have lived together for generations without much space to wander. All different ages and personalities mix closely together, often standing on one another's shoulders or holding one another up. People are physically as well as socially close, and that closeness is culturally cherished. However, those who don't fit within these confines, who need more room or a different kind of support, may balk at all this closeness. In the narrow bowl, loneliness can feel like a tight squeeze.

The tantalizing question is whether it's possible to create a third bowl that brings together the best of the other two. In this third bowl, the sense of common ground would be just as solid as in a traditional culture, but individuals would bond on the basis of personal choice, interests, and ideals, rather than primarily circumstances of birth.

This cultural container would preserve individual freedom of expression so people can be who they are and interact with others as they wish and need to, with solitude as desired, but it also would offer structures to prevent loneliness by engendering connection and trust and providing opportunities for gathering. Think broad and deep with pockets for bonding. Those pockets would catch people and give them a place to call home, so individuals don't fall through the cracks.

To create a third-bowl society, culture and structure clearly need to change. In Anaheim, California, I caught a glimpse of such change in action, with city leader Tom Tait at the forefront.

Tom Tait believes that one way to support our uniqueness while fostering a sense of belonging is to nurture a culture of kindness. Tom was a member of the city council in Anaheim when this idea first occurred to him more than a decade ago. He'd been noticing a mysterious poster campaign on walls scattered around the city. Each poster read: MAKE KINDNESS CONTAGIOUS. There was no ad that followed. No company listed as a sponsor. Just the message.

Tom saw his own struggles in this message. A self-described introvert, he'd long had a terror of public speaking. In school, he'd skipped any class that required an oral presentation. Yet he was drawn to public service, to the prospect of helping people. When the then-mayor appointed him to a vacant city council seat, he accepted, but he couldn't have done it without the support of friends he made in Toastmasters. They finally got him over his fear, and he wound up enjoying his time in office so much that he ran for a second term on the council.

The poster on kindness strongly resonated with Tom. "It caught my eye and lifted me up," he told me. "So I scheduled a meeting with the person responsible for putting those signs up. His name was Dr. Jaievsky."

Dr. Jaievsky's family had escaped the Nazis and fled to Argentina, where he was raised until he eventually emigrated to the United States. He told Tom that years earlier, while on vacation, his family had had a terrible accident that claimed the life of his six-year-old daughter, Natasha. He and the rest of the family were overcome with grief. But after they returned home and began going through her belongings, they found all of these beautiful notes she had written about kindness. When other children were playing games, she would sit and write. And this is what she chose to write about.

Inspired by his daughter, Dr. Jaievsky began to think more deeply about the role of kindness in healing.

"He was a holistic doctor," Tom recalled, "and he believed that in the same way healing in the body could be stimulated from within, cities, too, could heal from within through the power of kindness. That was a lightning bolt moment for me. I had ten years of treating symptoms during my time in city council in what felt like a constant game of Whac-A-Mole.

"Six years later there was an opening for mayor, and I was still thinking about kindness. I felt I had to run on this platform even though people might ridicule me. But when I announced my run and said I wanted to establish a core value of kindness in our city, I saw people's heads nodding. They understood it's what we needed." His vision of making Anaheim a city of kindness resonated so strongly that Tom won by a substantial margin.

One of the first issues he addressed in office was social disconnection—the wide bowl problem. "In our part of the country," he said, "the culture is privacy, big walls between houses, neighborhoods designed around cars which disappear into your garage, and secluded backyards." Many people didn't know their neighbors, even as they struggled to deal with hardships and illness on their own. Could kindness lead them to build relationships with each other? He didn't know, but he thought it was worth finding out.

Tom didn't even know most of his own neighbors, and he'd lived in the same place for ten years. So he initiated his "Hi Neighbor" program on his own street. Because it felt so awkward knocking on a neighbor's door to introduce himself after living there for so many years, he literally wrote a note: "Hi neighbor, I think it's important that we meet so we can look out for each other when needed." His wife, Julie, slipped this under each neighbor's door with an invitation to come over to their house one evening.

All but one of the ten neighboring families attended his get-together. After a few minutes of awkwardness, Tom piped up. "A kind act is the mortar that holds the bricks together," he said. "And it's important for keeping us safe. Community policing is based on neighbors knowing neighbors and being connected. The police also told me that criminals tend to know if neighbors are tight-knit and look out for each other, and they stay away from those neighborhoods. We're safer when we're connected."

The neighbors began talking about how they could help one another during an emergency. They talked about who had backup generators. They started to say hi to each other on the street, brought in each other's trash bins, and just helped out when they saw a neighbor in need. The way Tom saw it, these acts of kindness built social infrastructure, so he posted a "Hi Neighbor" template letter on the city's website for others to use as an outreach model.

He would say to his constituents that they were one day closer to the big earthquake, a terrorist attack, or some other disaster that may strike their community in the years ahead. He figured if a major event struck, it would take much more than the police and fire personnel to keep people safe. It would have to be people helping one another.

Tom's initiatives around kindness didn't stop there. He also launched the Million Acts of Kindness program in the Anaheim Elementary School District. Each school set an ambitious goal for kind acts for the students to meet each semester, and when they met their milestone, the entire school celebrated with a school assembly, which Tom attended as mayor. By the time they hit their district-wide target of one million acts of kindness, bullying was radically reduced, and suspensions district-wide were cut in half.

Tom envisioned kindness as the connective tissue that would bring his city together. It informed all his work as mayor, from hiring and employee evaluations to decisions on program priorities and policies. "I would step back and say, *How would a kind city respond to this problem?*" It meant accepting people's differences and fallibility while celebrating their shared community and human experience. Tom had tapped into the power of kindness to create civic structures and service initiatives that made his community safer, healthier, and more connected. Better together through kindness: this was a third-bowl approach.

When they were grappling with the opioid addiction crisis, for example, Tom asked his staff and the community to consider how they would deal with this problem with kindness. They ended up creating a successful program that engaged police officers to enter people into treatment instead of arresting them for substance use. "I wanted to send a message through the police that the community isn't here to judge you but to lend you a hand. I wanted to send a message that we're with you," Tom said. "In the first fifteen months alone, we had 270 people get into treatment. That all came from asking, *What would kindness do?*" What kindness wouldn't do was let those people drift off to fend for themselves or suffer alone.

The most impactful way to change the culture of his city, Tom found, was through his own voice. "To talk about a core value all the time and show it was important to me. That's what CEOs do. So why can't a mayor?" When he first started talking about kindness using his office as a bully pulpit, he admits, "It was like the ships were in port and nothing was happening for a couple of years. The culture wasn't changing. But then things started to click, and it was like the sails suddenly filled and the ships took off.

"Sometimes saying we need to be kind feels like it is stating the obvious," Tom said. "But it doesn't get stated, so I've had to talk a lot about kindness to make it part of our culture." Once people embrace the message, though, "kindness is contagious. Literally everything gets better if everyone is a little bit kinder."

Through such contagion, the social norms in a culture begin to shift, and it becomes more acceptable and normal to reach across social divisions to meet and help others, creating more of those third-bowl pockets for connection. When Tom visited the local schools to talk about kindness, for example, he shifted the perspective of many students. One was a boy named Sean Oliu. Now a senior in high school, Sean told me that Mayor Tait's talk back in elementary school "changed my mind-set about everything." A few months afterward, Sean won a singing competition. "*La Voz Kids*," he said, "was *The Voice* for Spanish kids and run through Telemundo—and I got a check for four thousand dollars. We didn't have any music programs in my school, so I thought, *Why don't we use this money to get a program started?*" Sean remembered what Mayor Tait had said about the power of kindness. "It was an easy decision after that." Then Sean began singing to raise money for other schools. He gathered a group of musicians—everything from mariachi to country music—to perform with him at fund-raisers. "I started a foundation called Kids Giving Back, which has continued this endeavor. In the last few years, my friends and I have raised over sixty thousand dollars, which has gone directly into schools to support music programs." As a result of Sean's kindness, some twenty-eight schools now offer music to their students—up from zero.

Eventually, people outside of Anaheim began to hear Mayor Tait's call. He connected with fellow mayors like Greg Fischer, of Louisville, Kentucky, who had launched an initiative to make his hometown a city of compassion. They met in India with the mayors of Mumbai and South Delhi to discuss how kindness and compassion could be part of their strategy to keep their cities safe and resilient.

Tom was invited to Washington, DC, to discuss how kindness could be used to build stronger connections and social resiliency from the ground up, and the US State Department Bureau of Counterterrorism invited him to meet with officials in Germany to discuss countering extremism by creating a culture of kindness. On that visit, he met a former neo-Nazi in Dusseldorf who told him it was a search for connection that initially had attracted him to the neo-Nazi movement, but what drew him away from prejudice were unexpected acts of kindness by the very people he'd been told to hate.

When Tom Tait now reflects on the many ways that he's been able to share the culture of kindness around the world, he's clear that the link between kindness and social connection is crucial. He told me about Dennis Hickey, a retired philosophy professor he'd met at a senior citizens' home, who cared deeply about kindness. "He told me there was another word I had to know: the German word '*mitsein*,' which means 'being with.' That's the higher level of kindness; that's where the action is. To be kind in the deepest way is to be with others and build connection with them."

Tom Tait has been able to strengthen the social fabric of his city—and set an example for others for a community that is both individualistic and collectivist—by showing people that everyone is worthy of kindness and that they all benefit when they are kind to one another.

Another person who's actively pursuing a third-bowl solution to disconnection is Dan Buettner, author of *The Blue Zones: Lessons for Living Longer from the People Who've Lived the Longest*.[18] Buettner has spent years identifying the areas of the world known as "blue zones," which have the statistically highest life expectancy or rate of people who live to the age of one hundred. And while he believes that most of their longevity is a function of an environment that nudges them into eating plant-based foods and moving naturally all day long, Dan has found that they also enjoy an unusually high degree of social connection.

In the blue zone of Okinawa, Japan, Buettner discovered an inspiring social system called the *moai*. The term, which means "meeting for common purpose," originally described a communal pool of funds that supported the whole village, but it's evolved to describe a social support network of close friends. In traditional times, Okinawan parents initiated a *moai* by bringing infants of similar ages together in groups of five, as if they were siblings. The families of these children supported one another, so the group grew up together and relied on one another, continuing as adults to meet daily or weekly. Today's *moai*s still help one another financially, when needed, but the "common purpose" now has more to do with companionship and advice. A *moai* is like a second family.

During his study of Okinawa, Buettner met Dr. Craig Willcox, an anthropologist and gerontologist, who had been involved in longevity research there years ago and had come to a similar conclusion about the key role social connection played in the health of Okinawans. "They live in tight communities," Willcox told me when reflecting on his findings about the Okinawan centenarians. "There is a lot of visiting behavior with people coming by each other's homes and bringing vegetables."

Willcox eventually moved to Okinawa and immersed himself in this deep and narrow bowl of culture. That included joining a few *moai*s over the years. Modern-day Okinawans are not necessarily placed in *moai*s as babies anymore. They often form their own groups later, usually around some common interest that serves as the initial basis for trust and connection. They may be from the same hometown. They might be classmates or from the same profession. Craig was part of a *moai* connected by the sea—one member was a diver, another a sailmaker, another worked on boat engines. There is still a financial component to *moai*s. Everyone chips in some money in the beginning, and it gets disbursed periodically, when one or another member has an urgent financial need. But the purpose of the modern *moai* is primarily social.

"If anyone passes away, every other *moai* member would show up" to the services, Craig said with certainty. "One of my *moai* buddies was mowing the lawn and chopped off a couple of toes. We visited him and cheered him on. Whether it's major or minor emotional crises, people help each other."

Despite the arrival of modernity, *moai*s are still alive and well in Okinawa, where Willcox estimates that many if not most residents, including young people, are part of these groups. What surprised me was that strong bonds form even when the *moai*s include community newcomers who, in many other cultures, might feel excluded and lonely. Craig attributes this to the strong emotional connections that are encouraged, where people talk to one another and share honestly and openly on a regular basis. This type of sharing is the connective tissue within *moai* culture, as kindness was in Tom Tait's Anaheim. Inclusive communal values like these are key to the creation of third-bowl cultures.

To see if the blue zones can be used as models for our own culture, Dan Buettner has established the Blue Zones Project in more than two dozen cities throughout the US. While I was surgeon general, my team reached out to him, and he was gracious enough to walk me through the work they were doing. His idea for American *moai*s was to bring people together around a common interest or activity, like cooking, or walking, or gardening. Then, Dan explained, "We nudge them into hanging out together for ten weeks. We have created *moai*s that are now several years old, and they are still exerting a healthy influence on members' lives."

Buettner's team connects people who share similar values as well as passions. Groups are initially organized for logistical convenience, based on geography and family schedules. Then everyone is given a list of questions about hobbies, musical preferences, even newspaper subscriptions, to help "stack the deck in favor of long-term relationship." The resulting communities become quite close-knit as members learn to sustain one another. Without necessarily realizing it, they are protecting themselves against loneliness at the same time that they're enhancing their health, happiness, and engagement.

My thoughts returned to Buettner's work in the summer of 2018 while I was on a fellowship retreat in Colorado Springs. It had been a year since I'd served as surgeon general, and I was still trying to figure out my next professional pursuit and how to balance that search with having two small children. Most of the time I felt like I was falling short on both fronts, and not having a close community of friends in Washington, DC, made for a lonely experience.

This was weighing on me in Colorado Springs when I ran into two friends, Sunny and Dave, who were also at the retreat. The three of us rarely see one another, but we connect deeply whenever we do. This time, no sooner had we started talking than we realized that we were all struggling with similar questions: what to do for work, how to do right by our families, and how to address the loneliness in our lives.

"I wish we saw each other more often," I said. They murmured in agreement, knowing that with our family and work commitments, we were unlikely to meet again any time soon.

That's when I realized we could create our own virtual *moai*. We agreed to meet once a month by video conference, during which we'd spend two hours (or more if needed) talking honestly about whatever was on our minds, including our joys and our challenges. We also agreed that we would be one another's source of accountability. This meant that when we discussed major challenges, we'd speak up if we felt each other's decisions didn't support our highest values. It also meant that when we made commitments for our health, such as diet, exercise, or meditation, we would keep each other honest in following through. Finally, we made a commitment to talk about the hard stuff that normally doesn't come up in routine conversations with friends: our fears, our health, and our finances.

All of these decisions turned our friendship into an intentional and valued source of connection in our ongoing lives. Instead of relying on fate or impulse to bring us together, we made an explicit commitment to be there for each other. The *moai* structure enabled us to act on that commitment. It minimized the risk that inertia would let us drift apart.

These choices made the difference for us between *having* friendship and *experiencing* friendship. And this experience has kept us honest in aspiring to live up to our highest values. In the first six months, all three of us used our *moai* to make pivotal career decisions. We made key commitments around our health and helped one another stick to them (I committed to walking at least ten thousand steps a day, cutting back on sugar from my diet, and doing a short daily meditation). We talk every month, but we also have ad hoc calls when issues come up such as a new opportunity at work or a challenge with our family. We also check in with one another regularly by text message to keep track of one another's progress, to ask for help if we're falling off course with our commitments, and to celebrate good things that happen in our lives.

A *moai* serves as a tangible, steady reminder to its members that they are not alone. It's one example of a simple strategy that can keep us connected in spite of the distances and demands built into our modern world. But the success of our *moai* also begs the question: Why is group friendship like this so rare today— especially within the culture of men?

Lonesome Cowboys

Even as the gap between the domestic and professional roles of men and women has begun to narrow, and even as we acknowledge that gender identity is complex for many individuals, traditional gender roles have created separate masculine and feminine cultures in most societies, which can affect how men and women experience loneliness and social connection. Studies have shown that men and women have roughly equal rates of loneliness.[19] But that's not to say that they express or experience loneliness in the same ways.

For Maxine Chaseling, male loneliness presented a singular challenge. Like Dan Buettner, Chaseling is what's known as a "social innovator."

The Chaseling home is in the town of Goolwa, an hour's drive south of Adelaide. Sandwiched between Australia's Kangaroo and Billygoat Islands, this historic port on the banks of the

Murray River is full of spectacular views of sand dunes and the rolling waves of the Southern Ocean. Looking out at the ocean, it's hard to imagine that following your line of sight due south for a few thousand miles will land you in the icy terrain of Antarctica. It's equally difficult to believe that this picturesque nook is the epicenter of a movement that's transformed the social lives of thousands of men around the world. But that is the change that Maxine Chaseling has catalyzed.

Maxine was doing community support work for Goolwa's elderly when, in 1987, a recession hit. A local factory closed, and many people had to retire early. That same year, her father's sixtieth year was marked by heart bypass surgery, which was successful but resulted in his sudden retirement. Maxine noticed a disturbing change in her father's mood. Overnight, he had gone from being Bill the manager to being Bill at home, and there seemed to be a void inside him that nothing could fill.

"We all knew he was unhappy and depressed," she recalled years later, but in 1987 psychological concerns were still heavily stigmatized in Australia. "Back then, it was impossible for me to say, 'Dad, you're depressed.'"

Bill's grumpiness was often directed at Maxine's mother, who just couldn't seem to do anything right in his eyes no matter how patient and understanding she tried to be. Maxine decided to intervene. She called the local Meals on Wheels and volunteered her dad as a driver to help deliver meals to people in need. The organization was ecstatic because they were in desperate need of drivers. There was only one problem: Bill had no idea these conversations were taking place.

Soon after the initial call, a representative from Meals on Wheels showed up at the house and rang the doorbell. Bill opened the door and was met with an enthusiastic handshake and an outpouring of gratitude for "stepping up for his community" and being the hero the community needed. He was confused, but the idea that the community needed him stirred something inside. So he joined the team. And he loved it.

Maxine was encouraged by what she saw: her father was becoming himself again. She decided to bump up her clandestine interventions to the next level: she called the police.

The local police oversaw the "neighborhood watch" program, and volunteers were often in short supply. After Maxine's call volunteering Bill (again without his knowledge), two uniformed policemen showed up and knocked on her father's door. "Bill, we really need you," they said. Would he help by being his neighborhood's coordinator? This official call for help had a powerful effect on Bill. It gave him a sense of purpose and connection. It convinced him that he still *mattered* to other people. He said yes to the policemen, and he enthusiastically took on his new role. Bill remained the neighborhood coordinator until the day he died.

Thanks to Maxine's initiative, her father's postretirement years became busy and fulfilling, and Bill was restored to his social self. Although he never learned how Maxine had influenced this change, her mother knew and was eternally grateful.

Meanwhile, Maxine took a closer look at other elderly men and women in Goolwa. She worked, at the time, at a community center called the Heritage Club, which offered social services such as group exercise classes, massages, and cooking lessons. There was a lounge as well, where people could meet over tea. Most, if not all, of the participants in Heritage Club programs were women. This didn't surprise Maxine, since she expected women to be more sociable than men, but she wondered what the men were doing instead.

It didn't take her long to find out. She simply needed to look out the window, where she found them in the parking lot, alone in their cars, reading the newspaper, waiting for their wives. Many spent hours like this several times a week, year after year, until they died. Their much-healthier wives then survived them as widows.

Suspecting that social disconnection was contributing to the men's declining health, Maxine thought the guys would benefit just as much as their wives from the services provided at the club.

But when she started going out to the parking lot to invite the husbands in, the answer was always a steadfast no. Women might need social programs, they told her, but men? Never!

"They were very defensive and proud," Maxine told me. "They felt if they walked in the front door of any community service operation, they were saying 'I am a sick person.'"

The mind-set of the men she encountered reminded her of her father: good at heart but stubborn, isolated, and resistant to help.

Maxine began to imagine a different space, where men could socialize together without feeling labeled as sick or lonely. She also recognized that the older men she wanted to help would not listen to advice from a woman. There was what she called "a huge barricade around the men. We can help create the environment that helps them, but we can't get them in. They are the only ones who can get past it." This would take a man's help.

A few weeks later, Alf Stokes showed up at the club to fix a cupboard. A retired carpenter with kind features, Alf had a habit of chewing on a big, unlit cigarette. He traveled with a large cattle dog, which he tied to the front of the club before coming in. Maxine described Alf as a "blokey, blokey bloke." He was the perfect man to lead the men's project. She explained it to him, and then he disappeared. Days later, she said, "I knew Alf was back because I saw his dog outside the door." He had come back to help.

Maxine and Alf both knew that the men they were trying to help were more likely to connect with one another while doing something that didn't directly focus on themselves—something like watching a game or working together. So, in 1993, they built a "men's shed" next to the club. There, men could work on carpentry, this being one of Alf's skills. They created a separate walkway from the parking lot so the men wouldn't feel conspicuous approaching the shed. They also kept Alf's dog tied to the front entrance to signal when Alf was inside. After that, men started to wander down the walkway whenever they saw the dog out front.

"We just came down to see what Alf is doing," they'd often say—then stay for hours. Initially, most just watched Alf work, but as they got more comfortable, they'd pick up some wood and start sawing, sanding, and carving. The shed was near the river, so the men began to help neighbors repair their wooden boats. Others in the community started bringing over household items for the men to help repair. The men even lent a hand to the railroad workers fixing a nearby line.

Maxine discovered that the men in the shed communicated differently from the women in the club. The men would talk occasionally while they worked, but they rarely had the sorts of long, confiding conversations that women did. Men's talk seemed to Maxine like surface conversation, yet it ended up creating an environment of comfort and familiarity.

In his book *The Men's Shed Movement: The Company of Men*, Barry Golding described it: "Women talk face to face while men talk shoulder to shoulder."[20]

As time went on, the men's group grew to ten. The shed became their refuge from a world where they often felt like they weren't understood and didn't belong. They got so comfortable being there that their wives had a hard time getting them home.

What made the shed so appealing, Maxine reflected, was that it simultaneously enabled "retired men to be productive, reclaim their networks, and enjoy themselves." Most important, Maxine deliberately took a back seat to allow the volunteer men to own the shed.

A few years after the shed opened, Maxine left Australia to work with UNICEF and the Institute for Medical Research on a variety of other health issues, but the movement she'd helped launch took off on its own. Over the next twenty years, nearly one thousand men's sheds sprouted across Australia, some spontaneous and many following Goolwa's example. Sheds began to appear in Ireland, the Netherlands, Denmark, New Zealand, Canada, the United States, and the United Kingdom. "Shoulder to shoulder," tens of thousands of men around the world to date have benefited.

I was curious to see a men's shed in action. So, on a warm fall afternoon, I pulled up to a nondescript building in the Camden Town section of London. I had come here to meet Mike Jenn, a lean, unassuming older man, balding, with tufts of white hair, a soft beard, and a relaxed expression on his face that somehow seemed to say he had the big picture in mind.

The neighborhood was packed with multiunit apartment buildings and offices, but in the middle of the day, it appeared deserted. Mike walked me up a concrete staircase to a door that could have been the entrance to anything from an office to a storage unit. As soon as I stepped over the threshold, I could hear the buzz of bandsaws, and my nostrils filled with the smell of fresh-cut wood. The space was the size of a typical modest London apartment but packed with machines, tools, and wooden pieces at various stages of production. On a small balcony overlooking the building next door, a few tree stumps were ready to be sliced and carved. I saw a partially finished decorative box with layers of beautiful colored wood. And there were handcrafted jewelry boxes and table centerpieces that were smoothly sanded and ready for use. Sawdust blew through the air and settled on every surface in the shed, but no one seemed to mind.

The shop was full of men ranging in age from their midfifties to early eighties, all working intently in their shared workspace. They measured their wood carefully and sanded with precision. I watched an elderly man with a fluffy white beard line up a long piece of wood in front of an automated saw that was rotating so fast I couldn't even make out the blades. I held my breath, hoping he wouldn't cut himself. But he cut the wood with ease and gave me a reassuring smile.

The first people who'd joined the Camden Town Shed came through word of mouth. Mike asked members of the shed to chip in what they could to help pay rent and expenses. They also began to sell the products they created to help support the shed. (One of the few rules the shed has is that you cannot use the shed to make things that you will sell for a profit.)

One of the men who joined the Camden Town Shed in those early years was Mick, a quiet, soft-spoken woodworker by trade with a tall, broad frame and hunched shoulders. Mick entered an apprenticeship when he was young, which is where he developed his skills with wood. I asked Mick what his social life had been like before he joined the shed. "I had some family around, and I would drink at the pub, where there were other guys," he told me. Later in life, he developed throat cancer, likely related to his smoking and heavy drinking. His treatment was intense and took a toll on him physically and mentally. At some point, his doctor sat him down and told him there was no point in treating him further if he was going to continue smoking and drinking. So what was he to do? He decided to join the Camden Town Shed where working with wood became his substitute for cigarettes and alcohol. Most of the other men didn't have his skills, so he taught them how to saw, cut, sand, and join pieces together. In return, they taught him about the internet and technology.

The members of the Camden Town Shed don't see each other much outside the shed, and even when they are there, they aren't sitting down to have profound, revealing conversations. So what, in fact, was happening between them?

"The shed gives men the opportunity for banter," Mike told me. "Banter is really important for men to form connections with each other."

As if on cue, Mick began ribbing one of the other men about his smoking. "He disappears every few hours and says he's taking a break, but I really know he's smoking," Mick quipped with a smile. The other man grinned, too.

Mick never used the word "lonely" to describe how he felt before he joined the men's shed, yet when I asked him to name the most valuable thing that he got out of the shed, he said it was the relationships. They filled a hole in his life that he had felt, even if he couldn't put his finger on it exactly.

A few years after Mick joined the shed, he began to notice that his eyes and skin were turning yellow. He had developed jaundice, a condition that occurs when the bile ducts are blocked, most commonly by a stone although sometimes by scarring or cancer. He was taken to the hospital for further tests and treatment, and it was discovered that he, in fact, had a new cancer. This time it was lymphoma. He underwent a course of chemotherapy, which required a lengthy stay in the hospital. And guess who came to visit during his hospitalization? His friends from the shed. Unlike his prior experience with throat cancer, he now had friends who came to support him. And it meant the world to him.

In England and other countries around the world, national shed associations continue to focus on health, which was Maxine's top priority. Sheds in Ireland have focused on addressing diabetes. Other sheds support men with Alzheimer's. The UK Men's Shed Association shared with me that participants reported a 75 percent decrease in anxiety and an 89 percent reduction in depression, along with a marked drop in loneliness. In a 2013 survey in Ireland, 86 percent of men said they felt more accepted in the community as a result of being a part of a men's shed, 97 percent said they felt better about themselves, and 74 percent said they felt happier at home.[21] In 2010, the Australian government recognized that isolation and loneliness among men were both unique and on the rise, and men's sheds were officially adopted as part of the country's National Male Health Policy.

It occurred to me that one reason for the men's shed movement's success is that it doesn't require men to admit that they're lonely. As Maxine noticed and other researchers have found, men are less likely than women to admit to feeling lonely.[22] They'll suffer in silence as if it's required of them, and, over time, their loneliness will deplete their energy, change their personalities, and erode their health.

This pattern repeats in almost every culture. Often with the best of intentions, parents the world over raise their sons to be tough and in control and to avoid acknowledging or talking about their feelings. But research has shown that boys don't necessarily start out this way. In one study, six-month-old boys were more likely than girls to show "facial expressions of anger . . . and to gesture that they wanted to be picked up." They cried more and were more likely to express joy when looking at their mothers.[23]

This unabashed delight in attachment withers, however, when boys are taught that they need to behave like "real men." Unlike girls, who tend to grow up confiding their innermost thoughts and feelings to one another, young men generally have fewer approved channels for social intimacy.

Dr. Niobe Way, a professor of developmental psychology at New York University and a leader in the field of adolescent development, says you can see the consequences of this training in the schoolyard. When we spoke, she described how in the early grades, boys will walk with their arms around one another and huddle close together as they talk. Little boys and girls tend to talk about their friendships similarly—with excitement, enthusiasm, and passion. In childhood, boys will develop deep, meaningful friendships with emotional honesty and intimacy. But as they approach puberty, they learn that social closeness is not okay.

"When I share with twelve-year-old boys the story of one of their peers who confided he feels sad and deeply hurt about friendships that are lost," Niobe told me, "the boys typically laugh. But when I tell them 85 percent of the boys I talk to say the same thing in private, they are silent. And then they start sharing about their friendships and challenges. All I have done is normalize emotions."

But when no one steps in to encourage this normalization, growing boys tell themselves they don't need to confide their feelings in friends anymore. They begin to mold themselves to a model of manhood that they believe will be desirable to women and acceptable in society. This version of masculinity, delivered through the media, as well as by their families and local culture, emphasizes independence, physical power, and emotional stoicism.

One emotion that this model allows men to express is anger. That's because anger so often ignites displays of power and toughness. As such, it's one of the few emotions a man can express and still feel masculine. But unlike feelings such as sadness, joy, and love, which invite sympathy and comfort, anger tends to push others away. So the more "manly" a boy appears, the more emotionally disconnected he can become from others.

Dr. Michael Kimmel, a sociologist specializing in the field of masculinity, does not see emotional suppression as a uniquely Western aspect of masculinity. He says virtually all cultures around the world frame traits like ambitiousness and assertiveness as masculine and qualities such as vulnerability and love as feminine. Most of these cultures also regard these feminine stereotypes as weak and inferior. The price of this emotional mutation is steep for both men and women.

For Niobe Way, growing up with brothers gave her a front-row seat on their relationships. She recalls the time when her younger brother was snubbed by his best friend. One day the two boys were nearly inseparable, and the next day his pal refused to play with him anymore. Her brother was deeply pained at the time and left wondering why his friend would cast aside their friendship. Even now, decades later, the memory of that childhood experience still makes him feel sad.

This kind of betrayal in friendship—or in romantic relationship, for that matter—can hit boys particularly hard because they don't know how to talk about it. They're left feeling ashamed and vulnerable, which adds shame on top of their pain and confusion, since vulnerability is "for girls." This compression of sadness, confusion, and shame may be one reason why teenage boys in the

US are three times more likely to kill themselves as girls the same age. And the darkness doesn't end with adolescence.

In 2016, the World Health Organization (WHO) reported that men accounted for most of the estimated 793,000 suicide deaths worldwide.[24] The BBC also reported that men are three times more likely to die by suicide in Australia,[25] three and a half times more likely in the US,[26] and more than four times more likely in Russia and Argentina.[27] In virtually every country, men are more likely to take their own lives than women are. This, in spite of the fact that women are more likely to be diagnosed with depression.[28]

Mara Grunau, executive director at the Centre for Suicide Prevention[29] in Canada, says that women are protected in part because they're encouraged at a young age to communicate their emotions. "Mothers talk way more to their girl children than their boy children," she told the BBC in 2019, "and they share and identify feelings." But boys are told to tough it out and hide any sign of vulnerability, and they are also less likely to go to the doctor or seek help.[30] We are forcing boys into a mold of "toughness" that actually leaves them emotionally defenseless.

As Niobe Way observed, when men feel emotionally isolated, they're as likely as women to feel lonely. But the harder it is for them to acknowledge their feelings, the more likely it is for their loneliness to come out as verbal abuse, short temperedness, impatience, and irritability.

Women and Loneliness

Unlike masculinity, which has traditionally revolved around power and rivalry, femininity in most cultures is rooted in relationships. Girls historically have been raised to be attentive wives, loving mothers, and helpful friends. In their 2018 essay "Cartography of a Lost Time: Mapping the Crisis of Connection," psychologists Drs. Carol Gilligan and Annie G. Rogers teamed up with communications professional Normi Noel in describing "the more puzzling aspects of women's psychology: the tendency for women to become selfless or voiceless in relationships, to care for others by diminishing themselves, to use their gifts for empathy and relationship to cover over their own feelings and thoughts, and to begin not to know what they want and know."[31] This nurturing role can make women a powerful force for building connections and weaving our social fabric. Yet when relationships falter or fail, girls and women tend to blame themselves. The resulting shame and loneliness are even more acute when women have blurred their sense of self in service of those relationships.

University of Houston professor Dr. Brené Brown has examined how shame and loneliness become particularly closely twinned for women. In *I Thought It Was Just Me: Women Reclaiming Power and Courage in a Culture of Shame*, Brown describes shame as "the intensely painful feeling or experience of believing we are flawed and therefore unworthy of acceptance and belonging."[32] The experience of shame is deeply "entangled in a web of layered, conflicting and competing social-community expectations. Shame leaves women feeling trapped, powerless and isolated."[33]

It might seem as if some women are immune to these forces. When women are confident, successful, and socially engaged, they can appear especially invulnerable. Keeping up that appearance, however, can itself contribute to loneliness when these women feel they cannot reach out in times of need.

Gina Clayton-Johnson was one of these women. As a University of Southern California undergrad, she became a youth organizer for the NAACP. She led campaigns on campus policing, state sentencing laws, and voter registration. Social justice was her passion and civil rights activists were her people. When she entered Harvard Law School, she quickly began connecting with like-minded friends who reaffirmed her commitment to criminal justice reform. Loneliness was not even on her radar. But midway through her first year of law school, Gina learned that someone close to her had been sentenced to twenty years in prison. The news not only broke her heart, it also drove her to secrecy.

"Something told me I couldn't share this with the people at Harvard," Gina told me years later.

That something was shame. Gina so respected her professors and colleagues, so wanted to be part of this community, that she didn't dare tell them her secret for fear they'd think less of her— for fear that they would reject her, even though this was the very community that worked to help people like her incarcerated loved one. The irony wasn't lost on her, but she still couldn't bring herself to tell anyone.

That all changed when after graduating and starting work at New York City's Neighborhood Defender Service of Harlem, she was assigned to represent an elderly grandmother named Sondria. Sondria was being evicted by the city under the claim that her home was a hub for criminal activity. The claim traced back to Sondria's grandson, who'd been arrested by the police and gave his grandmother's address in a moment of panic, even though he lived elsewhere. Despite Sondria's clean tenancy record of almost twenty years in that apartment and community, the authorities accused her of violating tenancy laws and moved to terminate her tenancy in a legal proceeding.

Gina knew many women like Sondria. They spent much of their lives toiling away to support loved ones who were incarcerated. Many felt they had little power to affect the world around them, especially within the criminal justice system. And, like Gina herself, they carried a sense of shame about their predicament. One by one, the links that gave them a sense of belonging and hope had eroded or broken, leaving them largely defenseless. When Sondria asked how long it would be before she was evicted, Gina sensed that her client, too, was giving up.

Searching for a way to persuade Sondria to stand up for her rights, Gina decided it was finally time to share her own secret. She looked Sondria in the eye and told her that she, too, had a loved one in prison. She shared the sense of embarrassment she'd felt when the news arrived, the four years of hiding the truth from her classmates and colleagues, the loneliness that ensued as she kept one of the most important parts of her life sealed off from her community.

As she shared her story, Gina could see a light of recognition glimmer as Sondria realized she was not alone. She was tired and worried, but Gina's sincerity and vulnerability connected with her and forged a bond of trust. This young lawyer understood what she was going through.

The power of connection was mutual. Like Sondria, Gina felt seen and heard in a way she hadn't in a long time. It required taking a risk and being vulnerable. It required faith that she wouldn't be rejected for telling the truth. But it felt good to finally bring herself—all of herself—to this connection.

Gina's belief and conviction rubbed off on Sondria, and she agreed to fight. It took many hard months, but together they prevailed. Sondria was able to stay in her home, and Gina found the inspiration for the work to which she would dedicate her life—bringing women with incarcerated family members out of isolation to support one another and advocate for more humane criminal justice policies.

When women like Gina Clayton-Johnson feel torn between hiding some shameful part of themselves or losing their community, they often choose to bury other true feelings along with the shame. Rosalind Wiseman, author of *Queen Bees and Wannabes*,[34] watched a similar struggle play out many times during the decade that she spent studying friendship in children.

"Girls have a feeling of constant comparison," Wiseman told me. This comparison exposes them to the shame of social failure and increases their risk of loneliness. "There's a fear of missing out, yet you can never keep up."

Lots of teenage friendships are healthy, of course, and Wiseman emphasized that they can be invaluable. "Many girls will make it through their teen years precisely because they have the support and care of a few good friends. These are the friendships in which a girl truly feels unconditionally accepted, understood, and sometimes even challenged when she's doing something that's not good for her—like dating someone who doesn't treat her with respect." And through these high-quality friendships, girls learn how to form and maintain nourishing relationships later in life.

At the same time, she went on, "Girls' friendships are often intense, confusing, frustrating, and humiliating." The joy and security of "best friendships" can be shattered by devastating breakups and betrayals. And the very importance that friendship plays in the identity of young women can make them vulnerable to hurtful relationships that they mistake as friendships. When girls can't navigate the social currents, that resulting shame can extend far beyond childhood. "Girls can develop patterns of behavior and expectations for future relationships that stop them from having healthy relationships with others as adults." And that can place them at heightened risk for loneliness.

That said, Wiseman takes care to point out that boys and girls *both* need meaningful relationships. "Sometimes we make judgments about girls' friendships being deeper, but that is absolutely not backed up by the research. When we look at girls who are talking all the time on Instagram, we might think those relationships are more intimate than boys who aren't talking so much. That's not true. Boys' friendship breakups are equally as devastating to them."

Despite the different cultural expectations that men and women absorb as they come of age, the truth is that people don't fall neatly into categories of social behavior or attitudes. Gendered norms may be deeply influential for some people (often with particularly complex effects on the lives of gay and transgender individuals—a subject deserving of an entire book), but others are more affected by factors such as personality or the particular attitudes within their families. It's important to recognize, however, that the broader cultural layers surround us all, dovetailing with other cultural imperatives to shape the ease, frequency, and quality of our social connections, as well as our relative risk for loneliness.

Together, the various aspects of cultures set the stage for our expectations of others, and they drive our own social behavior and aspirations. Cultural values reflect prevailing attitudes about what matters and how to direct our lives—attitudes so pervasive that they sometimes override our personal desires and priorities. Yet few of us challenge our cultural norms, even when their influence leaves us feeling lonely and isolated. Why is that?

In part, it's because we still carry the default wiring of our ancestors within us. For countless generations, human beings were bound to the land where they were born and the members of their immediate tribe. Culture was inherited and adopted without question, and belonging was not just about togetherness; it was also about defense against predators and enemies. In other words, culture was bundled up with fear of known threats and others who *might* be hostile. As a result, our wiring signals us that we need to belong to our people in order to feel safe, and that we need to avoid or shun others, for fear they can't be trusted. We see these instincts still playing out in the social behavior of teenagers, and we see them contributing to xenophobia, racism, and political hostilities. Evolution is slow to catch up with rapid societal change.

But societal change is every bit as real as the signals flashing through our emotional wiring, and therein lies the tension. We no longer live in a world of isolated and insular tribes and villages. We no longer are likely to stay in one location with the same group of people for our whole lives. We no longer have any rational justification for attacking or excluding others simply because they don't look like us. Nor are we condemned to wander in the wilderness alone forever if we don't fit into the community where we're born. We're still wired as if all those conditions were true, but they're not.

The simple reality is that we no longer have the luxury of thinking and acting tribally. Not only is it becoming harder to isolate ourselves from members of different cultures, but isolation costs us in terms of perspective and experience, which are ever more valuable resources in our global society. My view is that we have veered too far away from the group and toward the individual—throwing culture out of balance in the process—more out of benign neglect than anything else. We've emphasized freedom of individual expression without also ensuring that the underpinnings of community are protected and strengthened. Now we need to recapture our investment in the collective elements that matter—our relationships, our community organizations, our neighborhoods, our social and cultural institutions—and we must do this while continuing to protect individual expression.

We may have to make some sacrifices to be part of a community, and that's good. Giving and serving others doesn't just strengthen our communities; it enriches our lives and strengthens our own bonds to the community and our sense of value and purpose. It protects us against loneliness. But in order to come together, we shouldn't have to deny or hide the parts of us that make us who we are. As Tom Tait proved in Anaheim, kindness can play a vital role in this balancing act, which makes it an essential element of third-bowl cultures. Kindness can bridge the divides between us, healing our society even as it relieves our personal loneliness and brings us together.

Building such bridges for connection may never have been more important than it is right now. This urgency can only partially be explained by culture, however. The other reasons, writ large, are the pace, variety, and pressures of global change.

CHAPTER 4

Why Now?

Lots of people want to ride with you in the limo, but what you want is someone who will take the bus with you when the limo breaks down.

—Oprah Winfrey

This world of ours . . . must avoid becoming a community of dreadful fear and hate, and be, instead, a proud confederation of mutual trust and respect.

—President Dwight D. Eisenhower, Farewell Address to the Nation

The experience of loneliness may be as old as humanity, but the current moment feels like an important inflection point. Two decades ago in his book *Bowling Alone*, Robert Putnam famously described the erosion of social networks and social norms in the US that began in the latter third of the twentieth century. His research found that various measures of social engagement had declined precipitously—including religious participation, membership in community organizations, and the frequency with which people were inviting friends to their homes.[1] According to Putnam, many of these trends have only worsened in the years since his seminal publication.[2]

If you ask people today what they value most in life, most will point to family and friends. Yet the way we spend our days is often at odds with that value. Our twenty-first-century world demands that we focus on pursuits that seem to be in constant competition for our time, attention, energy, and commitment. Many of these pursuits are themselves competitions. We compete for jobs and status. We compete over possessions, money, and reputation. We strive to stay afloat and to get ahead. Meanwhile, the relationships we claim to prize often get neglected in the chase.

Modern progress has brought unprecedented advances that make it easier for us technically to connect, but often these advances create unforeseen challenges that make us feel more alone and disconnected. Thanks to advances in transportation, it's easier than ever to visit friends and family, yet increased mobility also means that more and more of us are living far away from our loved ones. Thanks to advances in medicine, many of us are living longer than we ever imagined—but inevitably, we lose many of our friends along the way. And thanks to advances in technology, we can enjoy all the conveniences of community without directly interacting with other people. We can have whole meals delivered without setting foot in the restaurants that produced them; stream movies online and watch them alone at home instead of in a crowded theater; and order nearly anything imaginable from online shopping sites, never even seeing the messenger who deposits the goods at our door. Many of us also telecommute, interacting with customers and colleagues virtually, if at all. Human connection is being edged out, or at best left to fit in around the edges.

As a management consultant, Amy Gallo had to confront many of these changes while traveling around the world. Today Amy is a contributing editor at *Harvard Business Review*, but early in her career she worked for a consulting firm based in New York, with a special focus on the unofficial networks and communities in organizations that govern how people work together in practice. Despite her specialty in workplace connection, however, she often struggled with a personal sense of profound disconnection, especially when her assignments sent her thousands of miles from home.

For one project she spent four months in South Korea, where she knew no one, didn't speak the language, and lived in a hotel. What saved her, she said, were three American colleagues who were there from the same consulting firm. The irony is that this random group's loneliness became their common ground. "These are people I probably wouldn't have chosen to be friends with," she said, "but being thrust into the situation where we all felt so disconnected, we formed quite an emotional bond together."

Another job required Amy and her colleagues to visit DC every couple of weeks, so each time they checked out of their hotel, they'd book rooms for the next trip. One week, only one room was available. Amy's female colleague suggested they share it.

"I must have looked at her like she had four heads," Amy recalled, "because that was the last thing I wanted to do." The two women liked each other, but their connection to that point had been superficial. "I joke that she probably would have shared the room with anyone. She's such an extrovert that way, and I'm not. But I just thought, *Oh well.*"

When they roomed together, they found that they had more in common than they'd realized. In fact, they liked each other so much that they opted to room together over the next six weeks on that project and wound up becoming friends and remain close to this day.

When I asked what it was that made this connection stick, Amy said, "I really felt like I could be myself. We talked about work, of course, but we also talked about life. She had gone through a bad breakup. We talked a lot about what we wanted from career and life." Such openness and mutual support are rare in today's hectic world—especially among globe-trotting businesspeople who do much of their work remotely.

A major cause of loneliness for business travelers, Amy explained, is the transactional nature of interactions on the road. She was talking not only about customers and clients but also the everyday contacts that occur during travel. "The flight attendant maybe acted like she cared about me," Amy said, "but it was her job to, and the same with the bellman at the hotel. It was all about getting from one place to another, paying people to do things for me and then going to another place. And sometimes I would have traveled with colleagues or met clients that I liked, but there was just no emotional component to it."

The problem of estrangement isn't limited to businesspeople or to world travelers. In exchange for efficiency, we're all letting more and more genuine human contact slip from our daily lives. I remember being jubilant when online grocery delivery services arrived on the scene. I told Alice that they'd liberate us from all that time trekking back and forth to the store. But those grocery store visits were when we met friends in our neighborhood sorting through produce or trying to make sense of baby food options. They were where we got to know the clerks who helped us track down hard-to-find items, where we commiserated with fellow parents over crying children. These seemingly small interactions were an important part of what kept us connected to the larger fabric of our local community. They contributed to our sense of belonging.

The biggest challenge we face in staying connected may be the sheer pace of change. Humans are built to adapt and evolve, but we need time to process new information and systems of behavior, to adjust to new societal rules and expectations. New technologies used to take a long time to test, develop, and catch on. As Rita Gunther McGrath wrote in *Harvard Business Review*,[3] before 1900, it took decades for the telephone to reach half the households in America. A century later, cell phones made that leap in just five years. And the pace is constantly accelerating. It took manufacturers approximately sixty months to design a car in 2008, and just five years later the design cycle was about half that. This dizzying speed means that, like the fabled Sorcerer's Apprentice, we barely have time to get used to one innovation before it's replaced by multiple new apps, devices, or platforms. Technology dares us to keep up.

This unspoken dare creates an underlying tension within the social fabric. Those who can't keep up get left behind, while those who can are constantly chasing the next new thing. They do this not just out of curiosity but because "keeping up" has become synonymous with having a competitive edge. Whether we realize it or not, the pace of change has created the impression that we have only two choices: adapt quickly to stay marketable, employable, and desirable; or fall back and lose out. This sets up a state of competition between tradition and innovation, between old and young, between online and physical communities, and between transactional and human interactions. These pervasive tensions make modern loneliness different than anything previous generations ever experienced.

Shifting social networks now often preempt family networks. We have robots that function as companions for our elderly, and virtual playmates that replace human friends. Games in cyberspace keep kids in rooms by themselves instead of engaging in face-to-face interactions with their peers. And this all has happened so fast that few of us even realize what these changes are doing to our social lives, skills, and spirits. In fact, we are being tossed like twigs in a stiff breeze, unable to get our bearings as we unwittingly lose sight of what matters and who matters to us. We still have the wiring for connection within us, but the more time and attention we lavish on racing to be current, the greater the risk we run that our innate social systems will falter and fail us due to neglect.

Online All the Time

When I first joined Facebook, Twitter, and Instagram, I thought they'd be great ways to stay connected to friends and engage in community conversations. I remember the first days of finding long-lost classmates and friends on Facebook and feeling happy to see their faces in photos smiling back at me. But while it was nice to be able to reach a wide group of friends online, I found that we weren't really having the meaningful dialogues I craved. Instead, as I absorbed the thrilling adventures, impressive career promotions, and stunning achievements reflected in my friends' posts, I felt inspired 25 percent of the time and inadequate 100 percent of the time. As one friend put it, checking your social media feed is like comparing everyone's best days to your average days—and you always come up short.

I noticed something else that disturbed me. I originally began posting on social media to share experiences and reflections with friends. But soon I found myself preoccupied with how many people would like, comment, and share my content. I remember posting a reflection on 9/11 during one of the anniversaries and feeling the genuine emotion that I'd poured into the piece dissolving as I kept checking to see if people liked the post. It turned an authentic act of expression into a hollow exercise. Chasing validation like that made me feel bad about myself.

Finally, I decided to take a break—no posting and no checking my feed. Social media participation had become a discouraging performance, and I was done with it. I deleted the apps from my phone and logged out of my accounts on my computer. After dealing with the initial few days of twitchiness as I instinctively tried to check my feed and wondered if I was missing something, I started to feel less distracted and less concerned about seeking digital validation from the outside world. I can't emphasize enough how freeing this was.

After many months off, I reengaged on very limited terms. I decided to only post if really moved to do so (like when Alice gave a moving, heartfelt talk in Louisville, Kentucky). And perhaps more important, I decided not to check for comments, likes, and retweets. I dramatically reduced the number of people I follow so my feed focuses more on posts that enrich my sense of connection and understanding of the world. I'm still seeing if it is possible to achieve a balance where I can interact with social media on my terms. The jury is still out.

The jury is also still out on the overall psychological costs and benefits of society's increasing symbiosis with digital technology. In January of 2019, researchers Drs. Amy Orben and Andrew Przybylski at the University of Oxford[4] published surprising findings that digital screen time has a negative but overall very small effect on the well-being of adolescents' social behavior. After crunching the data on more than 350,000 adolescents, they concluded that smoking marijuana and bullying do far more damage than use of digital technology. Przybylski and his colleague Dr. Netta Weinstein had previously shown that the amount of time spent in front of screens makes a difference in overall impact.[5] According to this "Goldilocks hypothesis," the mental well-being of adolescents does not appear to be harmed if they're spending one to two hours per day in front of screens, but much more than that can be detrimental. Interestingly, kids with zero screen time seemed worse off than those with moderate use, possibly because in a world where everyone around you is online, having no participation could lead to a sense of being left out and isolated.

In 2017, University of Pittsburgh professor Dr. Brian Primack and his colleagues found further evidence that high levels of social media use can be harmful, in this case contributing to loneliness. They studied 1,787 subjects between the ages of nineteen and thirty-two. One group of these young adults spent more than two hours a day on social media, the other just half an hour or less. All were asked to use a scale to describe how much or how little the following statements applied to them:

❖ I feel left out

❖ I feel that people barely know me

❖ I feel isolated from others

❖ I feel that people are around me but not with me.[6]

The Pittsburgh researchers found that the heavy social media users were twice as likely to feel lonely as those in the low-use group.[7] These results echoed concerns raised in a similar study, which found that heavy social media users are more likely to be depressed.[8]

All these findings raise the old chicken-and-egg question of which comes first. Are lonely, depressed people trying to *escape* into social media? Or does too much social media *make* people lonely and depressed? It could be the case that social media use is driving the outcomes of concern, but it will take more research to prove that. And use of these platforms is so prevalent and begins at such a young age that establishing rigorous research controls is challenging.

Amy Orben emphasizes that "we are really at the very beginning" of understanding the full impact of technology on people. When we spoke, she noted that much of the data on digital media usage is proprietary corporate data that isn't often accessible to the research community. This makes getting answers about the impact of technology more difficult. She also suggests that *how* we are using our screen-based devices may be more important than *how much* we are using them. A few minutes of harmful content for a susceptible child in the wrong circumstances could be devastating whereas an hour of screen time as part of a rich family experience might be very positive. "The problem is we're focusing so much on time spent on screens but not focusing enough on the content, type of technology, or motivation to use it," she said.

As we learn more about these various dimensions of technology, it is increasingly clear that technology holds mixed blessings for us. Social media can help people find meaningful connections, especially when they come from communities that have traditionally been isolated or marginalized. But in the wrong circumstances, it can exacerbate loneliness by amplifying comparison, enabling bullying, and substituting lower- for higher-quality relationships.

Balancing our use of these platforms, however, is not a simple matter. Social media has woven its way into our social and professional lives. If you're a reporter, you can't afford to turn off Twitter entirely. If you're looking for a new job, having a profile and being on LinkedIn may be essential. If your family and friends use social media to announce major life events or get-togethers, and you're not on that platform, you can find yourself in the dark.

Add to that the fact that today's social media platforms are developed with a highly sophisticated understanding of human behavior and brain science. Software engineers use all manner of techniques—from autoplay on YouTube to streaks on Snapchat, to interaction notifications on Instagram, Twitter, and Facebook—to keep bringing us back and to hold our attention on their platforms for as long as possible. In most cases, the economic measure of a successful app is not the quality of human interaction online but sheer quantity of usage. The more time we spend on the platform, the more revenue it generates, usually in the form of advertisements. In other words, our time is social media's money. In this way, apps have become the quintessential products of the attention economy.

One might ask, *Isn't it the responsibility of the user to exercise willpower and moderate their use?* In theory, yes. But in practice, to do so we must overcome deeply ingrained behavioral instincts that have been honed over millennia.

To greater and lesser degrees, we're all novelty seekers, and the internet is all about novelty. As soon as we click on a link, we're transported into a new site, a new product, a new virtual experience. As soon as we send a message or publish a post, followers and friends react with nearly instantaneous speed. This pace, made possible by online technology, creates a personal sense of urgency and importance, as if the world were waiting with bated breath for our next post. It also generates anticipation, which is why we feel a stab of rejection whenever we post and responses lag. The internet's feedback loop is as seductive as a new suitor and relies on the brain's very same reward systems as romance and friendship do. For some, the effect is so compelling and the ease of use so convenient that virtual relationships gradually replace face-to-face contact.

How often have you meant to spend five minutes checking your friends' posts only to end up spending an hour? You message a friend on Facebook, then bounce from profile to profile, checking out the cats, meals, and travels of people you barely even know. We may tell ourselves these online forays are just diversions, but they're stealing time that we could be spending in real life with family and friends.

This theft of time is abetted by the seductive and dangerous myth of multitasking. Technology—smartphones in particular—has promoted this myth like never before. All of a sudden, we can talk on the phone, send emails, pay our bills, order our groceries, and travel across town, all at the same time. It seems easy. And efficient. It creates the illusion that we can satisfy our curiosity in a dozen directions at once, simultaneously hearing a friend's story about his new baby, checking out a neighbor's vacation photos, picking up a text about a parent's trip to the doctor, and Googling the latest news about our favorite sports team. In fact, when we multitask, we're splitting our attention into smaller and smaller fragments, reducing efficiency and diminishing the quality of engagement we bring to each task.

Research has found that humans are incapable of attending to multiple activities at once. What we're actually doing when "multitasking" is switching back and forth very rapidly between tasks, attending to each one separately but briefly. As MIT neuroscientist Dr. Earl Miller explained in a 2008 interview on NPR,[9] "Switching from task to task, you think you're actually paying attention to everything around you at the same time. But you're actually not."

In the middle of a conversation, for instance, when stealing a look at our cell phone, we may hear and remember the words that are spoken, but we won't process the words and nonverbal cues nearly as quickly or completely. One reason for this is that tasks involving communication compete for the same pathways within the brain. "Those things are nearly impossible to do at the same time," Miller said. "You cannot focus on one while doing the other."

All this flipping back and forth actually costs us *more* time and energy in the end because it takes an average of twenty-three minutes to fully reengage[10] with our original subject of focus. In combination with technology, it also distorts our sense of the value of actual contact with friends. It's easy to passively scroll through our feed and see what friends are doing, or text for a quick update that creates the illusion we're keeping up with our friends. It requires much more energy and time to make a date, get ready, and physically go out to meet those same friends. But before we know it, days, weeks, or months can go by without a sincere or meaningful conversation. When that happens, it can feel like even harder work to see friends in person. But that interpersonal work delivers social benefits that the illusion of online friendship rarely does.

Stanford sociology professor Dr. Paolo Parigi[11] has been studying the effects of online reputations on personal relationships, and his findings are as complex as they are surprising. His subjects are users of networking services such as Airbnb and Uber, and his premise is that online reputations, which users build through services' apps, function as a form of social introduction. In the peer-to-peer marketplace, before you and your Uber driver or Airbnb host ever meet, you have a wealth of preliminary information about each other, which is distilled into a rating. This, in effect, crowdsources your trust in each other.

One real benefit of this ratings system, Parigi said in a 2018 interview,[12] is that it overrides superficial biases and increases the diversity of interactions in our daily lives. "What we found was that if you were interacting with someone who was different from you, but had a good reputation, using [the] Airbnb style of reputation (ratings and reviews), you were more likely to trust that person." However, the trust that forms as a result of these interactions is highly limited.

One reason for this is that the reputations we build online are conditional. Uber passengers feel comfortable trusting drivers to get them safely where they need to go, but not to housesit for them. Airbnb hosts trust their guests to be responsible with their belongings, but not to tend their elderly parents. App ratings produce what Parigi calls "thin" reputations, as opposed to reputations developed through direct personal familiarity over time.

"There used to be a process through which you would discover these commonalities," he explained in the interview. "And this process of discovering was the process that made the friendship. Now, this process has either been accelerated or removed. The information is available to you right up front. And so, there's no discovery process."

Parigi put this idea to the test with the hospitality networking app CouchSurfing, which connects travelers with hosts who allow them to stay in their homes without charge. The original assumption behind this service was that free stays would form the basis for lasting friendships. And there's no question about the popularity of the platform. Since launching in 2004, the CouchSurfing community has grown to fourteen million travelers and four hundred thousand hosts. But what about those friendships?

Parigi compared them with friendships that developed organically between offline hosts and travelers. "What we found is that when the couch surfer had more information about that other person he or she was going to meet, the resulting friendship after they met was weaker than in a world where the couch surfers did not have that amount of information about the unknown other." Virtually front-loading the relationship with social information, it seemed, was a trade-off that eased entry but made the resulting connection "less binding."[13]

In contrast, the effort that the group with less up-front information had to put into learning about each other from the ground up actually paid off in friendship. It's not just what we know about each other that counts, it's how we get to know it. And time and attention, with a little struggle thrown in, can make a real difference in strengthening connection.

What this means, Parigi says, is that technology might make us less isolated, but the more of these easy connections we substitute for old-fashioned hard-won friendship, the lonelier we'll feel. He explains, "This is to me the tension of modern or contemporary life. . . . You have a lot of connections, but do they mean what they used to?"

MIT professor Dr. Sherry Turkle is even more emphatic. She says, "We're losing the raw, human part of being with each other."[14] Turkle has spent the last three decades researching the psychology of people's relationships with technology. Her books have focused on the importance of conversation in digital cultures and technology's influence on relationships between friends, lovers, parents and children, and community, intimacy, and solitude. When we're on the digital tether, she says, we're not fully present in either our virtual or our physical life. Also, we're not fooling anyone. Others can tell when we're not paying attention, and it makes them less likely to share as much or as deeply.

No wonder the constant presence of our phones and other communication technology has been shown to reduce the emotional quality of our conversations. As Andrew Przybylski and Netta Weinstein found in their experiments, the mere sight of phones during conversation negatively impacted "the extent to which individuals felt empathy and understanding from their partners."[15]

This is concerning given how many of us bring our phones to the dinner table and family gatherings. No doubt, we try to be subtle about it. We put our phones facedown, move them off to the side, even cover them with napkins. We've also tried to convince ourselves that there is an acceptable etiquette around texting during conversations. I've been told that if you're texting but maintain eye contact with the person talking, then it isn't rude. I've also heard that, as long as someone else in the conversation is maintaining eye contact with the person talking, it's okay to look down to check your messages or send a text. But none of these strategies protect the integrity and quality of our conversations.

This increasingly common phenomenon of people snubbing each other in favor of their phone even has a term: phubbing. A 2015 study that surveyed 453 US adults found that 46.3 percent of respondents said their partner had phubbed them. A second survey found that those whose partners phubbed them reported more fights and less relationship satisfaction than those where phubbing was less frequent.[16]

The way in which we use technology can not only distract from in-person interactions, but it can also create distance between us and others. Not having to look people in the face when we're commenting on social media shields us from having to deal with their reaction or the pain our words may cause. That said, it is also common for social media to allow users a window into the lives of other people they may not have been able to glimpse. In doing so, it can give us opportunities to understand and engage in positive ways with a greater number of people. Simply put, there is a difference between doling out a harsh zinger to put someone in their place in an online forum versus reaching out and offering support to a friend who just posted about a personal hardship. It all comes down to how we choose to use social media and digital technology.

While the impact of technology on empathy may be mixed, what's happening to empathy in the population at large seems to be more clear. In 2010, researchers at the University of Michigan found empathy scores among college students had dropped about 40 percent from 1979 to 2009, with the biggest drop coming after 2000.[17]

The good news is that we have the capacity to recover. Dr. Yalda Uhls showed this with a landmark study that she designed while pursuing her PhD in psychology in 2012. Alarmed by the 2010 data showing that young people between eight and eighteen spend over seven and a half hours each day of the week using screen-based media outside of school,[18] she wanted to know what would happen if we replaced screen time with face time. So she studied one group of about fifty public school students who were attending a weeklong outdoor education camp where television, phones, and computers were not allowed. Another group of fifty, still at school, were instructed to continue their media use as usual. The students in each group were tested before and after the study period to assess their capacity for interpreting emotional states in still photographs and video. What Uhls found is that the camp group had a significantly greater boost in scores than the control group on both tests.[19]

Whether the impact of camp was creating distance from technology or spending time together in nature, Sherry Turkle points to Uhls's findings as evidence of resilience. "In only five days in a sleepaway camp without their phones, empathy levels come back up. How does this happen? The campers talk to each other."[20]

But detaching from technology is more difficult if we use it as an emotional escape, to avoid sadness, conflict, disappointment—and the hard, deep work of relationship. Instead of meeting in person to talk about misunderstandings or find shared solutions to real problems, we can just slip into cyberspace and spend hours among "friends" who won't ask the hard questions. It is an easier path—but one that ultimately leads to more loneliness.

While loneliness rates vary in studies, researchers have found that adolescence and young adulthood into the early thirties is a period when loneliness can rise (in addition to peaks observed in the fifties and eighties).[21 22 23] For this reason, clinical psychologist Dr. Catherine Steiner-Adair interviewed 1,250 children, adolescents, and young adults for her 2014 book *The Big Disconnect*.[24] The social tragedy of youth in the digital age, Steiner-Adair told me, was summed up for her by one particularly eloquent young woman: "It's so ironic. We're the most connected generation in history. But we suck at falling in love. We don't know how to flirt. We get shit-faced and hook up. And we don't even meet up before that; you text somebody at two fifteen a.m. *Hey, what's up?* Everyone knows it's a booty call. You don't even go out for a drink. And the really sad thing is we don't know how to be vulnerable. We don't know how to pick up the phone and say, 'Hey, I really like you. Hey, I'm feeling sad. Hey, would you like to go out on a date?'"

Steiner-Adair says many of these children have grown up on the receiving end of their parents' disconnection. "Little kids, middle school, high school, adults, young adults used the same words—sad, mad, lonely, angry, frustrated—trying to get their parents to be present and emotionally tuned in to them, because their parents are so digitally distracted." Yet the kids end up modeling their own behavior on their parents'."

Distraction is not the only reason that technology can interfere with high-quality connections. As I found before paring back my Facebook usage, social media also fosters a culture of comparison where we are constantly measuring ourselves against other users' bodies, wardrobes, cooking, houses, vacations, children, pets, hobbies, and thoughts about the world. It's a bit like a continuous high school reunion, where everyone is "sharing" their accomplishments, victories, and delights, vying to prove their worth. Some may simply want to share joy with friends, but the net result often is a curated portrait of seemingly perfect lives, which in turn can make us feel anxious, depressed, and worse about ourselves by comparison. And the most susceptible are young people, who are still in the process of defining their identities and goals.

When we're making comparisons online, we're not just rating ourselves. We're also comparing our various options in possessions, jobs, activities—and potential friends and partners. The digital pipeline presents us with a seemingly endless supply. Swipe left. Swipe right. Over and over and over. Certainty about our choices can quickly falter when the virtual supply chain promises to present us with ever better, brighter alternatives the next time we log on. Once we've selected our roommates, friends, and intimate partners, we'll have to do the messy offline work of getting to know one another's true complexity, and we might not love what we find. The allure of the "perfect" match, then, is a powerful deterrent to commitment. But perfection is an illusion that technology and modern culture cultivate at the expense of humanity. The perpetual cruising, the endless chase for the ideal companion is bound to leave us anxious and lonely.

The irony is that our capacity for solitude also is diminished by technology. Social media's constant presence creates the illusion that we never need to be alone—and that something must be wrong with us if we _feel_ alone. Yet we still need solitude, as well as the time and space to cultivate its benefits. We need regularly to free our minds to wander and explore without being directed by network algorithms and autoplay ads. Solitude allows us to get comfortable being with ourselves, which makes it easier to _be_ ourselves in interactions with others. That authenticity helps build strong connections.

To be real is to be vulnerable, and this takes courage, especially if we believe that others will like us more if we hide or distort who we truly are. Technology can promote this belief by making it easy to pose online as someone braver, happier, better looking, and more successful than we really feel. These poses, in fact, are a form of social withdrawal. They may let us pretend that we're more accepted, but the pretense only intensifies our loneliness.

Not all the effects of social media and technology are negative, of course. Technology can also facilitate _better_ connections. It all depends on how it is designed and used. Platforms like Skype allow students to attend classes across the country and businesspeople to confer with clients and colleagues on other continents. Social media can also allow people who are isolated due to disability or illness, or because they belong to marginalized groups, to find communities with which to connect. They can help us reconnect with long-lost friends. And they give us all a way to more easily share important moments like the birth of a child or the loss of a loved one with our friend networks, linking us to sources of support.

The point is that the more our lifestyle evolves to maximize efficiency at the expense of human interaction, the more focused we must become in directing our use of technology to facilitate deeper personal connections.

I learned the positive power of Facebook firsthand in its earliest days, when I decided to search for two old friends from business school. I didn't know where they lived or what career paths they'd pursued after graduation. All I had to go on were their names and those of our mutual friends, but thanks to the magic of Facebook, I eventually found Vinni and Shareen and sent them a message. They replied (I found out they were married and lived in Washington, DC), and over the next few years, we stayed in touch by email and phone. I started to visit their hometown for work, and whenever I traveled there, I stayed with them. They became my surrogate family—and I had Facebook to thank for that.

Modern communication technology can also bring our actual families closer. I remember as a child mailing blue single-paged aerograms to faraway relatives in India and filling every possible space on the paper. It took two weeks for the aerograms to be delivered, and we had to wait an additional two weeks or more for a reply to make its way back halfway across the world. Today, thanks to video-conferencing technology, my children can share a virtual meal anytime with their grandparents across the country. When I'm away on an overnight trip, I can still admire my son's latest artistic creation or cheer on my daughter as she toddles around the house.

John Cacioppo would say that all these examples show how technology can serve as an online way station to connect people offline. He pointed out to me that, while turning to one's social media feed as the *destination* typically leaves people feeling more distant and dissatisfied with their own lives, the prosocial use of media platforms as a link to human engagement offline has been shown to decrease loneliness.

There are many variations to the way station model. Streaming movies online can mean sharing a favorite film with an elderly relative who lacks the mobility to get to the movie theater. Telecommuting from home can give you time for a walk with your neighbors. Shopping online can free up time to volunteer in your child's school.

Other way station models begin as a purely personal exchange, but then morph into movements that foster high-quality connections among people both online and off. This was Dr. Hala Sabry's experience.

Hala is an emergency room physician and mother whose social media odyssey began late one November night in 2014. Married, with one child at the time, she was pregnant with twins and very anxious. The road to this point had been tortuous and painful. She'd spent five years undergoing infertility treatments, including eight cycles of in vitro fertilization and multiple doctors and clinics. She felt blessed to now have the prospect of three kids when for so long she'd feared having none, but that night, in the thirty-first week of her pregnancy, she suddenly began to feel her heart racing, her breath becoming short, and a pressure building in her chest. Her first thought was that she was having a pulmonary embolus, medical speak for a life-threatening blood clot that travels to the lungs and is more likely during pregnancy. Eventually, though, Hala figured out that she was having an anxiety attack.

Despite having fought so hard to have the large family she'd always dreamed of, she was suddenly gripped with self-doubt. What if she was doing the wrong thing by having these twins? What would happen if she was unable to juggle work and three small children? The demands of her work were intense, and she often felt no one around her understood what she was going through.

Hala had gone into medicine at the urging of her father, a physician from Egypt, who wanted her to have a stable job, since she was the eldest of his children and would need to take care of the whole family if anything happened to him. Becoming a doctor seemed like the best idea. Tragically, her father died at the age of fifty-two, just as she was starting her first year of med school. But she was determined to live up to his faith in her and soon fell in love with medicine.

Once she began practicing, she was often told that she'd have to choose between a successful career and motherhood. She described that during her first maternity leave, she was passed over for a promotion that went to a less qualified man. When she asked why, she was told they assumed that she'd want to be a mom since she just had a child. Now, as anxiety seized her, she wondered how much harder it would be with *three* kids? Her husband worked full-time as an aerospace engineer. They were going to need a second nanny, but how would *that* work?

She had no one to ask. There were moms' forums online, but she worried that even posting such a question about how to make things work with two nannies would make her seem terribly privileged. In the midst of her panic attack, she began to ask herself what she would tell her patients if they were going through this. She did not want to take common benzodiazepine anxiety medications like Ativan or Valium because of the risk during pregnancy. And talking to a therapist didn't feel like it would give her everything she needed. What she needed was to connect with other female physicians who could relate to her situation in a non-judgmental, supportive context.

She could think of only one person who might understand: Dina. Dina was a physician and the mom of three-week-old twins. The women had known each other since childhood, but they weren't close friends, and it was eleven p.m., but Hala decided to text anyway, to ask how Dina was managing child care.

As luck would have it, Dina happened to be up breastfeeding and called Hala right back. They had a long conversation about their mutual uncertainties and frustrations. When Dina said she was struggling with all the same questions, Hala decided they might both benefit from connecting with a few other physician moms, so she went on Facebook as they were talking and created a private group. After Dina promised to post questions, too, so Hala wouldn't feel overly elitist or incompetent, they invited twenty other women to join the group. To their astonishment, all twenty were awake and immediately answered Hala's question about nannies— and asked if they could invite other friends into the group. By the time Hala finally went to bed, her chest pain was gone.

Wouldn't it be great if the group grew to a hundred by the time I woke up? she thought as she drifted to sleep.

By the next morning, the Physician Moms' Group (PMG) had over two hundred members. One week later, the group had grown to one thousand. By the end of the month there were three thousand members. Five years later, the group has grown to more than seventy thousand.

I first learned about the PMG from Alice, who joined shortly after we were married in 2015. She would often tell me about the range of posts, asking for everything from medical advice on children's rashes, to recommendations for diapers, to opinions on which dress to wear for a date night. But what makes this group so extraordinary is the real impact the women have on each other's lives *offline*. They've organized to help each other as friends, and they meet offline throughout the year in small groups and at annual retreats that Hala describes as "a three-day sisterhood."

When Hala and I spoke by phone, she was huddled in her car outside her Southern California home. "If I go inside, there will be pandemonium with my kids and I won't be able to focus on our conversation," she said with the practiced wisdom of a veteran mother of five (she had another set of twins a few years after starting PMG). You could tell by the way she spoke about her family that they were her foundation, yet it also was clear that she felt a deep sense of responsibility to the many others she was serving. And that includes the members of PMG.

Creating a community of people who lift one another up hasn't been easy. Hala has had to establish norms to ensure that the group interacts with one another with respect and dignity (the lowest point for her was during and after the 2016 US presidential election, when there was great anger on both sides). She has a team of twenty-seven volunteer moderators who help her monitor conversations for violations of those norms. On occasion she's had to remove people from the group, and in a group as passionate and personal as PMG, such action can generate harsh responses. Once a disgruntled former member called a media outlet, which ran an unkind story about Hala and the group without even calling her for her input. She received hate mail and threats. At times, she even thought about quitting. But the positive impact that PMG was having on the lives of so many women always brought her back.

I asked Hala if there were any stories that really stood out. After a pause, she replied, "There are so many."

A few years ago, one of their members posted that her husband had just taken his life and now, with no one to talk to, she was feeling suicidal. Hala was about to go to sleep when she noticed the post. The group had created a protocol for responding to people with suicidal thoughts, so she messaged the woman right away and connected with her by phone. Five volunteers from PMG immediately stepped up to become her in-person support team. They set up a meal train. They took turns visiting so she was never alone on weekends. And they became friends. The power of community saw her through, and today she is thriving.

On another occasion an obstetrician member posted that she'd just delivered a baby to a mom who had a rare but potentially fatal complication: an amniotic fluid embolism, where some of the amniotic fluid that surrounds the baby *in utero* makes its way into the mother's bloodstream. Within minutes of her post, a group of critical care doctors began replying and suggesting interventions. It turned out the treatment the new mother needed wasn't available at the mother's hospital, so someone else in the group stepped in and arranged for a transfer to *her* hospital, which was nearby. In the end, the patient's life was saved. "*MOMS SAVING MOMS*," Hala posted the next day.

Hala also shared the wrenching story that began with a post about a baby in hospice, posted by the physician mom of this ill child. She posted poems and stories dedicated to her six-week-old that tore at the hearts of everyone in the group. They offered to help. When the baby died, group members offered to cover the bills, but the mom declined. Then they learned she had two other children. So they tracked down her local library, where the children's wing was being renovated. Chipping in whatever they could, they made a collective donation, and today there is a plaque there outside the children's reading room bearing a quote from one of the mother's original posts to the Physician Moms Group about her beloved child.

Before forming PMG, Hala recalled, she had one child and one job and was so stressed out. Now she has five kids and is busier than ever. But because she's so supported by the group, she is more emotionally available to her family and to her patients. "I am such a better doctor now," she told me. "In this group, you strengthen your purpose as a friend, as a sister, as a mom and wife. You use vulnerability to empower yourself."

I kept thinking about Hala's story for days after we spoke. What was so striking to me was not only the scale of impact that she was having on so many lives, but the positive effect she was having on her own life as a result of serving others. She never said she'd been lonely before this experience, but it was clear that social connection made possible by technology had enhanced her work and family life. Given that our connections with people are both our greatest source of fulfillment and also the ultimate performance enhancer, it is incumbent on technology companies and a new generation of humanistic entrepreneurs to imagine and design technology that intentionally strengthens our connections with each other instead of weakening them, that prioritizes quality in our interactions over quantity, and that supports a healthy and engaged society.

On the Move

In the film *Brooklyn*, a young woman in the 1950s left her small hometown in Ireland, where everyone knew everyone, and booked passage on a ship across the Atlantic to Brooklyn. She was homesick and lonely but lived in a boardinghouse with other immigrant women who shared meals together. She met people at a dance, at her work, at a class suggested by a local pastor, and gradually built a new community of people who looked out for one another. None of those steps along her journey was easy or comfortable. The transition took years, but this slow pace gave her and her fellow immigrants the time to make friends with those going their way.

Today intercontinental transportation takes just hours. For those with means, migration can happen overnight, and technology theoretically allows them to keep in touch with those left behind. But what about their need for community in their new life?

There's a Chinese saying that just as distant water cannot help you with a fire nearby, we need close neighbors even if we have faraway relatives. Tom Tait related a similar sentiment, seeing social connection as an essential element of disaster preparedness for Anaheim. Wherever we find ourselves living, we need one another. I learned this lesson painfully through the example of my uncle Rajesh.

I was in middle school when Rajesh came to stay with us in Miami. This was not unusual, since we frequently had visitors from India. My parents and these guests would stay up for hours sharing stories, and I loved hearing about a country I knew only from a distance. Rajesh was different. He didn't have many stories to tell, yet he left the strongest impression on me.

A gentle man with a quiet voice and a kind expression, Rajesh spoke rarely, and mostly about engineering. "I build bridges," he told me when he realized that I didn't know what a civil engineer did.

He was middle-aged and slightly stooped and wore suit pants and a button-down shirt that always seemed big on him. Though he tried to slick down his jet-black hair, it inevitably ended up flopping down over his thick glasses. Rajesh didn't smile much, but he wasn't mean-spirited or cross. There was an opacity to his expression that was hard to penetrate or interpret.

Even though he was older, Rajesh was drawn by the prospect of living the American dream and building a life of greater opportunity and prosperity for his family. So when the opportunity arose—when he was granted a visa after years of trying—he felt compelled to come. His plan was to build a secure foundation, then bring his wife and grown children over from India. I remember thinking how brave it was to leave a stable life and begin a whole new one all alone in an unfamiliar country. Of course, Rajesh was hardly the only person to make such a journey. Generations of immigrants, including my parents, had come before him, and millions more were on the move all over the world, many in harsher circumstances. But those were distant tales. Rajesh's story was unfolding right in front of me.

After I got home from school each day, Rajesh and I would keep each other company. Our house was undergoing major renovations, and we'd walk the construction site together. "You see that concrete beam that was just poured?" he said one day.

"Yes," I said, "they're leaving it to dry and harden and then they can build on top of it."

Rajesh shared a step I had missed in my explanation. "Before they build on it, they have to pour water on the concrete at intervals. Most of the strength of concrete comes from watering during the days after the concrete is poured." For some reason, that fact always stuck with me.

But Rajesh's awkwardness made new friendships challenging. We took him to house parties, but social interactions didn't come easy to him. Nor did the logistics of his new environment. Rajesh had no car and the unfamiliar suburbs of Miami were not simple to navigate. The day he discovered a bus stop near our house, he decided to catch a bus the next morning and explore the city, but when I came home from school that afternoon, I found him still sitting at the bus stop. Miami's public transportation was less than reliable at the time, and Rajesh had waited there all day, but no bus had shown up. Looking back, the image of him waiting there was a heartbreaking metaphor for the loneliness of migration.

Rajesh was intelligent and experienced, and he spoke English, but he had difficulty with the American accent and idioms, so communication was hard. My family ultimately helped him secure a job through a family friend's architecture firm, and Rajesh moved into a house that he shared with a young man in his thirties, who largely kept to himself, and a middle-aged Russian woman and her young son. Having never had to adjust to housemates before—much less three of them with completely different cultural backgrounds from his own—Rajesh mostly stayed in his room when not working.

Even as a kid I found this sad, but days turned to weeks, then months, and Rajesh never complained. When he learned to drive, my father gave him our aged blue Chevrolet Caprice Classic so he could get to and from work on his own. He appeared to be enjoying his job, which gave him the chance to immerse himself in the field he loved: engineering.

One day we learned that Rajesh had borrowed money from his boss to pay for his daughter's wedding in India. Like many traditional Indian fathers, he considered it his duty to give his child a spectacular wedding. But shortly after his daughter was married, Rajesh lost his job. He was told that his skills weren't a match with what the firm needed. He began searching for new positions, but interviews were tough to get, and the few he received never led to offers. Still, he could not bring himself to go home to India and face his community there as a failure.

On a Sunday afternoon about six weeks into his search, our phone rang. My sister and I were home alone, and I picked up the receiver.

"It's Sofia," Rajesh's Russian housemate said in a deadpan voice. "He hasn't come out of his room today even though we knocked, and we're not sure what to do."

I remember thinking that he must not have heard them. Rajesh was extremely hard of hearing. He'd slept right through Hurricane Andrew as it tore up South Florida in the summer of 1992. The rest of us huddled together, praying as the wind howled and twisting metal screeched in the darkness. Rajesh woke up the next morning and asked if the storm had come.

"Why don't you try really banging on the door, because he may not have his hearing aids in," I suggested to Sofia. She said she'd try, but when that didn't work, I got worried. Maybe he was sick. Or maybe he'd fallen and knocked himself unconscious.

I asked her to call 911 and have emergency rescue break down his door. She paused for a minute.

"Okay," she said and hung up.

The wait felt like hours, but it was only about ten minutes before the phone rang.

There was no emotion in Sofia's voice. "They broke down the door and found him hanging from the ceiling fan. He's dead."

I couldn't speak. I'd experienced the deaths of a few close relatives due to illness, but I had no idea how to think about or process suicide.

As it turned out, I wasn't alone. No one in my family had seen Rajesh's death coming, and his loss hit all of us hard. Worst of all was my dad and uncle having to make the dreaded call to Rajesh's wife in India to tell her the unthinkable had happened. We felt a sense of responsibility, given that we were the only family Rajesh had had in the area. We couldn't stop wondering what we should have done to better support him. Were there signs that we'd missed? This was one of my first lessons that we can't always tell from the outside how much pain people are in on the inside (a lesson that plays out all the time with people who are lonely but don't let it show).

Rajesh's death also caused me to reflect on the significance of my own interactions with him. I used to assume that he thought of me as a small child of little consequence. But if he was lonely, our brief conversations about the concrete and other seemingly mundane things were likely far more meaningful than I'd realized. The truth is, we never can tell when small interactions with others might be significant to them—or to us. Consider, for instance, the wisdom contained within Rajesh's description of the process of curing concrete. It took me years to see that, just as the concrete draws most of its strength from the water poured on it in the days after it's placed, each of us gains our strength not by virtue of being born but because of the love that is showered upon us in the days, months, and years that follow. That love comes through our relationships with everyone around us.

In the years that followed Rajesh's death, my family and I tried to piece together what had happened to estrange him from those sources of love and support. Part of the pressure on him certainly stemmed from his role as the male head of his family. He'd been under more stress than usual as he searched for a new job, especially since he'd borrowed the money for his daughter's wedding. He could have returned to a life of relative comfort in India, where he'd have a good job and be with his family, but he might have viewed that option as an admission of failure.

Rajesh was no stranger to hard times. He'd been raised in the same village where my father grew up, enduring poverty and illness, yet somehow Rajesh completed school and secured a coveted seat in engineering college. Against the odds, he'd worked his way up to a faculty position at a prestigious engineering school. There was, however, one glaring difference between

Rajesh's hardships of the past and his challenges in Miami: dislocation had stripped him of his core social network.

In India, Rajesh had been surrounded by family and friends who knew him well and would support him. He saw those people every day and had known them for decades. He lived with his family, and people came to his house all the time, which gave him the opportunity to see and talk to them even when he didn't seek them out.

In Miami, my father's brother was the closest thing to a friend Rajesh had, and a few months before Rajesh lost his job, my uncle had moved to New Jersey. One might think Rajesh would lean on his relationships in India for support, but in the 1990s a phone call to his wife could run several dollars a minute. That was simply too much for a man struggling to make ends meet. Plus, he might have been too embarrassed to tell his family about his struggles to find work.

In retrospect, it's clear to me that Rajesh must have been desperately lonely. He never said anything about it to us, but then again, we weren't his confidantes. He didn't have any in Miami.

Sadly, Rajesh's story is not unique. In 2018, the US Centers for Disease Control and Prevention reported that 54 percent of those who have died by suicide have no diagnosis of mental illness. Even worse, it is estimated that in 2016 there were 793,000 lives lost to suicide globally.[25] While global suicide rates are decreasing, in some countries the suicide rate has actually been increasing in recent decades. The United States is among these nations, having experienced a one-third increase in suicide mortality rates between 1999–2017 with rates being particularly high in rural areas, among men,[26] and in certain refugee communities.[27]

The Forum, a London charity serving migrants and refugees, conducted a small survey in 2014 where nearly 60 percent of its members viewed loneliness and isolation as the biggest challenges they face in living away from their home countries.[28] Reading the list of contributing reasons for their loneliness, I felt as if I were reading a detailed description of Rajesh's life in America:

- ❖ Loss of family and friends

- ❖ Lack of social networks

- ❖ Language barriers

- ❖ Lack of access to services and resources

- ❖ Loss of status

- ❖ Loss of identity

- ❖ Loss of job or career

- ❖ Cultural differences

- ❖ Discrimination and stigma connected to being a foreigner

- ❖ Isolating impact of government policies

The Forum report noted that life becomes especially difficult for immigrants when these circumstances overlap, as they did for Rajesh, with language barriers and cultural differences leading a cascade of losses, from professional status to identity and ever more increasing isolation and shame—with a heightened risk of illness and death. Those who are also elderly, impoverished, or struggling with other mental health issues are most vulnerable of all, but children, too, are at risk because they're often bullied and teased for looking and sounding different from their classmates.

That hostility is evident in racist and anti-immigrant rhetoric in Europe and the US, and in violent attacks on immigrant communities. To be a refugee or asylum seeker, to be foreign—noticeably different from the majority around you—can mean being stigmatized and threatened, out of sync and out of place. As one woman told The Forum: "I felt remarkably unwelcome in the UK. There was a distinct feeling that you, as a foreigner, were not welcome."

The Forum has found that keeping people active and connected with activities like mentoring and volunteer activities can make a dramatic difference in reducing immigrants' loneliness.[29] However, the surging pace of migration makes it very difficult for support organizations to keep up with the need.

According to the UN International Organization for Migration, 3.5 percent of the world's total population, or 272 million people, lived outside their home countries in 2019. They included more than twenty-eight million refugees.[30] Another sixty-six million adults in 2015 planned to move permanently to another country within the next year for reasons that included religious and ethnic persecution, war, violence, and human rights violations. Climate change, too: eighteen million people in 135 countries were displaced in 2017 by weather-related disasters. And these data don't even include the millions of "internal migrants" around the world who relocate far from home within their own countries.[31]

China alone has an estimated 241 million internal migrants, most between the ages of sixteen and forty, who move from the countryside to cities to work in factories and construction.[32] Like overseas immigrants elsewhere, these rural transplants face an intense pressure to succeed, coupled with both unofficial and official discrimination in the cities, where they're denied many of the services granted to urban citizens.[33 34] China's migrants are known as the "floating people," or *liudong renkou*. And together with the country's single "empty nest youth," who are less mobile but just as emotionally isolated, they represent a new so-called loneliness economy that's spreading throughout Asia.

Thanks to the loneliness economy, karaoke, a popular group activity in Asia, can now be performed in a karaoke booth for one at the mall. Hot pot, or shabu-shabu, is a meal where a family or other group cooks their meal together in one large pot of boiling broth, but according to the *South China Morning Post*, a Hong Kong restaurant chain now features "one person one pot"—and it's seen its shares triple in a year. Lonely people can purchase robotic companions and pets, or they can play with virtual app-based friends, such as Tabikaeru, the Travel Frog, who stars in a popular Japanese smartphone game. Like a pal who's off on holiday, Travel Frog sends players photographs and souvenirs from different travel destinations. Some say that the fact that the frog travels alone is part of what endears him to his single human friends. As of early 2018, Chinese players accounted for 95 percent of the ten million downloads of Tabikaeru.

The loneliness economy has a more human face in Japan, where the population is aging and young people are delaying marriage and parenthood. Japan's birth rate today is the lowest it's been in modern history. Two out of five Japanese households are expected to be singles by 2040.[35] The need for company is so great that one popular service in Tokyo allows customers to hire companions to join them for meals or activities.[36]

Many of these loneliness economy offerings may seem extreme, but the fact that business is booming points to a need that all of us must attend to, no matter where we live. If we want to connect in a more dispersed world, we have to push past our instinctual habits and reticence. Transplants living far from their comfort zones may appear fine on the outside, but displacement can cause a series of stresses that build over time and can be lonely and isolating. A helping hand and a friendly word—coupled with the recognition that we all have more in common than meets the eye—can make a life-changing difference.

On Earth

One modern trend that's spurring global loneliness might seem like purely good news: there are more elderly people than ever, and they're living longer. Who doesn't want a longer life? Like technology and increased mobility, however, this trend is a mixed blessing. With advanced age come health challenges and other losses. Today's oldest seniors have outlived partners, friends, and loved ones—even grown children. Many have physical disabilities. And many live in relative isolation.

The problem can be particularly acute in rapidly modernizing countries like China and Korea, where those young "floating people" often leave their elders behind. Traditionally in these societies, seniors held a place of respect and honor. They lived at the top of multigeneration households, shared their wisdom and life experiences, and were integrated into the daily lives of younger generations. Left-behind seniors who were raised to expect this reverence and care, then, can feel abandoned and betrayed. They may fall into despair. In South Korea, rates of suicide among the elderly more than quintupled from 1990 to 2009, and as of 2017, they remained the highest among industrialized nations.[37] In Taiwan, seniors take their own lives twice as often as any other age group. And in China, suicide rates among elderly city-dwellers have more than doubled since the 1990s.[38]

Meanwhile, in the west, elders are more accustomed to living alone, but this can make it both embarrassing and challenging when they do need help. Their family members may not be accustomed to supporting them and may not be helpful. Social services are just beginning to address a need that's only going to intensify as last century's baby boomers get ever older. In the US, boomers make up around one-quarter of the population,[39] and the first of them hit retirement age back in 2011.[40] It is questionable even whether social services can begin to replace the role that extended family has played for the elderly—and vice versa—in eras past.

Older people can serve as an indispensable anchor for their families, reminding them of shared history, traditions, and rituals that help to secure a sense of belonging and identity. Yet the vast majority of Americans do not live in multigenerational households. And as the elderly increase in age, their peer group dwindles and their risk of loneliness eventually begins to rise.

Like so many in this age group, Anne has been struggling with loneliness ever since her husband died. That was two years ago. Now she lives alone in the modest suburban home where they raised their three sons. She's slim and petite, her gray hair in a fashionable bob. At eighty-eight, she seems strong on her feet. She walks regularly on a trail near her house in the California Bay Area, and she still drives. Though somewhat reserved, she loves to talk about her husband, James, and the family they raised together.

Back in the day, she'll say, the house was a hurricane of activity, and Anne liked it that way. Weekends were busy with neighborhood get-togethers, attending the boys' games, and entertaining James's associates from the newspaper where he worked. James was gregarious and generous, and Anne was engaged in the community. Then came grandparenthood. Their sons were attentive, and all settled nearby, so Anne never felt much loneliness after the nest emptied.

It helped that she and James were physically active, healthy, and deeply committed to each other. Married since 1956, they remained very much in love. And Anne cherished the mutual support they gave each other. "It was like there was someone there who's got your back. They'll be there for you no matter what."

James's retirement gave them more time to spend together. James took up painting, and both of them loved having their grandchildren over. They also had plenty of friends.

Yet as they grew older, many of these friends succumbed to cancer or heart disease, and their social network shrank. Then, in 2012, James's health began to slip. He started to feel out of breath and weak. After he had a fall, he needed constant care, and the stress started to impact Anne's health as well.

Finally, they decided to move James into a facility that could give him around-the-clock care. Anne hadn't lived alone in nearly sixty years, and it took some time to adjust, but she kept herself busy managing James's care. She took him to appointments and spent most days at his side. As the months passed, more of their old friends died, and so did many of the residents of the care facility.

After about two years in the care facility, James passed, too. He was eighty-nine.

As much as Anne had prepared herself, his death stunned her. It hasn't gotten easier with time. Her sons take turns coming by, and they help with the house and the yard. The grandchildren, most of them now teenagers, come when they can, but they're busy with sports and friends and all the many cultural and technological changes that, for them, are as easy to manage as breathing.

For Anne, change is increasingly difficult, which is a real problem because age changes everything. "It's like you've been vibrantly planning ahead," she says, "and then you're not anymore." It's easy to feel left out, and it's hard to catch up.

As sharp and youthful as her mind is, Anne's low voice is getting raspy with age. She was recently diagnosed with breast cancer, though it's slow-moving and doesn't yet warrant aggressive treatment. She has less energy and isn't able to do as much as she used to. And she doesn't know how much longer she'll be able to maintain her independence.

"It's a bit of a lost feeling," she says. "Wow, mortality has always been there. But it always seemed so far off." It makes her feel lonely to face it alone.

Sophie Andrews is well acquainted with seniors like Anne. Andrews is the president of Silver Line, a call center for the elderly in the UK whose motto is: "No question too big, no problem too small, no need to be alone."

The Silver Line has fielded two million calls since starting in 2013 with the number of calls increasing 10 percent every month, all by word of mouth. "There's such a stigma to loneliness," she said. "For many people, we're the only place they can talk to someone."

There's a pattern to the calls that the Silver Line receives. Daytime calls are informational. Callers want to know how to find a service or connect with other seniors. In the evening, Andrews said, "We become like a friend on the sofa . . . People call to say good night." Later at night, "people are more emotionally challenged. They're lonely. Then in the morning, they call to say good morning, to have someone to talk to."

But the Silver Line can only help those who call in. And many seniors, especially those who survived World War II and have always prided themselves on their self-reliance, view any request for help as an admission of failure. Their reluctance to reach out is often intensified by the fear that they'll be viewed as a burden by their families, that they'll be forced to move into a new living situation, perhaps leaving homes and familiar surroundings that have become entwined with their identity. Faced with the threat of losing their cherished independence, many seniors "choose" instead to suffer in silence with their loneliness.

Others, though, are discovering that there's social strength in their rising numbers. This was the thought that occurred to a group of aging friends in Boston back in 1999. *What*, they asked one another, *if we joined together as one another's support system?*

This was the beginning of what's come to be known as the Village Movement, now encompassing more than 350 local senior-driven nonprofits across the country.

The one thing the Beacon Hill founders knew was that they did *not* want to move—or be forced to move—from their own homes into a nursing home. So they formed a membership community called Beacon Hill Village with the mission of helping one another to "prosper from directing our lives and creating our own future." As a Village, they secure help with the daily challenges of life, from rides to doctors' appointments to grocery shopping and housekeeping. They also share referrals to trusted professionals, from plumbers to financial advisors. And perhaps most important of all, they gather regularly to share programs of mutual interest, including workshops, concerts, and volunteer activities.

Beacon Hill inspired hundreds of other Villages around the country, including San Francisco Village, which has a network of small, hyperlocal Neighborhood Circles organized by zip code. This organizational principle fosters a strong local, neighborhood connection that's especially valuable in San Francisco, a city where increasing gentrification and displacement threaten to further isolate older adults.

When I spoke with Kate Hoepke, the executive director of San Francisco Village, she told me that their programs are specifically aimed at helping members "navigate today's changing cultural and economic San Francisco" so that they stay engaged and involved not just with one another but also with the city around them. Programs include mentorship exchanges with high school students and gig economy classes. Many are organized and hosted by the members themselves, which taps into the culture of reciprocity that is a core part of the Village ethos.

"As a member," Kate told me, "one may ask and give help. Reciprocity means that you are depending on others to age in place. That sense of collective need is part of what fuels social connection at San Francisco Village."

At seventy-one, Judy Jacobs has been a member of San Francisco Village for several years now. She likens it to college for older people. "You're going to get out of it what you put in."

In the beginning, she recalled, she took a workshop on brain health. "It met every week, and some of those women are now my closest friends. It's like we're a gang. It's because we saw each other every week."

Some of the most valuable programs, Judy's found, are those that help members learn to tell their stories, whether through writing or art or oral storytelling. "People want to share their story," she said. "I think that all of us want to know that we matter and that we've touched each other's lives."

There was something so universal about what she described, a moving description of the human yearning to connect.

On Edge

Alas, one more change stoking the current trends of loneliness is the politicized climate of distrust and division that hangs over much of the world. While many factors play into this polarization, social disconnection is an important root cause.

In the same way that healthy connections help us work through challenges in a relationship, strong human connections can help us work through societal challenges. Communities around the world are dealing with pressing problems like climate change, terrorism, poverty, and racial and economic inequities. Addressing these issues requires dialogue and cooperation. But even as we live with increasing diversity, it's easier than ever to restrict our contact, both online and off, to people who resemble us in appearance, views, and interests. That makes it easy to dismiss people for their beliefs or affiliations when we don't know them as human beings. The result is a spiral of disconnection that's contributing to the unraveling of civil society today.

It's a vicious cycle. When we're disconnected, we have a hard time listening to each other. We tend to judge quickly and assume the worst about people who disagree with us. This makes working together to overcome challenges increasingly difficult. Then the more problems we face, the angrier we get, which fuels the cycle of fear and distrust that stokes alienation and a sense of estrangement from society as a whole. How did it come to this?

One factor is our social geography. Today a majority of Americans live in the suburbs, and the numbers are growing.[41] But according to the Pew Research Center, 68 percent of current suburbanites are white, compared with just 44 percent of city dwellers. That sets up a racial disconnect between urban and suburban populations.[42] Even in urban centers, people often live in neighborhoods that are segregated by race or socioeconomic status.

Meanwhile, many people have seen their real wages remain stagnant amid rising income inequality, and millions of Americans in cities, suburbia, and rural areas alike are struggling with poverty and without good-paying jobs. This has steeped fear and resentment not only among those who feel that they've lost status they're entitled to, but also among those who feel that they've been too long excluded from their fair share. We hear this resentment boil over online, in street protests, on talk radio, and in government. In 2018, one major poll found that 79 percent of American adults are concerned that the "negative tone and lack of civility in Washington will lead to violence or acts of terror."[43] The poll found that sentiment was shared by strong majorities across the political spectrum, ages, income levels, education, and regions. This pulsing undercurrent of anxiety pushes us all to our set positions, talking with one another less and accusing one another more, understanding one another less and feeling ever more isolated.

Yet it doesn't have to be like this. Thanks in part to technology, we have more means today than ever before to engage and discover our common ground with people who are different from us. There is a growing movement afoot to restore civil discourse and engage people in healthy debate to overcome the prejudices and the divergent viewpoints and lived experiences that divide us. The goal is not to resolve these problems overnight but to help us face them together.

Dr. John Paul Lederach is an international peace builder and expert in conflict resolution who's given a great deal of thought to the mechanisms that pull people together and tear them apart. "The challenge of the remainder of our century," he told me bluntly, "is how are we as a global family going to attend to the basic fundamentals of creating the right of belonging? There isn't a community that doesn't face this."

So, what's needed?

For Lederach, the first step is to promote a *mutual* sense of belonging. That means meeting and serving people where they live, by physically going to their homes or neighborhoods. "When you go to where people live and you sit with them, you actually begin collective empathy—you see the world from how they perceive and live it," John Paul told me.

Accessing this vantage point is especially important, he said, when meeting people who are different from you, with whom you want to build connection in spite of fear or distrust. Only this way can we truly begin to appreciate the context of one another's lives.

John Paul's remarks reminded me that the relationship between doctor and patient used to be much more intimate and informed when doctors still made house calls. My own experience in residency doing home visits taught me their value. I remember visiting a frail elderly woman in her house outside of Boston. We'd seen each other several times in clinic, but my visiting her at home shifted the power dynamic. Now I was paying her a call. I'd made the effort to get there. This was *her* turf.

The trust she afforded me grew as she felt more seen and understood as a person and not just as a patient. At her home I met members of her family and saw other reflections of her life as a whole—pictures of special moments with her family, the books on her shelf, memorabilia that sat on her side table. My appreciation for her as a whole person grew more in that one visit than it would have in ten clinic visits.

I learned more about her health, as well, because she was more comfortable telling me about her concerns, including issues like family members she was worried about and problems she was having with repairs in her house. These challenges weren't medical, but they nevertheless affected her condition. The fact that modern medicine has largely done away with house calls doesn't change the fact that the best way to see patients as whole human beings is to meet them where they live.

"A lot of our isolation," John Paul said, "is the degree to which people feel invisible. Invisibility brings with it a deep ambiguity of not being located. So, when you come and show up and have concern and conversation from their location, you're rehumanizing the situation that has lost that connection at a very deep level."

That humanization is the beginning of belonging, and when we share space together we promote a *mutual* sense of belonging. This is one reason why communities have historically made sure to build intentionally shared spaces into their towns and cities. Throughout the world, dwellings have clustered around public squares where town-wide events from markets and bazaars to concerts were held. In colonial times, American communities were built around the village green, where children played and everyone got to know one another. When Sir Ebenezer Howard became one of the earliest modern urban planners in the 1880s, his idea of utopia was a self-contained community surrounded by parks and separate from industry and agriculture. These towns would be managed by the citizens who shared an economic interest in them, forging a distinct sense of community belonging. This ideal was another casualty of the rise of suburbia and the dominance of car culture over people culture.

When people occupy the same space, John Paul said, spending time there and sharing both the responsibility and the rewards from it, everyone becomes grounded together. He pointed to the community gardening movement as a perfect example. Around the world, people are growing fruits and vegetables together, creating a shared stake in public and private plots of earth. "That sort of imagination helps [address] a deep sense of ungroundedness, which seems to be a part of our modern society."

What John Paul described points to an important challenge of our time. Given the many trends like migration and virtual work and commerce, which make community harder to build and prioritize, we need *physical* common ground even more than ever in the form of spaces where we come together to live, work, play, and belong.

But what about feuding groups who *refuse* to share space, whose distrust for each other has ignited into fear and anger? That fear and anger blunt our empathy and concern for one another. They increase the distance between us, fueling a sense of disconnection. Historically, this was how wars fomented, since it was easy to demonize an enemy one was never going to encounter personally except on the battleground. But this formula for conflict has ramped up with the advent of 24/7 broadcasting and social media.

Today's technology creates the illusion that we *do* know our enemies. We see them, we hear them in our own homes every day, at any hour we choose to look. The versions that we "know" are often deceptive and unidimensional, yet we believe what we see and hear even when the videos are completely fabricated. As a result, the people we learn to fear seem both closer and even scarier than they ever used to. Whether we're talking about Republican vs. Democrat animosity or conflicts in the Middle East, a sense of imminent threat makes our world feel less safe and hospitable. It erodes our sense that we all belong here.

This anxiety may not initially feel like the loneliness we associate with isolation. It can feel like passionate—if negative—engagement. But the natural response to protect ourselves in the face of threat is to close down and prejudge others, instead of opening up and giving them the benefit of the doubt. We can't listen to another point of view nearly as well when we're angry and scared—we all know this from our personal conflicts. And that drives us apart. Too often, we're also filled with contempt, which poses a big obstacle when we try to come together.

Much of this, according to a 2014 series of studies published in the *Proceedings of the National Academy of Sciences*,[44] is fueled by a cognitive bias known as "motive attribution asymmetry," which tells us that our beliefs are grounded in love, while our opponents' are based on hatred. The studies found that this bias applies to Israelis who believe *they* are fighting out of love for their people, while Palestinians are driven by hatred—and vice versa. The same bias infects both Democrats and Republicans in America, who believe that their own fervor is driven by "love of this country" while wondering why the other party "hates us."

The contempt that results from this type of bias is visceral and righteous, feeding not just intolerance but also the same emotional stew that makes loneliness so toxic. If you must deal with people who believe you're driven by hatred, you're bound to feel rejected and frustrated. But if you're confronting someone *you* believe is driven by hatred, then your stress levels spike out of fear and distrust.

In the same way that having a stressful job or dealing with financial hardship can drain us of the energy we need to nourish our personal relationships, so, too, does the stress of generalized fear and anger take a toll, which I think of as an emotional tax. This insidious but dangerous tax may register as weariness and despair over the nightly news. It may sap the energy we have available for constructive engagement. It may compromise our tolerance and patience even in interactions with family and friends.

This emotional tax can blind us to the presence of positive relationships and make us feel either as if we're disconnected from everyone or as if all our encounters are negative. Whether in a condo building disagreement, a city council debate, or deliberations in national legislative bodies like Congress, such alienation makes it exceedingly difficult to find realistic solutions to conflicts. Almost all problem solving requires compromise, and we're much more likely to seek and accept compromise if we can identify with the people on the other side of a dispute.

Otherwise, we'll just dig in our heels and demand an all-or-nothing outcome, which only deepens the conflict and our own alienation.

John Paul Lederach is extremely familiar with such standoffs from his peace-building work in Colombia, the Philippines, Nepal, and several countries in East and West Africa. I wondered if some of the methods he uses to mediate disputes in war zones could be applied at home.

I asked him how we can move beyond our differences to engage in the meaningful dialogue that allows us to share space without exploding.

"We need to befriend," he said. "We need to come at friendship as a verb."

How does he define that friendship?

"Authenticity," he said. "Authenticity is about reaching and revealing, being real with each other. A level of honesty and commitment to relationship that permits people to stay in connection in spite of difference and diversity."

In conflict zones, John Paul told me, people are not only deeply polarized but they have traumatic long-term knowledge of threats and abuses against other members of their families. In places like Nepal or Colombia, he said, the grudges and accusations go back multiple generations. Groups have been raised to view each other as threats. Those antagonisms calcify over time and are very difficult to soften.

"One of the things we're working on," he said, "is trust and cohesion. Enough trust that people can reach and reveal—they can have a greater honesty or authenticity to where their concerns and fears can sit. Reaching is going beyond that fear of the other—or the stigma the in-group has placed on the other."

"Reach and reveal," John Paul says, "are the pillars that create the capacity for civic engagement and democracy, that have to be present for there to be a vibrant community. I think the real quality of friendship is that you *stay* connected, in spite of difference."

But how can we apply this to our homegrown conflicts?

He gave me an easy prescription from his other work, as a professor at the University of Notre Dame. "My proposal to students is that they look across their classes and campus and locate a person who is somewhat different. Then find a way to reach out and see if they'd be willing to go out to coffee or tea."

The purpose of reaching out, he emphasized, is not to try to change their mind, "not to try to put forward your view or hear them so you can develop better arguments."

No, he said. The purpose is simply to meet and find common ground so that you can build the trust you need "to reconstitute the fabric of friendship." To do this, it's important to "start small but to commit to a higher quality of presence in relationship."

And to demonstrate this commitment, John Paul gives his students three basic challenges:

1. Listen to understand.

2. Speak from the heart.

3. Stay at it. For the rest of your life. Persist.

"I have this phrase 'moving together,'" John Paul said. "You don't worry about moving the whole, you worry about getting a few people to move together against gravity."

Moving together against gravity. I could hardly think of a better description for the unlikely relationship that was pivotal in moving Derek Black, the child of KKK believers, to turn away from white nationalism and to embrace people across cultures.

Matthew Stevenson, one of Derek's first friends outside the movement, is an Orthodox Jew who hosted Shabbat dinners at New College when he and Derek were students there. Both went on to graduate school, Derek in history and Matthew in business, but their friendship remains a pivotal accomplishment in both their lives.

"How did you begin to bridge the divide?" I asked when we spoke in 2019.

Matthew recalled living across the hall from Derek in the dorm. "He would play guitar and played country-and-western. I'd sometimes go along and listen to him play or sing along. This was before anyone knew anything about Derek's background, but I was wearing a yarmulke, so I was pretty open about who I was."

Derek remembered watching a movie with Matthew and other people in his dorm room, and they had a class together. They were friendly to each other but not yet close. Derek still considered himself a white nationalist. He just didn't talk about it.

When Derek's secret finally got out, he was in Germany for a semester abroad. An upperclassman back on campus posted an online photograph of Derek with the tag: "Derek Black: white supremacist, radio host . . . New College student???"

"When the story came out that Derek's father was the founder of Stormfront," Matthew said, "obviously it was a big shock." The campus was in a furor. Most of Derek's classmates were irate that they'd been misled. Yet, when Derek returned from Germany, Matthew reached out and invited him to his Shabbat dinner. And he persuaded other friends to join them—without confrontation.

"That took courage," I said. "What were your expectations?"

Matthew's reply was simple but profound. "I have a fundamental belief that at the root of every person is a spark of the Creator. There's something that binds everyone. Even if they are behaving in ways I find reprehensible, we still share a common humanity. And that can't be erased. Even if someone is doing things that are really against me or harming me or society, I feel somewhat of a responsibility to that person."

When I asked how he'd come to this extraordinary world-view, Matthew said that his mother had been an alcoholic and took him with her as a boy to Alcoholics Anonymous meetings. "I saw a lot of people who had been in very dark places in their lives. There was a guy who unintentionally ran over his son when he was drunk in the driveway. Many of those people I saw transform their lives, from tornados of vulnerability to beacons of hope."

He paused. "So there wasn't a doubt in my mind that people like Derek can transform."

Just as John Paul Lederach would have recommended, Matthew reached out not to persuade but to befriend. "I told everyone at the dinner not to bring up his political views, because I didn't want it to become a shouting match. I thought it would be a unique opportunity to get to know him. My guess was that Derek didn't have many opportunities growing up to get exposed to the people that white nationalism condemned."

I asked Derek how he remembered that first dinner.

"I expected there would be a group confrontation," he admitted. "But then there wasn't a confrontation."

"I knew we had common interests, like music and history," Matthew said. "I don't think I would have invited Derek had I not had those previous interactions with him, and I don't think he would have accepted."

To my amazement, Derek said he was moved to accept in part because it was a Shabbat dinner. "This changed the context of the conversation and how we were interacting. This is a sacred moment that you shouldn't mess up that way."

And then there were more Shabbat dinners. And Derek became one of the regulars, along with students of color and others who were immigrants, Jews, or members of the LGBTQ+ community. Afterward, Matthew and Derek would hang out. Matthew didn't go to parties on Fridays because of Shabbat. "And Derek wasn't really welcome at parties, so we'd end up spending lots of one-on-one time together, just talking in my living room. But white nationalism was the elephant in the room for two years."

I couldn't help asking, "Did you ever have an urge to discuss the elephant in the room?"

"I was very curious," Matthew admitted. "I had experienced getting spit on, shoved for anti-Semitic reasons when I was traveling. It wasn't an abstract idea to me. But I figured that if I brought it up, it would lead to defensiveness. I thought it was more important for him to come to those dinners than me satisfying my curiosity."

"Initially," Derek said, "it was important that we didn't argue because we wouldn't change each other's minds. I can see why it took so long to be open about it."

"What *did* you share?"

"Derek's father had been sick," Matthew recalled. "When my mom was diagnosed with cancer, we spoke about that experience. We spoke about religion and spirituality, but we never specifically broached the topic of white nationalism. I didn't want it to define our friendship, so I figured I'd wait for Derek to bring it up."

Matthew did nudge the issue, however. After he learned that Derek was scheduled to join his father and speak at a Stormfront conference, Matthew asked him, "What are you up to this weekend?" Derek told him he was going to Tennessee for a family reunion.

One person who was not concerned about engaging directly with Derek was Matthew's suitemate Allison. She had originally stopped coming to the Shabbat dinners when Matthew decided to invite Derek, but eventually she came back. Because she was white and not Jewish and therefore not a person targeted by white nationalism, she felt she needed to take on the role of talking explicitly with Derek about his beliefs. "She would ask me how I could hold my beliefs and also go to these Shabbat dinners. Wasn't there a conflict there?" Derek recalled. Over countless private conversations, she asked him to examine and explain his beliefs.

In time, those beliefs began to shift. By the end of college, many of his closest friends were precisely the kinds of people he had been told to hate earlier in life. "It became more and more incompatible. I got to the point where I had to condemn my own family beliefs and leave it." Allison, who had become Derek's girlfriend by then, told him it wasn't enough to quietly give up his beliefs. He had to announce it explicitly.

Derek publicly renounced white supremacy by writing an article that went viral. That was when Derek and Matthew finally talked. Derek related how the conversation finally began: "I remember asking you, 'I'm pretty sure you're aware of my family stuff, but we've never talked about it. Are you aware?' And Matthew responded, 'Yes. Obviously.'" Over drinks at a bar, they unpacked everything that had happened in the past two years—Derek's past, as well as his journey, and the profound impact those Shabbat dinners had had on his transformation.

Still, for Derek, it took time to fully own the person he had become. To his surprise, he found that it helped to tell his story to journalist Eli Saslow for a book about his transformation. "I thought the reaction would be quite negative, since I had come from something so negative. However, I realized that I could explain what had happened." When he looked at the story from all sides, he found a deeper understanding of both the forces that had shaped his childhood and the forces that had led to his change. "I could be open with the good and the bad. And in the process of doing that, it was actually more comfortable."

Derek's transformation has come with a personal cost, though. The feelings of anger and hurt that his family experienced after his public renouncement of white nationalism are still raw. When we spoke, he was down in Florida visiting his parents and walking that long road to rehabilitating the deeply damaged relationship. This is a reality of being human . . . that we have the capacity to love people—family, friends, and strangers—even if we profoundly disagree with them.

I was speaking with sociologist and author Dr. Parker J. Palmer one day when I realized that the layer of trust, acceptance, and common ground that Matthew and Derek established before they ever talked politics exemplifies what the French historian of the 1800s Alexis de Tocqueville described as prepolitical association.

Palmer, who founded the Center for Courage and Renewal to facilitate fellowship across divisions and differences, was describing de Tocqueville's observations of our society and political system in *Democracy in America*. "He said that American democracy could not thrive without the prepolitical layer of voluntary associations in which people gather in various forms of community—family, friendship groups, classrooms, workplaces, religious communities, and civic spaces." What happens in these gatherings, Palmer said, is that people "remind themselves of their connectedness with one another and create a million microdemocracies upon which the macrodemocracy depends."

By "macrodemocracy," he meant more than just voting. He meant civic engagement and participation. If I'm connected to the children in my neighborhood, I may be motivated to go to a school board meeting, even if I don't have kids. If I have friends who can't drive, I'm more likely to engage in a campaign for better public transportation. If I participate in a community garden, I'll probably pay more attention to zoning changes that might open up or eliminate green space. Being connected to others gives us a stake in more than our own interests. It expands those interests to include our whole community and thus increases our motivation to work together.

By the same token, the absence of connection that accompanies loneliness makes us less likely to participate in civic engagement. We tend to ignore or shrug off problems that don't affect anyone we know. Why help clean up a park in a stranger's neighborhood? Why pay attention to rent control issues if we know no one who rents? Why even bother voting if we don't know anyone who might be affected by the ballot choices? This is why the kind of microdemocracy that de Tocqueville described matters so much: because it gives everyone a shared stake in the future.

What Matthew and Derek and their college friends established was indeed a microdemocracy. Without it, they might never have been able to overcome their political differences. And Derek would have continued to ignore and denigrate the views of anyone who contradicted the white nationalist mind-set. Derek had remarked on this, too, when he told me his college friendships had transformed his view of the link between community and persuasion.

As a white nationalist, he'd assumed that persuasion was a matter of reason, data, and arguments, and that people joined communities after being persuaded. Thanks to Matthew, he came to understand that the reverse is actually true: "You find your community first, *then* you get persuaded."

This simple insight has enormous potential ramifications for many of the entrenched conflicts that are tearing our society apart today. The way to get people to find common ground on reproductive rights, climate change, and criminal justice is not necessarily to talk first and hear everyone's arguments. Instead, it's to establish relationships between those who disagree—relationships where people meet first as fellow human beings, not as political positions. Derek's right: once we find points of shared value and concern, our minds and hearts open to each other. And that's when we, too, can "move together against gravity."

Our politicians used to understand this. Until fairly recently, members of all parties in Congress would meet at school functions because their kids went to the same schools. They played softball or met at the gym. They attended many of the same parties. But now representatives travel back to their districts on weekends, their families often stay in their home state, and socializing across ideological lines is viewed as betrayal. As a result, Palmer's "prepolitical layers of association" have frayed and increasingly are being replaced by "postpolitical" connections that require agreement *before* connection. This imposes disconnection, making it ever more difficult for politicians to work with each other. Meanwhile, the entire country is stuck in gridlock.

Sadly, Palmer said, many Americans today subscribe to Derek's original view: "As long as you act, look, think like us, you can join." And when this is the price of belonging, the only alternative is: "You can say or do anything you want, but no one is paying any attention."

He seemed to be describing the difference between traditional and individualistic cultures. "But it sounds," I said, thinking of the third-bowl model, "as if you think there's a third way."

The Center for Courage and Renewal,[45] Palmer acknowledged, was trying to craft a different way of being together in community. "Being alone together. A community of solitude where people are paying attention." What happens in this community is that people tell their stories, and others bear witness—seeing them, hearing them, allowing them to feel known and visible in a safe shared space, without being challenged by the others. Palmer was talking about creating another structural element of third-bowl culture, much as Buettner did with *moai*s and Tom Tait did with kindness.

The power of personal stories, he emphasized, should not be underestimated. They humanize large complex issues and bring seemingly overwhelming problems—and solutions—down to scale. They bring people together as partners in solving problems that they might not otherwise realize they have in common. "The big story of a social issue is too chilly for human habitation. Connecting to the little story of an individual life warms the big story up—and allows it to shed light on the big story, which helps people understand the significance of their own experience." In other words, only by sharing our individual stories can we connect and begin to heal our divided society.

But it's not easy to get people today to quiet themselves and restrain the impulse to interrupt and challenge, to listen with respect and openness to unfamiliar stories. That's why Palmer's center sets clear rules for togetherness. "One of the rules is that you can't correct each other, but once people get into it, they love it. It clears the field for a completely different kind of conversation."

It's a conversation of fellowship, he says, because after people have been "alone together," they feel less threatened by each other. "Strangers do not have horns. They do not bring danger. They carry news from another place that we need to know."

By redefining what it means to "be alone together," Parker said, we can overcome our prejudices and bridge the gap between love and fear. "When you create a safe space where people can tell their stories, people break out of their social isolation."

But "safety" is the watchword. A community of this sort needs a facilitator, and that person needs to understand the risks and have "the courage to throw themselves in front of something bad happening before there is a train wreck—because if there is a train wreck, most of the people will not trust the safe space again and won't come back."

Palmer told me this is why the center discourages leaders from describing their gatherings with terms like "family" or "friends," both of which presume a close affiliation that can threaten or discourage people who feel different. "It worries me a lot when I hear churches talking about 'the church family,'" he said. "You shouldn't collapse yourself into the family imagery. You have the opportunity to be a *bridge* between private and public life."

To illustrate what he meant, Palmer told me about some of the clergy who'd taken the center's leadership training and returned home to create sponsored safe spaces where teenagers and police could meet alone together—with potentially lifesaving results. "By telling each other stories, the next time they meet on the street, it's a different kind of meeting. The results are felt outside the walls of that experience."

Palmer admitted that this approach is unlikely to work with members of society at extreme polar opposites. With rare exceptions like Derek Black, extremists tend to be so invested in their positions that their only interest is in conversion, not conversation. But in Palmer's estimation, extremists left and right account for less than 40 percent of the population. "Max out those numbers, and you still have 60 percent in the middle, which is more than enough to make significant positive change."

The bottom line is that we all long to connect. "There are two basic human yearnings," Palmer said. "To feel at home in one's own skin and to feel at home on this wonderful earth. To only connect with your own ego is to be in a very lonely place. Our sense of self is a communal construct. Whether you put it theologically or biologically, we are created for community. Without community, we struggle. It's as if we didn't have oxygen to breathe."

CHAPTER 5

Unmasking Loneliness

Who knows what true loneliness is—not the conventional word, but the naked terror? To the lonely themselves it wears a mask.

—Joseph Conrad, *Under Western Eyes*

Loneliness is the great masquerader. It can appear as anger, alienation, sadness, and a host of distressing emotional states. It also can attach itself to other sources of those emotions, exacerbating the effects of trauma and intensifying pain while preventing healing. The resulting web of hurt, fear, and despair can make it almost impossible to locate the true source of anguish, but if we look closely at stories of pain like Anthony Doran's, we'll often find loneliness lurking just beneath the surface.

To Anthony, the men of Alpha Company were family. They'd met during their first assignment at Schofield Barracks Army Base in Oahu and bonded over their common sense of purpose in the wake of 9/11. Many, like Anthony, had enlisted after watching the Twin Towers fall. They spent twelve months working, training, eating, and sleeping as one small group. Together they built not just physical strength but also such interdependence that they could count on one another without hesitation. At the end of training, Alpha Company boarded a military transport plane to start a one-year tour of duty in Afghanistan—the best year of his life, Anthony would later tell me.

What he never could have predicted at age twenty-three, he said, was that war would give him such a sense of belonging. "You know you'd be willing to die for the guy to the left or the right of you," he said. "The bonds are that strong." Also, they were proud of the work they were doing. They believed in their mission and in one another.

In Afghanistan, Anthony would accompany FBI personnel tracking cells to capture insurgents hiding in burned-out buildings. He was sent to organize and protect Afghans risking their lives to vote in the country's first democratically held presidential election. Some days, his team went out on humanitarian missions to distribute food and supplies. The heat index could reach 127 degrees, which the soldiers had to endure in full gear. Each day they faced the real possibility that one or all of them wouldn't return. Yet that very knowledge held them together.

Without a doubt, Anthony recalled, it was the connection he felt to his fellow soldiers that got him through each day. And that connection was what he longed for the minute he got back on American soil in 2006. He still does, more than a decade later. "I miss being around all those guys. Most of us would go back in a heartbeat just to feel that camaraderie."

Even though I'd heard similar sentiments from other soldiers, Anthony's emphasis still gave me a jolt. The bond he'd felt—and lost—with his fellow soldiers meant so much to him that he'd risk his life all over again to revive it. Why couldn't he and his company sustain their connection in the theater of peace, as well as war?

Like many vets, Anthony had thrived within the structure and mission of the army and, by comparison, found civilian life chaotic and purposeless. War had given his days meaning and shape, and without it he was lost. Back home in New Jersey, nobody could relate to his experience, and friends and strangers alike struck him as self-centered and frivolous. He wrestled with depression and severe bouts of anxiety.

He tried turning to his army brothers, but whenever he called them, he felt like he was intruding. He got the impression that others in Alpha Company had slipped easily back into their old lives. They were enjoying their families. Finding jobs. Like so many trapped in the depths of loneliness, Anthony underestimated the emotional isolation of others in comparison with his own.

"It seemed like they had it all together," he said. "I didn't find out till later that some of them thought the same about me."

The reality was that the military code of toughness had trained them all to mask the truth about their emotional state. The mentality was to be strong and stoic. That stoicism had served them well when facing the danger and uncertainty of war. They'd learned not to express feelings or talk about personal problems, and the stigma against asking for help was particularly powerful in the service. "You just don't do it," Anthony told me. "We were highly trained in combat, but we weren't trained how to deal when we got back."

Anthony's experience in the army reinforced his childhood conditioning. His father was an Irish-American police officer who worked twelve-hour days and then picked up extra shifts to make ends meet. The four Doran boys were each expected to "be a man" and keep their feelings bottled up from a very young age. This meant that Anthony had no way to express, much less manage, the painful symptoms of post-traumatic stress that he was experiencing.

Feeling increasingly isolated and without anyone to talk to about his experiences in Afghanistan and back home, Anthony began drinking and using drugs to numb the pain—first opioid painkillers a doctor had prescribed for back pain and eventually heroin. Twice he nearly overdosed, one time leaving a suicide note. Arrested repeatedly for buying illegal prescription drugs, he was in and out of more treatment facilities than he can remember.

Then his older brother Joseph, who had served in Iraq, lost his own battle with addiction and died from an overdose of heroin. To his parents, the loss was nearly unbearable, but Anthony didn't mourn. He was too numb.

Soon he was homeless, living in his car. Eventually, all his exhausted family could do was let him come back to his childhood bedroom.

One cold January night in 2013, with his parents watching TV in the living room, Anthony holed up in bed with a bag of heroin. Tired of the constant search for the next high, worn down by the aching feelings of self-hate, and, perhaps most painful of all, lonely for the connections with friends he no longer knew, he took comfort in the idea of disappearing.

Anthony threw a noose over the door and slipped it around his neck. But as he stepped into space and felt the rope cut off his air supply, he was gripped by a surge of dread. Much as he didn't want to live, he didn't want to die, either. Somehow managing to wrangle himself free, he collapsed on the floor, bruised and gasping but alive.

There was no epiphany, no grand promise to himself to change, no intervention from concerned family and friends. Just a decision to keep living with the ghosts that haunted him.

Unfortunately, his addictions persisted. More short-term recovery programs failed to help. Still grieving the death of their oldest son, his parents begged Anthony to try more treatment, but nothing got through until an anonymous donor provided a gift to a treatment facility—$150,000—that paid for him to spend nearly a year getting the inpatient care he needed.

He arrived at the facility in February 2013. At first, he just sat silently in group sessions, refusing to talk or share his story. But he was listening as others spoke. Bit by bit, he started to see threads of his own story in theirs. Slowly, he opened up, asking questions from time to time and occasionally sharing his own perspective. As he started to feel safe in this community, he allowed himself to be vulnerable and reveal the pain that he'd carried for so long.

It was a long process, but Anthony came to recognize just how insidious and powerful a hold loneliness had over him. He'd tried to use substances to deaden his despair, but what he really needed was human connection. As he began to build friendships within this new culture, he felt a renewal of the camaraderie he'd lost when he left the army. He learned to trust his new team at the treatment facility as he had the men of Alpha Company. With their belief and encouragement, along with the steadfast support of his family, he found the strength to face down his demons. Anthony became sober during that year, and he's remained so ever since.

Recognizing the power of human connection that brought him back from the edge, Anthony committed himself to helping others as he was helped. Today he shares his story and listens to those of returning soldiers, those dealing with addiction, and families of tormented veterans. He almost always finds a strong undercurrent of loneliness in their stories. He wants others to know they are not alone. And in the process of serving them, he strengthens his own sense of purpose, reversing the downward spiral of loneliness and finding new meaning and direction.

The Masquerade of Pain

Dr. Frieda Fromm-Reichmann, a Jewish German psychiatrist born in 1889, may have been the first to notice the tendency of loneliness to lurk behind and beneath other confounding conditions. Her interest in loneliness seems to have started with a young patient who was completely catatonic when treatment began. It wasn't until Fromm-Reichmann, in a sympathetic tone, asked her to describe her misery, that the patient lifted one finger as a signal.

Fromm-Reichmann replied, "That lonely?" And this simple response changed the young woman's demeanor. She continued to communicate through finger gestures for a couple of weeks before completely emerging from the anxiety and pain of her isolation.

This success was a turning point for Fromm-Reichmann, who began to see severe loneliness as much different from simple "aloneness" or the unique experience of mourning. Crucially, she recognized that patients suffering from loneliness were often unwilling to admit to being lonely. "I think that this may be in part determined by the fact that loneliness is a most unpopular phenomenon in this group-conscious culture," she wrote.[1]

Some lonely people, Fromm-Reichmann observed, would end up alienating those closest to them with their antisocial behavior. They would rage or withdraw, hurl insults or feign indifference. Though craving human company, they pushed people away. She might have been talking about Anthony Doran.

As evolutionary research has taught us, the main reason for this behavior is fear, sometimes amounting to terror, that becomes embedded in the trauma of loneliness. It's a fear of being hurt, aimed at those who might reject us. And it's a fear of being abandoned, which can turn to anger—and even violence—at those perceived to be leaving or ignoring us.

For years, researchers have observed a connection between loneliness and violence. In one study, when researchers planted the idea in subjects' minds that they'd be alone in later life or that their fellow subjects had rejected them, the excluded people tended to react by lashing out or by deriding those they believed had rejected them.[2] Examinations of the backgrounds of violent criminals from mass shooters to serial killers have turned up evidence of loneliness.

Extreme violence is a rare response to the common human experience of loneliness, and violence has its origins in many more factors than loneliness alone. But if loneliness is a factor in leading some people to violence, can connection help turn those individuals away from violence? To find out I paid a visit to the Anti-Recidivism Coalition (ARC) in Los Angeles.

Founded in 2013, ARC provides a variety of housing, employment, and educational support services to hundreds of formerly incarcerated individuals. It also provides them with a safe community of supportive people. The goal of the organization is to help people rebuild their lives while living "crime-free, gang-free, and drug-free." And ARC has proven its value: As of 2018, an estimated 11 percent of ARC members return to prison, as compared with around a 50 percent recidivism rate for the state of California.[3]

ARC's headquarters are located close to Skid Row in downtown Los Angeles. Just blocks from the glitzy billboards and tall reflective buildings of the civic center, this area consists mostly of warehouses and parking lots. The exterior walls of many of the buildings I drove past on the cold and rainy day of my visit were covered in red, blue, and black graffiti with words and images artfully etched onto peeling plaster. I was thus unprepared for the newly constructed building that houses ARC. With its light-filled open plan and hardwood floors, ARC's offices feel more like a Silicon Valley start-up than a nonprofit social services operation. The glass-partitioned conference rooms are continuously filled with meetings. The place buzzes with energy as ARC members, interns, policy researchers, therapists, and volunteers stride through the halls and gather in groups, talking, laughing, and problem solving.

That day I met several ARC members willing to share their life experiences with me. The first, Richard Lopez, was in his late thirties, covered with tattoos, including on his scalp. But he was dressed in khakis and a button-down dress shirt, and except for the tattoos, he could have passed for a corporate consultant on casual Friday. Although his violent past is evident in his criminal record, he spoke of his nine-year-old son with the tenderness and unmistakable love of a doting parent. He radiated pride at the fulfillment he's found since leaving prison, yet his face betrayed a deep, lingering sadness.

Richard grew up in the housing projects of Wilmington, California. Originally built in 1942 to house temporary shipyard workers during World War II, the Dana Strand Village was filled with drugs, gangs, and violence by the time Richard was born. "Kind of like its own little world within its own little world" was how Richard described his childhood neighborhood. "You could drive by it and won't realize that within the housing complex there's a shootout going on."

Sandwiched between his siblings in birth order, Richard felt he had to compete for attention and affection. His father had a long-standing problem with alcohol, which, charitably speaking, distracted him from parenting; he rarely knew what his children were doing or where they were. Meanwhile, Richard's mother worked all the time—until one day during his teenage years when she abruptly left the family.

Richard came to feel like he didn't belong in his own home. "I would sometimes tear up when I entered the house because I felt something was missing," he said, the ache still evident in his voice. "I was lonely but didn't know it."

Searching for a sense of belonging and acceptance, he turned to other young men who were experiencing a void at home. As with so many boys who feel they're not allowed to express sadness or vulnerability, their loneliness often manifested as anger, which they channeled into crime. At thirteen, Richard was arrested for stealing a car. For the next five years he was in and out of Los Padrinos Juvenile Hall. The minute he got out, he'd reconnect with his friends on the street, most of whom were now in gangs. At first he refused their pressure to join. He hated the gangs he'd grown up around. But one day when he was walking with friends, a car pulled up beside them and members of a local gang inside demanded to know where Richard and his friends were from. The coded words were meant to determine their gang affiliation.

Something shifted inside Richard in that moment. He looked his questioners in the eye and stated loudly and proudly the name of another local gang to which he said he belonged. His friends were dumbstruck. The car left them in peace since they didn't have a conflict with the gang he named. Richard still remembers how excited his friends were that he had finally joined the family.

Richard has tried in the years since to figure out why he felt compelled to, essentially, join a gang on the spot. As best he could tell, it was the pent-up desire to belong that finally took over. This reflection reminded me of Derek Black's remarks about his childhood within the white nationalist movement. A gang may have a lot of negatives, Richard said, but it also provided a community and a sense that he mattered.

"When you do get jumped into the gang, the love that you get at that moment, it kind of overwhelms you because everybody's hugging you," Richard told me. "Everyone is like, 'Welcome to the hood, man. You did good, man. You part of us now, man, you family.' And as a naïve young adult, I was like, 'Okay, I feel loved.' Like I felt so loved that I had to return that love. And in gang life the way to return that love is to produce violence, to go out there and cause havoc."

Richard still yearned for a sense of belonging with his family at home. But joining a gang created even more distance between him and his siblings. He couldn't bear to tell them he'd joined a gang because he knew they'd worry. So he put his gang life in a box and put it away when he got home. The more things that happened to him in the gang, the more he stuffed in the box. Pretty soon it was overflowing with pain and regret. Not being able to share this with the people who were supposed to be his closest relationships made him feel even more estranged and alone.

The way Richard describes it, his loneliness turned to anger, and his anger turned to violence. In 2005, he was arrested for attempted murder. Police had found him with a firearm and ammunition. He only received 180 days for the firearm charge, but in 2007 he was arrested for assault after a fight with members of a rival gang. The previous strike on his record dramatically increased his punishment. Richard was sentenced to fourteen years and four months in a maximum-security state prison.

"Unspeakable things happened there," Richard told me, dropping his voice.

Yet it was in the isolation of a prison cell that Richard began to change. Soon after he landed there, his girlfriend sent news that he was going to be a father. He was both overjoyed and heartbroken, knowing that his son might grow up as he had, without the presence of a loving father.

"That was the beginning of my transition. I began to read more. I began to pray more. I started going to school, got my GED, began college. I started getting certificates in a bunch of subjects, including parenting. I just started to engage in it all, and I loved it."

When I spoke with Richard, he'd only been out of jail for six months, after serving ten of the fourteen years. He already had built a new life with his family, had a job that enabled him to pay rent, owned a vehicle, and had a bank account. He owes a lot of this to ARC's portfolio of jobs, housing, and other reintegration programs and its social support groups.

But Richard's emotional recovery is more gradual. "Every day I fight, you know, mentally, to beat that monster down that tells me I can't escape my past. The loneliness still affects me today."

Though he and his wife love each other, he found it hard to talk to her about some of the experiences he'd been through. Like Anthony Doran coming home from war, Richard felt people just wouldn't understand if they hadn't been in a gang or in prison. It didn't help that his tattoos—a vestige of his past—scared people away.

The one person he came to feel completely comfortable talking to was his nine-year-old son. Conversations with his son were free of judgment. They let him feel normal. For Richard, his son was a godsend. "Our conversations are what get me connected back to my human roots. Because for so many years I was dehumanized. I wake up every morning and tell him I love him, and he tells me he loves me, too. And that feels incredible."

I was struck by the number of times Richard mentioned the word "love" in our conversations. He considered love to be the opposite of loneliness. Love was the solution to a lack of connection. And he'd realized that loving oneself and loving another were inextricably linked.

One of the last things he told me was a bit of advice he would offer to his younger self: "Surround yourself with people who are going in the right direction. And there you'll find that love you need. Because if you surround yourself with those who are doing the negative, you're going to get love, but it's a love that's fictitious, it's fake. It's only temporary."

I was intrigued by Richard's parting words but a bit puzzled as well. He joined a gang to fill a gaping emotional hole in his life, and it worked. The gang became his home and garnered his loyalty. He put his life on the line for fellow gang members, just as Anthony Doran had for the soldiers of Alpha Company. So why did Richard describe the love that came from the gang as "fake"?

Phillip Lester helped me understand.

In many ways, Phillip and Richard lived parallel lives. Phillip now is forty years old, tall and lanky with long dreadlocks and a soft-spoken demeanor, but when he was sixteen, he was tried for four attempted murders and ended up serving two different stints in prison, totaling twenty-one years. Phillip grew up in South Central Los Angeles, the place that inspired iconic movies like *Boyz n the Hood* and *Colors*.

Phillip's grandmother raised him and gave him the love and stability he needed in the beginning. But then the gangs moved in. People were wearing different colors and flashing hand signs. And violence followed.

The first time he was in a shoot-out, he was eight. "Me and my uncle were standing on the street corner," Phillip said. "Some guys pulled up and asked where we were from. My uncle went immediately to go shoot, backing up towards the house, and they were shooting, too. It wasn't like I was scared, though. I was just like, 'Oh shit, is this like really happening?' I didn't even know the gravity of it. My grandmother's house wound up being targeted on several occasions by drive-by shootings. I got shot in my grandmother's yard twice. Her son, my uncle, got killed in her yard as well."

As the gangs took over the neighborhood, they became the new normal, and Phillip eventually joined one. But he found that relationships within the gang were different from friendships on the outside: love in the gang felt conditional.

"What I had to realize is that individuals are not loyal to you; they are loyal to the code. I could have known you since elementary school, but if you have decided to do something that is taboo, like snitching, it instantly goes out the door."

When I asked Phillip and Richard to reflect on the connection between loneliness and violence, Richard replied without hesitation, "I think loneliness and violence are in a weird way brother and sister. Where I grew up, you had a bunch of lonely people running around looking for an outlet. You become very hostile to those around you when you're lonely. I would find any little thing to set me off and use that as an excuse for a violent act." He described the effect of violence much the way Anthony had the effect of opioids. "The violence covers the loneliness for a quick minute, but once that high wears off, the loneliness would come back much stronger and hungrier. There's no way you can escape it. It becomes a dominant force in your life. You can run in circles trying to figure it out, you can pacify it with alcohol or drugs or with anything you can imagine under the sun. But in the end, it's still there. You've got to face the man in the mirror."

Richard's analysis also reminded me of Maxine Chaseling and her experience with older men in Australia who were struggling with loneliness but whose feelings manifested as frustration, anger, impatience, and general grumpiness. The most common target of those feelings were the men's spouses. No wonder many wives in these situations ended up feeling frustrated and at their wits' end.

The repeated expression of anger—whether through emotional or physical violence—leads to a certain hardening over time, for all involved. Phillip pointed out that this makes connection even more difficult. "It's like a certain part of your humanity becomes numb. Some of us carry that detachment throughout our lives, and you find yourself in a lonely, isolated place because you feel people don't understand you." Loneliness can beget violence, which perpetuates loneliness.

So what stops the cycle? For Richard, it was the love of this family. For Phillip, it was the ARC community. In the years he'd been out of prison, Phillip had become deeply engaged in the mission of the coalition, both helping others and receiving help through support circles. No longer part of a community that demanded violence, he began to see a different way to form and secure a sense of belonging and togetherness. At ARC he could show up and feel seen in an honest and nonjudgmental way. "Just the genuineness of the people here," he said. "This is home. You know, they recognize you for who you are."

Phillip's comments about helping others at ARC echoed Anthony Doran's vow to help his fellow soldiers and other vets struggling with loneliness and despair. It resonated with Richard's commitment to help his son grow up safe and loved, and also with the quiet but evident need of men's shed members to be of service to each other and their communities. The common thread of service that ran through these lifesaving connections reminded me of an observation that John and Stephanie Cacioppo made when working with active duty US Army soldiers on improving social resilience. They found that acts of kindness and generosity were among the most powerful exercises for reducing loneliness and improving well-being.

"A small favor implicitly creates a sense of obligation to return the favor," John and Stephanie wrote in the *Harvard Business Review*.[4] "When the initial act is perceived as kindhearted, the social norm of reciprocity stimulates a sense of gratitude and mutual respect, promotes cooperation, and strengthens the trust and bonds between people."

That's what was happening when Frieda Fromm-Reichmann showed kindness and interest in her catatonic patient's true feelings. It was as if this simple act of grace began pulling the mask off loneliness and laying the groundwork for relationships.

Faith traditions have always understood this connection. That's why service plays an elemental role in every major religion. Congregations are expected to hold and help one another just as our ancestors' tribes once did, and in so doing, they feel closer to God. Crucially, it's understood that, through this triangle with divinity, *both* the giver and the recipient reap the rewards of service.

As the Bengali poet Rabindranath Tagore wrote, Gautama Buddha taught his followers to seek "liberation that comes not by abjuring work but by the practicing of self-giving through right action."[5] The Hindu Upanishads declare, "The Divinities rejoice when somebody's happiness owes another's sacrifice given voluntarily."[6]

In Christianity, Jesus is revered for his generosity and devotion to the poor and needy, and charity is considered a core virtue. Most Christians believe that helping others is an expression of faith.

And in Judaism, the commandment of *tzedakah*, or justice, shares the same root as *Sadaqah*, the Muslim word for giving. Beyond donating time and money to the poor, rabbis emphasize "*gemilut hasadim*," meaning loving kindness, as the spirit of giving. They also hold up the ancient Jewish phrase "*tikkun olam*," meaning to repair or heal the world, which has been referred to by presidents including Barack Obama and Bill Clinton as a vision for service.

In Islam, too, service is written into scripture. And while the rich are expected to give in service of the poor, the Quran wisely provides guidance so that the poor can be of service, too. Revealing the importance of human connection as a fundament of faith, the Prophet Muhammad recommended the simple act of smiling as a valuable gift of charity.

Like the Prophet Muhammad, the twelfth-century rabbi Maimonides understood that the primary purpose of charity is to elevate the relationship between giver and recipient. That's why Maimonides taught that the quality of interaction is at least as important as the content of the charitable service. Humiliation, superiority, and dependence have no place in compassionate giving. Or, as sociologists Christian Smith and Hilary Davidson put it, in giving we receive, and in grasping we lose.[7]

The point that this makes is essential. The practice of service need not be onerous, distracting, or draining, but it must be kind. Ideally, through service this kindness becomes a deeper part of who we are, woven into our character. This is what India's great spiritual leader Mahatma Gandhi meant when he said, "The best way to find yourself is to lose yourself in the service of others."[8]

Researchers lately have picked up this thread from a neuroscientific perspective. One of them is Dr. Steve Cole.[9] Service, Cole told me, is tied together with purpose and meaning, and all three play potent roles in social connectedness. But service, in particular, may offer a major key to healing the trauma of loneliness.

At its core, Cole pointed out, the hypervigilance associated with loneliness is egocentric. Severely lonely people feel so threatened that they are preoccupied with their own emotional safety and have little energy for empathy or concern for others. And yet, he said, "We value a lot of things besides our own individual health and security." Those concerns might include nature, art, politics, or poverty, and they might motivate us to volunteer at the local museum or food bank even when we're feeling lonely. "That's why getting threatened people to focus on things that they care about turns out to be a pretty good trick from a neuro-biological perspective."

In 2016, Dr. Naomi Eisenberger and fellow researchers reported that the experience of helping others lowers activity in the brain's stress and threat centers, including the amygdala, dorsal anterior cingulate cortex, and anterior insula. At the same time, *increased* activity is seen in the parts of our brain associated with caregiving and rewards (our ventral striatum and septal area).[10] This indicates that helping others reduces our stress even as it increases our sense of well-being, making it an important antidote to the pain of loneliness and disconnection.

Another study, published in 2017 in the *Journal of Gerontology*, confirmed this effect by comparing rates of loneliness among widows and currently married women from a pool of nearly six thousand Americans.[11] Not surprisingly, the widows generally tended to be much lonelier than the married women. However, there was one notable exception: widows who started volunteer-ing in some service activity for an average of two or more hours a week were no lonelier than volunteers whose spouses were still alive. Helping others effectively erased the loneliness caused by loss.

This shouldn't really surprise us. Helping others helps us feel competent and purposeful, and it gives our actions added mean-ing by extending their value to others. In short, helping others makes us feel we matter, and mattering feels good.

What doesn't matter so much, Cole says, is the specific type of service we perform. There's no "best" or "one size fits all" way to help others. The goal doesn't even have to focus on people. When we're lonely, we may feel too intimidated to join a group that works directly with underprivileged kids or seniors, but our love of animals might lead us to a rescue shelter. Our concern for the environment might inspire us to pitch in when groups clean up the beach or forest. Our love of literature might draw us to the public library where we can volunteer shelving books. Any form of service will do, as long as it feels genuinely and personally meaningful.

According to Cole, when we have a strong sense of purpose and meaning, "it shifts the balance between these two powerful brain systems—one involved in avoiding danger or threat and responding to it somehow, and the other one involved in seeking and discovering and wanting." Once activated, the seeking, discovering, and wanting system can overrule the threat-avoidance system. This creates a sort of "therapeutic state" that transfers the focus off oneself—which can be a relief.

This relief, in turn, serves to ease our encounters with others who also are helping or being helped, so that everyone can work together toward a common goal while gaining a mutual sense of purpose and meaning. This mutuality is what's happening socially and emotionally when we're working alongside others at the library or animal shelter.

This also is why volunteer organizations, activist movements, religious groups, and programs like those created by ARC play such a critical role in lifting people out of loneliness. They provide safe opportunities to rekindle a sense of meaning, value, and purpose while also connecting with others.

To be clear, just caring about an issue isn't enough. Nor is the simple act of joining a group. The real therapeutic synergy occurs when we come together with others to take action to achieve a common goal. "It's less about meeting other people, at least at first," Steve said, "and more about finding purpose and taking part in something larger than yourself."

We're social creatures, after all, and our bodies know it's not normal to be completely self-absorbed. So our brains reward us neurobiologically when we join forces to accomplish something positive. In other words, *doing good makes us feel good*.

The effect on loneliness is indirect, Cole stressed. "Focusing on a goal or mission may help get lonely people back engaged in things where they will then learn for real that other people are not always threatening. As a result, they may build social relationships and social capital that will give them the resources they need to feel okay."

What Steve was suggesting was that service operates like a back door out of loneliness into social revival. While I found this true to my own experience, when I stepped back to think about it, I realized that one well-known organization has been employing this therapeutic "back door" for nearly a century.

Driving Addiction

Bill Wilson, a cofounder of Alcoholics Anonymous (AA), was as clear on the therapeutic role of service between AA members as he was on the relationship between loneliness and addiction. This three-way association is as true for addiction to opioids, gambling, gaming, and food, as it is for alcoholism. Wilson, however, was the pioneer who connected these three dots, and his goal was to help alcoholics.

"Almost without exception," Wilson wrote, "alcoholics are tortured by loneliness.[12] Even before our drinking got bad and people began to cut us off, nearly all of us suffered the feeling that we didn't quite belong. Either we were shy, and dared not draw near others, or we were apt to be noisy good fellows craving attention and companionship, but never getting it—at least to our way of thinking. There was always that mysterious barrier we could neither surmount nor understand."

Wilson understood this because of his personal experience with addiction. A few months into his sobriety, it struck him that if he was going to remain sober, he would need to connect with someone else who was struggling with alcohol—someone who could talk to him as an equal, particularly when the urge to drink resurfaced with a vengeance. That someone was Dr. Bob, who'd been struggling with his drinking as well. The relationship they built not only inspired AA, but it was the basis for a form of service called "sponsorship," where alcoholics serve as trusted, confidential mentors to help each other stay sober. As described in AA's pamphlet on sponsorship, "We know from experience that our own sobriety is greatly strengthened when we give it away!"[13]

What this is saying is that service is a two-way gift. Sponsors "give away" their sobriety by drawing on all their struggles, triumphs, strategies, and perseverance to guide, encourage, and help their fellow members, but this service is not a sacrifice. It actually strengthens recovery for the sponsor as well as for the recipient. This is what Steve Cole meant when he talked about "finding purpose and taking part in something larger than yourself."

When loneliness leaves an aching hole in one's life, violence, drugs, and alcohol aren't the only unhealthy behaviors that people use to anesthetize the pain. Food, sex, and even work can also be used to mask the void. Often, these stopgaps are connected to loneliness, and sometimes to one another, in ways we cannot see. All can do us harm.

Dr. Bryan Robinson is a psychotherapist who's studied and experienced this firsthand when it comes to work. Through his own life, as well as hundreds of interviews, he's traced the trajectory from childhood to workaholism in his book *#Chill: Turn Off Your Job and Turn On Your Life*.[14] For Robinson, as for those he interviewed, loneliness played a starring role in this story.

Bryan's father was an alcoholic who never got help for his drinking. As a young boy, Bryan told me, he and his siblings would get blindsided when their dad came home and fights broke out. "When you're a child and you are bombarded with that kind of stress, your body is not prepared to integrate it. You develop hypervigilance waiting for the shoe to drop. And some people go to alcohol, some people go to food, some people go to work as a way to assuage that anxiety."

Work and duty became Robinson's twin refuges. In effect, he appointed himself the grown-up in the family. "In psychology," he said, "we call it 'parentification.'" He made it his job to protect his little sister. He did the housework. He aced his homework. "*Doing* gave me a false sense of control and stability."

He remembers consoling himself with stories that he'd make up about kids in trouble. "I would get them out of trouble. It was my way to try to control the chaos that I was drowning in. Talk about loneliness!"

From the outside, young Bryan appeared to have it all together. He looked competent, capable, and super motivated. "Underneath, it's all to maintain some kind of control. The paradox is, you become out of control with whatever coping mechanism you're using."

What he was doing *looked* a lot like service. In high school he wrote the church's Christmas play. He directed it. He designed and built the set. He acted in the lead role. "And, of course, what happens is everybody around you thinks this is great. They slap you on the back and give you accolades, when inside you're wounded." Instead of engaging with others through genuine service, in effect, he was using all this work to distance and mask the intimate loneliness he felt as a result of missing the love and affection of his parents. Yet work and the recognition he received couldn't fill that emptiness or allow him to better connect with others.

The pattern carried through college and graduate school and into Robinson's career as a professor, even when he found a life partner. "I worked day and night. I worked holidays and weekends. I didn't have any friends. My primary relationship was falling apart. I was having gastrointestinal problems, but I didn't really know what was going on." That's because all the external markers kept telling him he was a "success" even though he sensed the emotional hole in his life.

The more deeply he immersed himself in his work, the more he avoided doing the painful but necessary work of sorting through the fears and anxieties that were wreaking havoc on his internal life. As time went on, he purposely didn't seek out others, but not because he didn't think he'd enjoy their company. "If you don't let people in and you don't let yourself get too close, you can't get your heart stomped on again. Thus, aloneness seems to be the antidote against the threat of hurt, although it imprisons us."

Bryan recalls going to the beach on vacation and hiding his work so his family wouldn't catch him. "Sometimes I would put it under a spare tire or sometimes I just put it in the leg of my jeans, just like an alcoholic would hide a bottle. Everybody would say, 'Let's go for a walk on the beach.' And I would stretch my arms and yawn and pretend I was tired and say I was going to sleep, and once they were out of sight, I would pull out my project from the university and work feverishly to try to complete it."

He admits that not all work addiction is that extreme. But some cultures reward this behavior more than others. In Japan it's common enough that there's a special term for this condition: *karōshi*. It means "death from overwork." But in America, he said, "we don't really have a name that identifies it because of the denial in our culture."

Bryan's denial began to crack when he started attending therapy meetings to support a family member in treatment for alcoholism. "I didn't understand what was going on in my own situation, but it helped me start to realize that I, too, had an addictive issue." He went on to join Al-Anon, a support group that helps families and friends of alcoholics. There, the Twelve Steps encouraged him to surrender control, admit that life had become unmanageable, and take a "searching and fearless moral inventory" of himself.

"I remember leaving those meetings so serene and so calm," he said, "just simply by sitting there listening and hearing what other people are doing and how they're coping." Then he discovered Workaholics Anonymous meetings, where the only requirement for membership was the desire to stop working compulsively. "And it started to sink in that I was using my work the way my father used his bottle." And in doing so, he was pushing away the very people he needed most.

He began to practice yoga and mindfulness meditation. "That took me into a deeper place within myself and helped me make deeper connections about what I had been doing and what I could do differently. I got to know myself in a different way, in a deeper, more connected way."

Looking inside oneself, Bryan says, is not only something busy career professionals or lonely college students need to do. The same pattern of distracting busyness can affect anyone who's unable to turn off the noise enough to regroup, recharge, and re-center themselves. Once he began to reclaim space and time in his life, he found that he was also better able to let in the people around him and give attention to his relationships. "Being with myself and being with the people around me started to give me something I had never experienced before."

He discovered that he enjoyed Saturday-afternoon matinees and working in the garden with his husband, who loves to grow orchids. He also found a new appreciation for beauty and sound. Less preoccupied with what needed to be done next, he was better able to focus on the person right in front of him. "I was able to settle more in the present moment, which has a whole different effect on your system."

Bryan describes this crucial change as "leading from the inside out instead of being pressured from the outside in."

The first and most striking reward of this change was the improvement in his marriage. Bryan told me his early research showed that work addiction raises the divorce rate and that children of parents with work addiction are at greater risk of anxiety and depression. "When you're a work addict, your tasks become the most important thing. A relationship will often feel like an obligation," he shared. The spouses of people who are addicted to work understandably will complain that they feel lonely and neglected. What's broken is the reciprocity of true connection.

Bryan remembers his husband "was on his knees begging me to spend time with him. My view was, you are interfering with some of the most important things I will ever do in my life. How dare you? It wasn't empathic and it wasn't compassionate."

Today Bryan has reversed his priorities. "My commitment to the people that I love is at the top."

Disrupting the vicious cycle between work addiction and loneliness has also had an unexpected and positive impact on his professional performance. "The paradox is that I became more productive and more effective, the more I slowed down and was aware and connected." In a modern version of Aesop's fable of the tortoise and the hare, Bryan was proving that slow and steady really does win the race.

But the final benefit for Bryan was completely personal. "I was happier and more fulfilled," he says. "I'm busy, but I'm having fun. I don't feel like work is looming over me and driving me. I'm driving it."

Invisible Wounds

I couldn't help but notice how many of these stories of loneliness began with some level of trauma in childhood. Domestic violence, gang violence, murder, parental divorce, and abandonment are hardly conducive to happy childhoods and healthy kids. These early wounds can leave long-term scars, among them a great deal of social anxiety. As Bryan said, the threat of harm can form an internal prison filled with loneliness.

The tragedy is that one's earliest relationships can and should serve as the foundation for social strength. In an ideal world, every baby would be born into a clan that provided enough social interaction, guidance, and affection for the child to grow up with a secure identity and a strong sense of belonging. Close friends and relatives could be counted on to respond to the child with care and insight. From them, the child would learn both the value and the complexity of social interaction, how to form strong and healthy friendships, how to cultivate trust and grow up to be a reliable and effective member of society. As we've seen, however, the world is not perfect, and no family, much less any relationship, is ideal.

Public health experts often refer to traumatic experiences that occur during childhood as "adverse childhood experiences" (ACEs). The term encompasses physical, emotional, and sexual abuse; physical/emotional neglect; having a parent who's an alcoholic or a victim of domestic violence, a family member in jail, or a family member diagnosed with a mental illness; and the disappearance of a parent due to divorce, death, or abandonment.[15]

High levels of toxic stress from ACEs without the buffer of loving relationships can damage the structure and function of a child's developing brain. This can lead to problems with learning and behavior. Physiologically, it can impair immunity and growth and even affect us at a genetic level. Children with high ACE scores are much more prone to addiction, depression, suicide, heart disease, lung disease, and cancer. They are also more likely to have trouble building trusted relationships and are at greater risk for loneliness.

According to a 2018 *JAMA Pediatrics* study that surveyed American adults in twenty-three states, 60 percent of adults grew up with at least one ACE and 25 percent had three or more.[16] They may desperately want to connect and be accepted, but can't, because life has trained them to be afraid of being exploited or hurt by other people. "They start to look for any tiny sign of threat," said Steve Cole, who had helped me understand that with our emotional scars often comes a higher sensitivity to threat and rejection.

So, what's the solution? We can't just write these children off because they were victims of abuse and neglect.

And why is it that, for all the devastating evidence of the damage that early trauma *can* do to kids, there are many who somehow defy the odds and grow up to be whole and healthy, with strong and supportive social networks?

These two burning questions compelled University of California, Davis, professor Dr. Emmy Werner more than sixty years ago to launch a landmark long-term study of childhood resilience on the Hawaiian island of Kauai.[17]

Hawaii is known the world over for its palm trees and pristine beaches, for gentle trade winds, welcoming leis of fragrant orchids, and graceful hula dancers. But Hawaii's poverty rate is thirteenth in the nation, and its multiracial residents experience the same array of hardships as do mainlanders. Its benefit for Werner and her team, who launched their study in 1955, was that they could easily identify and track the health and development of all 698 of the children born on the island of Kauai that year. They would continue to follow these children at intervals until the age of forty.

What made this study truly groundbreaking was that it was most interested not in the damage that hardships such as trauma and illness could do as their subjects aged, but rather in identifying the sources of strength that allowed many of these kids to thrive *in spite of* their hardships.

Nearly a third of the Kauai children studied were born into poverty or faced problems including family discord, parental divorce, and family histories of substance abuse and mental illness. And two-thirds of the group with four or more of these risk factors developed serious problems like learning difficulties, behavioral problems, and mental health problems. But the researchers paid closest attention to that *other* third—the kids in the high-risk group who grew up to be "competent, confident, and caring" adults. Before turning forty, these hardy souls managed to marry and establish careers, and many became devoted parents themselves. Given the odds against them, what accounted for their resilience?

The answer was that the most protective factors in childhood were largely social.[18] Genetics definitely helped, in that children who were born with calm and agreeable dispositions naturally attracted care and support, but it was the social support that made the difference. Kids who were able to bond as babies with their parents or primary caregivers had one social advantage. Kids who formed close bonds with substitute parents within the family had another. These substitutes might be older siblings, aunts or uncles, or grandparents; *a child only needed one*. What mattered was that the surrogate be both nurturing and available and emotionally stable and mature.

As they got older, the nurtured kids learned to lean on trusted and trustworthy community relationships. Turning to teachers, pastors, neighbors, church members, or their friends' parents, they "recruited" helpful adults outside their own family for emotional support and advice in times of crisis. Still later, they found genuinely caring and stable partners who were friends as well as lovers, and together they built healthy marriages and raised healthy families.

Werner called the group that did well despite adversity "vulnerable but invincible." Within this group, there were significantly more women than men. She noted that the women in her study "relied on a larger network of social supports to help them cope with stressful life events and worries."[19]

The importance of these relationships in mitigating the negative effects of ACEs cannot be overstated. Werner made this clear in a 2012 interview when she was asked how important belonging and attachment were in explaining the success of those children.[20] She replied, "I think that is really the most basic thing on which you need to build everything else." And it doesn't take a special gene or trait to establish this attachment. It takes human connections and the social skills that we all learn through the sharing of love and kindness.

The Kauai resiliency findings have since been confirmed by other studies.[21] Today it's widely understood that one of the most important factors in preventing and addressing toxic stress in children is healthy social connection.[22] [23]

While a traumatic past may increase our risk of bad things happening, we are not destined to crash and burn. Adversity doesn't mean that we're destroyed. Werner's research and the work of others tell us that we can rescue one another. It is in our relationships with one another that we can all find healing and a better path forward.

One of the insights Phillip passed on to me at ARC was the adage: *If you build a kid, you won't have to repair an adult.* Reflecting on this comment after reviewing the Kauai study, I wondered what could happen if we were able to apply the lessons of Werner's findings at scale. Big Brothers Big Sisters of America provided a heartening answer.

The oldest and largest youth mentoring program in the United States, Big Brothers Big Sisters (BBBS) was started more than a century ago in 1904 as a way to reduce juvenile delinquency. Today the organization has a vision that all children can achieve success in life, regardless of their background. They help kids succeed by matching at-risk kids ("Littles") with adult volunteers ("Bigs") in one-on-one mentoring relationships. The kids may start as young as age five and continue through young adulthood, regularly spending time with their mentors in settings and activities of their choosing.

BBBS's 2018 survey of matches showed improvements for Littles in all seven areas: parental trust, attitudes toward risky behaviors, grades, educational expectations, confidence in doing schoolwork, sense of belonging among peers, and the presence of a special adult.[24] An earlier controlled study found that after eighteen months of spending time with their Bigs, the Littles, when compared to matched controls, were less likely to use illegal drugs, skip school, or hit someone. They were also more confident of their schoolwork and got along better with their families.[25]

This is powerful evidence of the difference that just one caring adult can make. Those of us who are blessed with wise and loving parents can generally credit them with much of our social equi-librium. My own were not only a refuge during lonely times but a source of guidance and an example of how to build relationships with self-confidence, compassion, and generosity. Even the most supportive adults, however, can't defend a child against social trauma that occurs outside their presence. When kids fall prey to schoolyard bullies, even the most loved child can experience a kind of shell shock.

I should know. I was one of them.

When I was in middle school, I remember spending eight in-terminable weeks in woodshop class with two classmates who called me "Gandhi" (and not in an admiring way) and mocked me constantly about my Indian heritage and darker skin. It was one of the more painful experiences of seventh grade and made me dread going to class. The leader of the pair was much bigger and stronger than his sidekick, who had an injured air about him and few, if any, other friends. In retrospect, I suspect the smaller boy's loneliness played a role in this dynamic, as he doubtless felt that his acceptance by the bully was contingent on his joining in the bullying. If he refused, he'd be rejected and become an object of derision himself. This dynamic mirrors the "fake love" of Richard Lopez's gang. Belonging is such a desirable goal that the threat of rejection can be a powerful group enforcement mechanism.

But my own loneliness doubtless also played a role in this dynamic. Researchers have found that bullies target lonely kids, who are less likely to have defenders.[26] At the same time, the experience of being bullied *makes* kids more fearful, with-drawn, and ever lonelier.

In a 2015 survey of research on loneliness and bullying, California State University professor Dr. Shireen Pavri cited the same cyclical effect that Steve Cole described. "Boys and girls who reported feeling bullied at least weekly, reported the highest incidence of symptoms such as feeling lonely, helpless, and left out."[27] Worse, the cycle often seems to turn in only one direction, so that children who are bullied become lonelier, but that loneliness doesn't improve right away if the bullying stops. This means that the social and emotional effects can last much longer than the actual bullying. Pavri further described research showing that "adults who were victimized as children reported lower self-esteem, higher emotional loneliness, greater difficulties maintaining friendships, and were at higher risk for continued victimization as adults."[28]

If bullying were a rare event, this wouldn't be so worrisome. But the rates and impact of bullying around the world are alarming. According to the National Center for Education Statistics, 21 percent of American children in 2015 said they'd been bullied during the school year.[29] A World Health Organization survey of adolescents in twenty-eight countries found that an average of 18 percent of boys and 15 percent of girls had been bullied in the previous thirty days. The more often students were bullied, the more physical and mental complaints they had, including headaches, sleeping problems, nervousness, loneliness, and feeling left out.[30]

Not every victim of bullying, of course, is permanently traumatized. Boys and girls who have a social circle, even a small one, that includes genuine and supporting friends, often can bounce back from the adversities of bullying. And, with kids as with adults, one of the most empowering ways they can cure their loneliness is through service to others.

Goucher College student Noah Block accidentally discovered this solution at fourteen, when he was required to choose a community service project for school. By then Noah had been subject to bullying for years. "In elementary school," he recalled, "my only friends were the special needs kids. When I was nine or ten, I remember feeling that I didn't want to wake up in the morning. I ended up talking to my mother. I told her I felt like killing myself, but I also wanted to try to get help."

The solid support of his parents helped Noah survive those dark years. Both were psychologists. They understood what he was going through, and they cared. When his school didn't act to protect him, they moved him to a different school. They acted as his allies, his sounding board, and his social mentors. But they alone couldn't cure his loneliness or change the schoolyard dynamics. And Noah had no expectation that community service would, either.

But when Noah volunteered at the YMCA Marin County Youth Court, his life began to change. The Marin County Youth Court is administered by the Restorative Services department of the YMCA in collaboration with the Superior Court system. It's an alternative to the traditional juvenile justice system and relies on nonadversarial, peer-to-peer restorative practices. Young volunteers like Noah serve as jurors, bailiffs, advocates, and judges. Their clients are kids who have broken the law and are willing to accept accountability. The clients' stories gave Noah perspective on traumas and struggles beyond his own, and he found that he sometimes could help.

One girl had stolen a bagel. "They almost didn't send the case to us because it was a ninety-eight-cent bagel," Noah told me. "But she started to open up and talk to us and ultimately shared she had an opioid addiction and experienced sexual violence in her family."

Another girl had been arrested for shoplifting baby formula and wet wipes for a friend who was too poor to get them for her kids. "We were able to get her connected to services that supported her and her friend."

The goal of Youth Court is to keep young people out of jail and get their lives and futures back on track. "The first step," Noah learned to tell young clients, "is always to ask for help. People are there. You just have to find them." The program taught him to tell himself the same thing.

"While we had different life experiences," he told me, "there was a common thread that brought us together to Youth Court, that allowed us to talk about our family lives, trauma, etc. I got to hear about what was happening to young people and got to also work with other young people who were passionate about these issues. It was my first experience building authentic friendships after being bullied."

One consequence of loneliness is a deep sense of helplessness and hopelessness, and that message is driven home by bullies, who strive to make their victims feel weak and worthless. What Noah discovered in Youth Court was that his life had both meaning and purpose. He had the power to make a real difference in the lives of peers who faced other kinds of danger and challenges than he had known. He learned this by connecting with these fellow youth, listening to their problems, and imagining himself in their shoes. He found that he possessed the compassion and wisdom to counsel them well, and in the process he gained invaluable perspective on his own problems. Just as he could see a way forward for these other kids in trouble, he could see a future for himself.

Now nineteen, Noah says his work on Youth Court "fundamentally changed me as a human being." Helping others healed him. It gave him a sense that he mattered and that he belonged in the world.

From birth to death, we all need a sense of place and people who will help us learn, grow, heal, and serve one another. The bonds that we form through service can not only break the downward spiral of loneliness, but can also provide the cure for trauma and the enduring source of security that every one of us needs.

My paternal grandfather embodied this truth. Despite living in bracing poverty in a small village in India and raising six children on his own after my grandmother died from tuberculosis, he still spent time each year traveling from village to village raising money for a youth hostel so that the children of his village would have a place to study. He himself had never even finished elementary school, but he was committed to helping the next generation of his village do better. His firm belief was that our bond to others was precious, and with it came a responsibility to help and serve. This belief not only defined him, but it gave him strength.

Sometimes people would suggest that he had his priorities mixed up. "Your own kids don't even have enough to eat," they'd say, "and you're out there raising money for other people's children. What's wrong with you?"

To which he would simply—powerfully—respond, "Those kids are our kids, too."

Although my grandfather passed away when I was young, my father often told me this story, and I've taken his gentle but powerful words into my heart. They remain one of the best definitions of "connection" I know.

Building a More Connected Life

CHAPTER 6

Relating Inside Out

The most common form of despair is not being who you are.

—Søren Kierkegaard

You can't really love someone else unless you really love yourself first.

—Fred Rogers, *You Are Special: Neighborly Words of Wisdom from Mr. Rogers*

The moment Serena Bian arrived at her dorm room—empty but for the leftover scraps of paper and bedding from the previous year's occupants—something felt deeply unnerving about the transition that awaited her. She was beginning her freshman year at the University of Pennsylvania and was brand new to Philadelphia. She knew no one here and suddenly wondered if she ever would. As this thought crossed her mind, Serena felt like she was losing herself. The memory still made her shudder when she told me about it six years later.

What Serena was experiencing was the first tremor of loneliness, and her response fit the classic pattern that John Cacioppo identified two decades ago. Her body was flashing a warning signal, just as if she were a stranded hominid on the tundra. She was separated from her people. She was in unfamiliar territory. The tribe she was about to meet might contain enemies. She needed to put her guard up, stay hypervigilant, and find her people soon. Unfortunately, Serena's people were hundreds of miles away, and she didn't know how to replace them.

Born and raised in suburban Michigan, she was the child of immigrant parents who'd left China in search of opportunity in the 1970s. Five foot six inches with a radiant smile that frequently punctuates her pensive expression, Serena today is a picture of quiet intensity and joy. The first time I met her I realized that, while she speaks with a gentle voice and soft tones, this young woman brims with curiosity, idealism, and a fierce belief in humanity. She told me that early in life, "I learned how to deal with cultural isolation as one of the only Asian Americans in a predominantly Caucasian environment." But that didn't mar her childhood. Far from it. She had lots of interests, and she felt "known" at her small, private school. As a teenager she developed a passion for sustainability and a fervent desire to protect the environment. "I became a beekeeper, made some fantastic friends, had mentors in school who believed in me." She also fell in love for the first time.

Yet like many new freshmen, when Serena got to college, she was in a state of flux. Shortly before leaving home she'd broken up with her boyfriend, so she arrived on campus overwhelmed by heartache, homesickness, and shock at this abrupt and friendless transition. "How was I supposed to leave the life I had spent eighteen years slowly building, to start all over again, in this foreign territory?"

What she hadn't expected and didn't yet realize was that she'd left more than her life behind; she'd also left her sense of herself—her identity—at home. Like most of us, Serena's childhood identity was forged within the "tribe" of her family, friends, school, and neighborhood. She hadn't yet defined herself apart from those relationships or that sense of belonging, so when she entered the utterly different context of college alone, it was as if she'd lost all the markers that helped her see herself. Suddenly, she felt invisible not only to others but also to her own eyes.

It didn't help when, during new student orientation, she was told that the first week at Penn was going to be "the best week of your life" because of the parties that throbbed across campus from sundown to sunup. For Serena, the "opportunity" to meet hundreds of new freshmen translated into a kind of ultimatum to lunge into this new college life.

Though naturally quite introverted, she tried to adapt. For two nights she braved the parties, only to wind up drunk among strangers. On the final night of orientation, which coincided with her eighteenth birthday, she found herself "walking with some random guy to inevitably hook up. As soon as I got to his room, it dawned on me how unlike me this was. I told him I wanted to go home, and luckily he was nice enough to walk me back to my dorm."

While the encounter ended up involving nothing more than flirtation, Serena was shaken by self-doubt and a profound sense of anxiety. Had she chosen the wrong school, or was there something wrong with her? Should she try to change to fit in, or should she just keep to herself, remaining on guard and defensive? What made it all harder was the lack of anyone she could trust to talk to about her fears and uncertainties. Everyone else seemed to be enjoying this frenzy. The distortions of loneliness made her perceptions of others as suspect as her view of herself.

"No one tells you how hard the first year of college is," she reflected when we spoke. "It's unrealistic to anticipate such a smooth transition when you're uprooted for the first time in your life." The real problem, though, is not knowing who you are as an individual the first time you're expected to meet the wider world *as* an individual.

If only she'd realized how many college students feel the same way. More than 60 percent report that they've felt very lonely within the past year, nearly 30 percent within the past two weeks.[1] In a 2019 survey at the University of California, Davis, half of college freshmen said making friends was more difficult than they'd expected.[2]

For Serena, the scale of her college posed an additional hurdle. Penn is like a city within the city of Philadelphia, and she felt like an insignificant face in the crowd. "The sheer quantity of students on campus who are going through the same experience can create a herd mentality. Keep your head down and stay a part of the herd. If you get left behind, oftentimes, no one sees. It's made doubly challenging when your class sizes are so big, it's difficult to develop personal relationships with your professors."

Those first few weeks, Serena would duck into bathroom stalls between classes to cry. After class, when other students made lunch plans, she made no effort to tag along. "It seemed that whenever I didn't make plans to spend time with people, I would feel lonely and left out. However, whenever I did make plans, there was something incredibly shallow about the interactions. We'd talk about Greek life, partying, getting anxious about school and grades." She longed for the deep conversations she'd enjoyed with her high school friends. But they knew her—and she knew them—from the *inside*. She hadn't yet established that kind of bond with any of her classmates in Philadelphia.

"It seemed like I was a total outsider. I would hear swaths of friends leaving for another party, while I stayed in bed and watched Netflix. I felt like a nobody."

As the semester progressed, Serena's experience of loneliness changed but without lessening in intensity. "I was busy all the time. If I wasn't studying for classes, I was signing up for new clubs, attending various speaker panels or conferences, or in a library or coffee shop doing my homework. I was partly able to distract myself from my loneliness because of the sheer work and extracurricular activities. Busyness is almost like a disease!" she said, echoing Bryan Robinson's description of work addiction.

But she still had no friends, and because the clubs at Penn are so competitive, few freshman applicants are accepted. Serena was no exception. Now college became a time of loneliness *and* rejection. "I felt so lost and just so deeply confused about everything in my life."

Serena's loneliness was often paired with self-blame and self-criticism: "I can't find my place among these people, so it must be my fault or something wrong with me." Again, she was far less alone than she realized. In the UC Davis survey, three-fourths of college students who found it difficult to make friends freshman year told researchers they thought that everyone else had an easier time making friends than they did.[3] This is the cruel pattern of loneliness at work, intensifying isolation and distorting self-consciousness.

Back at home during winter break, Serena met up with one of her high school mentors, who immediately noticed the flatness of her voice, the lack of life in her eyes. She leaned forward and asked, "Serena, do you think you might be depressed?"

"I realized then that I certainly was. A depression caused mostly from an experience of loneliness."

She no longer felt excited about sustainability and beekeeping. She no longer had any desire to meet new people. She'd lost sight of everything she loved, why she mattered, and what gave meaning to her life. It was as if she no longer belonged to herself—or anyone.

She sat down with her parents and considered transferring to a different school. Here, again, she had plenty of generational company. Loneliness and depression can be two important predictors of a college dropout.[4] [5] Forty-one percent of students who left or transferred out of the University of Washington in 2014, for example, said "feeling socially alone" was a factor in their decision to leave.[6]

But Serena ultimately decided instead to start therapy when she returned to Penn that spring. She got a bike and would ride to art museums and along the river, doing things that gave her pleasure and reminded her what she cared about. This helped her regain a sense of herself, but she still felt off-kilter and tentative when interacting with others. "I felt that if I left campus and never returned, there wouldn't be anyone that I would miss, nor would I feel missed by others."

That summer, however, everything changed. Back home, she got a job on an urban farm, where she could get her hands dirty with work she deeply loved, and she enrolled in a monthlong yoga teacher training that she described as "transformative."

"It wasn't so much the yoga that healed me, but rather the community." This group of fifteen spanned all stages and backgrounds of life. There were grandmothers, new fathers, working mothers, graduate students, and a couple who flew to Michigan from Hawaii just for this training. They were strangers, and yet the terms on which they came together jump-started their connections with one another.

The culture of the training felt completely different from that of college, Serena said. It was safe, warm, patient, and welcoming. "Instead of making quick judgments about a person, we took time to understand one another's stories. I learned from this community that at all moments in life, we are each going through our own struggles. I learned that while on the surface, it may seem like someone has it all together, that may not be the case at all."

The training program united these participants around a common set of values, such as kindness and honesty, and interests, such as the practice of yoga, that mattered deeply to every individual. In this way, the group reflected Serena's sense of herself and reinforced her sense of belonging. But these new relationships didn't define her like the close friendships she'd spent her whole life building; she was as new and singular to these strangers as they were to her. Each person had to come to the group in their own way, leading with their own sense of self. And it was in this process of coming to the group and revealing her true self that Serena found the inner balance and conviction she'd been missing on campus.

She realized that the yoga community's shared vulnerability was its primary source of strength. People weren't just allowed to be open and honest; they were encouraged to share and come together around their truest feelings and fears. "I rediscovered the power of uncovering our common humanity."

Serena learned, in the process, to appreciate her own humanity and to be more open, accepting, and forgiving with herself. She recovered not only a sense of her true values and core identity, but also the ability to project and honor that identity through her interactions and relationships with others. She felt centered and grounded, which gave her the confidence she'd been missing freshman year.

"When I left for my sophomore year of college," she said, "I was determined to make more connection on campus happen."

At first, she took baby steps, like inviting individual classmates out to coffee. But instead of settling for the usual small talk, she was candid about her freshman-year loneliness. To her surprise, nearly everyone she told said they'd experienced some form of loneliness, too. "Even the ones that seemed to have so many Facebook friends or thousands of followers on Instagram!"

Intrigued now by this discovery, Serena put together a brief anonymous survey on the college experience and gave it out randomly to seventy-two Penn students. "I was shocked by the number who reported the number one thing they wished they had at Penn was 'deeper/more authentic conversations and friendships.'"

At the same time, Serena became interested in the effect of physical space and architecture on human interactions and cultural change. She noticed that all the spaces on campus seemed to have a predetermined culture. "Meaning, whenever you are on Penn's campus, the predominant culture is that of competition, busyness, and social hierarchy." She wondered if it would be possible to create a physical space that "optimizes for deeply human interactions." In such a space, she imagined, people could interact as the participants of her yoga training had. They would feel free and safe to reveal their true selves, to share their personal passions and concerns—to "be real." They would treat one another with genuine compassion and kindness, as they'd like to be treated themselves. They'd lead with deeply held thoughts and feelings, instead of surface appearances. In other words, they'd relate to one another from the inside out, rather than from the outside in.

As an experiment, Serena rented an Airbnb off campus and invited a group of Penn students who were all strangers to come together for an evening of personal conversation and storytelling. She called it a Space Gathering.

"I actually just approached people on the sidewalk and asked if they'd be interested in spending a few hours with a group of other students getting to know each other and having intentional conversations." Most of the people she approached expressed the same yearning for human openness and honesty that Serena felt.

The first gathering brought together twenty students across various classes and social backgrounds. Because she wanted the experience to be free of small talk and distractions, Serena asked everyone to put their phones away upon entering and sit quietly until all had arrived. "We went through an exercise where we stared at each other's eyes for three minutes before launching into a series of introductions that were less about your stereotypical labels, and more about your story: What is one thing that is going really well in your life, and what is an area where you are struggling?" Then, for the next three hours, they shared their experiences and opinions of social life on campus, their passions and their fears. "The energy in that room at the end of the evening," Serena remembers, "was one of inspiration and hope."

How was it that, after only three hours, a group of strangers could feel so connected? Serena believes that the key lay in creating a space where people could put aside any preconceived social expectations and instead share candid stories without fear of criticism. "Each one of us has fears, aspirations, hopes. We go through more common experiences of things like loneliness, anxiety, depression, than we assume."

The first Space Gathering was so successful that Serena began to host them with new people every few weeks. Her goal was not to turn each group into best friends but to awaken them to their common humanity and, perhaps, to inspire them to treat other students with more kindness and compassion upon returning to campus. She wanted to adjust the culture's value system—one story at a time.

She also wanted to let go of her own judgments, which had so misled her freshman year. "I had to have the mind-set shift that people are good, and that everyone is going through some sort of battle. We're all just trying to figure this stuff out together. I had to let go of the fact that I couldn't clone my high school friends. I had to learn how to cherish each relationship for its uniqueness."

This shift helped her appreciate something new about herself, too. "I became much more open and super *curious* about others!"

Serena began to find people who shared her desire for deeper and more genuine connections. She met some of her closest friends sophomore year, and by the beginning of junior year she felt true belonging in her circle of connections. A few close friendships emerged from Space Gatherings, she told me, but the process was indirect. "I could make lots of casual friends from the Gatherings and turn them into trusted confidantes, simply because I had gotten to know them in such a deep way over a matter of hours." In other words, those honest conversations made it easier both to launch acquaintants and to build lasting friendships. Those skills extended to building and strengthening friendships apart from the gatherings, too.

For Serena, the lasting lesson is not that we all need to be best friends, but that we do need to develop cultures in which all are encouraged to express and share our true humanity. One way to do that is through the power of direct face-to-face conversation. So the culture Serena created took place mostly offline.

"After each gathering, I would ask each participant to recommend one friend—who was as different from them as possible—to attend the next gathering." It turned out that the hunger for human connection was so strong, the gatherings were populated almost entirely through word of mouth. By the time Serena graduated, she'd hosted some forty-five Space Gatherings and created a playbook for peers who'd stepped up to facilitate their own.

Penn's student wellness communications coordinator, Ben Bolnick, attended one evening, and he admitted to the *Daily Pennsylvanian* that Serena's Space Gatherings were filling a vital gap. "Something that all people need," he said, "is to reflect, to discuss, to flesh out ideas and concepts and struggles with other human beings. And sometimes we just don't get that often enough."[7]

Befriending Ourselves

What was it that ultimately allowed Serena to take charge of her loneliness? Her supportive parents, hometown friends, and yoga community certainly played important roles. But the most important factor, I believe, was the connection with herself that she rekindled during that pivotal summer. This firmly centered inner connection gave her the foundation to establish new relationships, starting from the inside out.

Serena's journey back to herself reminded me of a passage in the theologian Thomas Merton's 1960 book *The Wisdom of the Desert*: "What can we gain by sailing to the moon if we are not able to cross the abyss that separates us from ourselves? This is the most important of all voyages of discovery, and without it all the rest are not only useless but disastrous."[8]

Merton's insight resonates within Serena's own comment, "I felt like a nobody." When we feel socially disconnected, we often feel unknown. As Ami Rokach observed, it's like being invisible to the world around us. But the problem isn't only that others fail to see us accurately; the fog of loneliness also blurs our internal mirrors. It obscures our inner strengths, as well as the value that we have to offer, the meaning of our own lives, and the sources of joy and wonder that would normally make us feel connected to the universe around us. This blindness can allow us to drift off course, forgetting what we love about our lives and neglecting to accept and befriend ourselves with the compassion and understanding we deserve.

Sometimes, as in Serena's case, the disconnect reflects an abrupt change in environment. In her positive experiences of high school, Serena felt known and appreciated as a quiet, curious, imaginative thinker and naturalist. It would take time before her fellow students at Penn could get to know her personal passions and concerns. Eventually, she would discover that the campus was filled with people who shared them, but her initial discomfort with unfamiliar people made those individuals as invisible to her as she felt to everyone else. Many of us experience a similar abyss when we start a new school or job or move to a region or country where we're unknown and unmoored, especially if we're afraid of being judged for looking, sounding, or acting different from the surrounding culture. If we're so lonely and fearful that we fail to seek common ground with others in these new surroundings, the sense of culture shock can be profoundly alienating.

But we can get disconnected from our own instincts even without such dislocations. Our circumstances invariably change over time. We get older. We move in and out of professions and relationships. We have experiences and meet people that challenge our preconceived notions about ourselves and the world. At the same time, many of us are constantly seeking to "improve" or "reinvent" ourselves. Much of this change is natural, necessary, and healthy. We strive to learn, to grow, to expand our skills and deepen our knowledge—and self-knowledge. This is a vital and lifelong process. Along the way, however, external influences are constantly pressing us to change in ways that may not be natural or healthy. These external influences can infiltrate and distort our internal decision making.

Modern society bombards us with ideals, such as wealth, celebrity, and perfect fitness, that are seldom attainable and not necessarily desirable for most of us, yet are used commercially like lures. Claims are made for these lures that are rarely true. If we overvalue material ideals and superficial goals, then we risk losing sight of the goals that truly matter to us. We may also lose access to the friends and pursuits that give our lives depth and meaning, as my patient James, the lottery winner, found after becoming rich.

Some of the most pernicious ideals in today's media-driven world are social. Our social media feeds would have us all believe that our social lives depend on having hundreds of friends and followers online and a constant schedule of dates, trips, and parties. This pressure can make us feel out of step if we'd honestly rather watch a movie by ourselves or stay in on a Friday night.

Society also sets norms around ambition that suggest the more we criticize ourselves, the more motivated we'll be to do more and better. This self-criticism dovetails in a dangerous manner with the hypervigilance of loneliness. When lonely, we may feel compelled to beat ourselves up, castigating ourselves as Serena did, for our "failure" to be someone we're not. In the process, we tend to magnify our weaknesses, discount our strengths, and distrust our natural instincts.

This criticism can come out in judgmental, even damning, self-talk. Especially during moments of stress, we may say things to ourselves that we'd never say to a close friend. For example, after a disappointing date or meeting, do you console yourself with a pep talk, or are you more likely to curse yourself for falling short? If you gain a few unwanted pounds, do you promise to make better food choices and give yourself more time to exercise, or do you condemn your body and character?

Ingrained competition and mismatched value systems also can intensify negative self-talk, as I've witnessed in the trenches of medicine. One day during my internship, one of my fellow interns walked into our small group discussion and threw her papers on the table in frustration. "I feel like such a failure," she said, mostly addressing herself. "I'm never the first one to get the diagnosis in our morning case conferences, and I can't rattle off all the clinical trials the way some of our co-interns can. All I can do is sit with patients and make them feel better!" My friend was and is a gifted physician. But she was operating in a highly competitive culture that prized scientific and intellectual knowledge far above compassion. Medical school faculty in this program didn't get promoted because they were kind to patients and tended to their physical and emotional needs. More often than not, they gained recognition for publishing research papers or bringing in grant money to the university. Discoveries in the lab trumped human empathy and compassion, which left my friend feeling inadequate and dismissive of her considerable gifts as a healer. Because her profession seemed to disregard her talents, she began to lose sight of the aspects of medicine that she most loved. In the process, she started to undervalue herself.

Once we lose our internal compass, our emotional sense of grounding and identity can begin to slip. On a rational level, we may know we have worth, that we have light to bring to the lives of others, yet it's hard to ignore the messaging that insists we ought to be someone we're not.

Many of us then try to jump the gap, as Serena did at first, by posing as that other someone. We might fake being happy and busy as we mimic the behavior we observe around us. Or we might pretend to be above the fray, so confident and self-sufficient that we don't care or need to connect. The pose could be a full-time or a part-time performance. Perhaps we can be ourselves at home or with a few close friends, only to put on the act when we walk out the door. We might keep this up for months or even years. But such poses are exhausting, and the relationships that we form when pretending are inevitably disappointing. Even as we go through the motions of a "normal" social life, loneliness builds behind the façade, and the fog persists.

For Serena, the emotional tumult and distracting "busyness" of freshman year only served to estrange her from the personal qualities that, back home, had made her feel most true and valuable—her warmth, sense of humor, creativity, and generosity. In high school, her close relationships had given her a natural outlet for exercising these qualities and, in the process, strengthened her self-esteem and deepened her sense of herself. But she hadn't yet learned the importance of transferring that support from her friends internally to befriend herself.

In order to move independently through the world, we all need to learn to treat ourselves with the kindness, encouragement, and candor that we would offer a good friend. This is what we're doing when we give ourselves a pep talk on difficult days, when we treat ourselves to a calming walk to let off stress or tell ourselves to get to sleep early when we feel a cold coming on. We incorporate all the soothing, supportive messages that we've absorbed from others who love us and relay those messages to ourselves. This constructive self-talk reminds us who we are, what we love and value, and why we need to keep going—just as a close friend would do. But it takes time alone and consistent practice to develop the habit of being compassionate toward oneself, and Serena had never needed this kind of internal support when her close friends were nearby. So, with no one at college to remind her why she mattered, she was floundering. Like weakened physical muscles, her emotional strength and motivation felt harder to summon. By the end of her first semester at Penn, loneliness had estranged her from herself.

That magical summer brought her back together by re-engaging her solitary love of planting and beekeeping and by allowing her to slow down and reflect in the relative safety of her hometown and in her yoga group, where she learned to make new friends in a way that felt honest and meaningful. She was reminded how fulfilling it was to spend time with people who reflected back a view of her that felt true and whole. She may have felt antisocial and awkward during her freshman year, but that was the result of the pressure she felt on campus to act like someone she wasn't. Besides, a little self-doubt is normal during major transitions and by no means meant she was wrong or broken. But her yoga friends reminded her of the qualities that came most naturally to her and that she most valued in herself.

As Serena reclaimed the interests, passions, and values that gave her life direction and a sense of purpose, she began to feel grounded and confident again. She no longer depended on her family and childhood friends to show her who she was. To be sure, she remained deeply connected to them, but she also was able to see herself independently as a worthwhile individual apart from them. In the process, she reaffirmed that she was someone worth befriending, thus creating a positive feedback loop that allowed her to befriend herself.

Like a friend, she could see that her commitment to sustainability, her desire to form deep and significant human connections, her fascination with the interplay between environment and social behavior, all were part of what gave her value *and* showed that there was much more to her than she'd even discovered yet. Like all of us, she was a life in progress, destined to make and learn from as many mistakes as she achieved successes.

The shared vulnerability of people at her yoga training taught Serena that no one is perfect or perfectly attuned to everyone around them. Everyone has flaws and suffers failures. The key is to learn and gain deeper compassion, rather than anger or resentment, as a result of setbacks. This new wisdom, along with her deeper sense of herself, allowed Serena to treat herself and others more kindly, from a stance of friendship rather than fear. It gave her the courage to change aspects of her life back on campus that had contributed to her suffering, and it helped her feel grounded and centered even as she faced the inevitable changes and uncertainties of adult life that awaited her.

Self-Knowledge

The phrase "know thyself" was inscribed on the entrance to the ancient Greek Temple of Apollo at Delphi and on ancient Egyptian sarcophagi. In the New Testament, this advice took the form of a parable, embedded in what Christians take to be one of the most formative of Jesus's recorded teachings, the Sermon on the Mount: "Neither do men light a candle, and put it under a bushel, but on a candlestick; and it giveth light unto all that are in the house."

What are we to make of these instructions? First and foremost, knowing oneself is both more challenging and more important for connecting with others than it may seem. Indeed, it's often much easier to gain insight and perspective into others than into ourselves. That's because knowledge requires a degree of objectivity, which is difficult to summon when we are the subject of concern. It is also a lifelong process, as the very act of looking deeply into ourselves gives us insights that in turn affect who we are.

To begin to know ourselves better, we need to take a step back and allow ourselves to think about questions that reveal what we value and why we respond to the world and others as we do: *What do you most love doing, and why? What do you dread? How do you respond to stress? What are you most grateful for? What do you yearn for?* We need to examine our own personality, to consider how our particular traits and tendencies differ from, conflict with, and complement other people's. We also need to appreciate that humans have varying degrees of anxiety, social needs, and moodiness. To make sense of our own beliefs and interests, we need to understand the cultural attitudes that surround us so that we can assess what is "true" to us and what we may have accepted reflexively from others. These are just a few aspects of the self that can make self-awareness so elusive.

No one is born with self-knowledge, nor is this insight acquired overnight. We do tend to learn more about ourselves during pivotal phases of our lives, such as adolescence and early adulthood, when aspects of our character are tested and revealed in new and varied situations. This is what Serena was experiencing during her first two years in college. But it's not a passive or time-limited process. We learn who we are through regular reflection and by actively engaging with other people and challenges throughout our lives.

The idea of self-knowledge is not to shine with perfection but to gain insight and self-acceptance. Knowing ourselves doesn't require us to solve all our problems. Nor does it rule out change. Self-knowledge is not egotistical or self-aggrandizing. The goal is to examine our natural instincts, feelings, and behaviors honestly, to come to understand them better so that they inform our choices instead of colliding with them. We may still feel uncomfortable with certain traits of personality or behavior, but self-awareness can help us find constructive ways to address that discomfort.

When it comes to our relationship with loneliness, specifically, it's important to understand how our relative introversion or extroversion informs our preference for social interaction. These two terms describe the opposing ends of a wide spectrum. While there are relatively few extreme introverts or extroverts, most of us lean in one direction or the other. If we lean more toward introversion, we'll generally prefer less social activity than more extroverted people. One inclination is not "better" than another, but our culture can make it seem as if extroverts have a social advantage. Commercial images tend to focus on gregarious people as if they were the norm. Universities hold mixers for incoming students as if every newly arriving freshman must be eager to network with crowds of strangers. Politicians are required to meet and greet casts of thousands as if a gargantuan social appetite were a fundamental qualification for wise leadership. And social media users often seem to be basking in friends, dates, nights out with friends. If you accept these implicit messages, you might understandably think that extroverts have more fun.

What is true is that extroverts are naturally hungry for human company. If you're very extroverted, you'll prefer larger crowds and lots of social engagement. You probably love meeting new people, and when no one else is around, you may feel driven to actively seek out companionship. From stadium concerts to group outings, fun for you looks like one big social event.

For strong introverts, fun looks more like a deep conversation with one good friend in the corner of a library. Or it might look like a solitary browse through the library stacks. If you're very introverted, you prefer to spend much of your time alone, and when you do connect, you'd rather get together with one or two close friends than face a crowd. You like solitude.

To better understand the distinction, I sought out Dr. Susan Cain, author of a groundbreaking 2012 book about introverts: *Quiet*.[9] She explained that the difference between introversion and extroversion has a lot to do with how we naturally get our energy. Extroverts can feel drained and bored at the end of a solitary evening but invigorated after several hours at a large gathering, even if everyone there is a stranger. By contrast, introverts feel energized by solitude and quiet conversation, but large groups quickly exhaust them, even if they've had a good time.

"Introverts might not wish to connect by having more block parties or getting together with church groups," Cain told me. "It doesn't mean they don't feel elevated by connecting, but that just isn't their way of doing it."

Introverts and extroverts alike can get lonely, just not in the same way. "We all have different needs," Cain said, "and when those needs aren't met, we get lonely." So an extrovert may feel lonely if physically isolated for too long, while an introvert is more likely to feel lonely in a sea of strangers. To be clear, *everyone* needs meaningful relationships; it's just that the preferred pace, frequency, and intensity of engagement vary depending on where we fall along the spectrum.

No matter how introverted or extroverted we may be, it can be challenging to find the right balance between time with others and time alone. Some of this balance is dictated by the social realities of daily life. For the sake of work and family, most of us must participate in events such as meetings, group meals, and the occasional birthday party. At the same time, most of us will spend some portion of each day commuting, working, waiting, or simply daydreaming by ourselves. The important thing is to pay attention to our responses to these different situations. Which feels calming? Which unnerving? There are no right or wrong answers, but it's important to know so that we can find ways to honor our own preferences while also maintaining the connections that secure our personal and professional lives. The more clearly we understand our true nature, the less stressful it becomes to perform this balancing act.

As vital as self-knowledge is, however, alone it's not enough. Our sense of ourselves is bound to shift over time, and through our interactions and reflections, we'll come to learn more about who we are becoming and who we choose to be. Our identity, preferences, and needs will evolve, sometimes under stress and duress, and in order to stay whole, grounded, and securely connected with ourselves despite these fluctuations, we need an added stream of self-compassion. This is what makes self-acceptance possible as we come to know ourselves.

Self-Compassion

Dr. Jack Kornfield, one of America's most renowned Buddhist monks and meditation teachers, first introduced me to the concept of self-compassion sixteen years ago when I attended his class at Spirit Rock, the meditation center he cofounded in Woodacre, California. Jack's own introduction to self-compassion was his first meeting with the Dalai Lama many years earlier in Dharamsala, India. How, Jack and a group of fellow teachers had asked His Holiness, could they help people eradicate self-hatred or low self-esteem?

"He and his translators seemed confused," Jack told me with a laugh. "It was such a foreign concept in Tibetan culture to not be compassionate and loving toward yourself."

And that, in its gentle way, *was* the lesson. Compassion forms a natural bridge between self-knowledge and self-acceptance, and loving kindness toward oneself is the first path leading over that bridge. In the wake of this gentle lesson, Kornfield made the cultivation of inner-directed compassion and love the center of his life's work.

Self-compassion is what shields us from—or at least softens the blow of—the judgment and ridicule of people who don't understand us. It allows us to grow through our pain instead of being dragged down by it. It also helps us to see our light, however dim it may seem, instead of being consumed by darkness and self-doubt. Such a powerful force is not easily summed up, and is itself the subject of entire books, but we can start by recognizing the important role it plays in relieving loneliness and centering our sense of self.

To help people cultivate self-compassion, Jack employed a practice called *metta*, or loving kindness, meditation that is based on a central Buddhist practice. It's a form of meditation that melds the head (self-knowledge) and the heart (loving kindness).

Although one of the goals is to direct this union toward oneself, Jack explained, "I've found it's difficult for people to start with loving themselves because of our culture of self-criticism and self-hatred. So I will start people with someone they love or care about."

The meditation invites the emotion in through recited phrases such as: "May you be filled with loving kindness. May you be safe from inner and outer dangers. May you be well in body and mind. May you be at ease and happy."

As these phrases are recited, the person is invited to visualize the loved one. "The principle is to start wherever it's easy to open your heart," Jack told me. "You are cultivating the qualities of love that are in all of us."

Allowing the mind to immerse itself in gratitude and compassion can be a restorative and calming experience. "Sometimes other emotions come up," Jack said, "but you just let that be."

After repeating the meditation for a few minutes with one or two beloved friends in mind, the next step is to imagine them gazing back and wishing you the same love and kindness in return. "Think about how those two friends would want you to be well," Jack said. "Imagine them saying, 'May you be safe and protected. May you be peaceful and well. Now put a hand on your heart and take that in. As they wished it for you, wish it for yourself. Spend some time reciting the same intentions and inviting the same feelings for yourself. Once you've experienced that love within yourself, you can extend it to other people, including those you have a hard time with."

The practice, Jack said, encourages us to appreciate our good qualities and good intentions and forgive ourselves for those moments when we haven't lived up to our expectations or desires. While the research on kindness-based meditation practices like *metta* is in its early stages, preliminary studies have suggested that these practices can increase compassion, self-compassion, and positive emotions.[10][11]

Moments of Pause

Metta meditation, like other forms of self-reflection, requires time and solitude. It takes patience and quiet to train our attention inward, to focus our thoughts and feelings and locate inner sources of genuine purpose and value. When we engage in this type of focused solitude, psychologists have found, it correlates with increased creativity and intimacy. It activates the parts of the brain responsible for incorporating meaning into our lives. It also strengthens our sense of identity by giving us the space to connect with ourselves.[12]

The problem is that we live in a world that is perpetually racing, daring us to keep up. Technology, media, global news, fashion, economic competition, climate crises, political conflict—and, in far too many places, war—compel us to keep moving, changing, working, striving, and competing to stay ahead of the next unexpected challenge. Most of us are pressured at work and at home. Finances and health challenges are just a couple of the concerns that can preoccupy us at the expense of the quiet we need to regroup and center ourselves. We are besieged, online and off, by demands for our attention, our responses, our decisions and commitments. Amid all this turbulence, solitude can seem boring, wasteful, or simply impossible.

It takes a concerted effort to reclaim our opportunities for solitude today. What's required is the white space that allows us to deliberately suspend our mental clutter and fully experience our feelings and our thoughts. For many of us, this will mean strictly limiting distractions to protect periods of quiet. According to developmental psychologists, we need to be free of interruptions such as texts, emails, and news feed alerts, in order to access our deepest thoughts and feelings. Today such freedom does not come easily, but this makes it all the more important to intentionally reserve time for solitude on a regular basis.

Solitude doesn't require a retreat to nature or a vow of silence. The practice of self-reflection can take the form of meditation or prayer, a nature walk, or simply a few minutes of silent contemplation in a park, during our work commute, or before we go to bed at night.

These moments of pause allow us to tune in to ourselves, which simultaneously prepares us to tune in to others. By allowing our minds to wander without an agenda or destination, we learn to read our emotions and sensations, to listen to our bodies and trace our thoughts. We relax. We reflect on the significance and consequences of our actions and choices. We make sense of the responses we receive from others. It can be challenging when difficult thoughts surface, such as disappointments or the pain of a recent conflict. Most of us have a tendency to retract from such experiences and try to avoid thinking about them. That's what

Serena was doing when she packed her freshman year with distracting busyness. But it's important to make time to reflect even on our pain so we can learn from it. Often, it's this very reflection that hastens decisions, which lead to relief.

Solitude on its own won't give us knowledge and compassion—it depends how we use that time with ourselves. But it gives us the opportunity to listen to ourselves, to hear the ideas, inspiration, feelings, and reactions that arise, and hopefully to approach what arises with kindness and compassion even when the thoughts that come up are painful or unflattering.

Moments of pause are especially powerful when combined with gratitude and feelings of love. I had a medical school professor who struggled with the demands of being a mother, doctor, teacher, researcher, and administrator. Finding time to meditate or go on a retreat was a near impossibility for her, but whenever she washed her hands before seeing a patient, she would let the warm water run over her hands for a few extra seconds and think of something she was grateful for—the opportunity to be a part of the patient's healing, the health of her family, the joy of teaching a student earlier that morning. She was one of the first people to teach me that the power of gratitude can be delivered in the smallest of moments . . . and those moments have the power to change how we see ourselves and the people around us.

If we ever forget the power of pausing, we need only remember the lesson of our heart. The heart operates in two phases: systole where it pumps blood to the vital organs and diastole where it relaxes. Most people think that systole is where the action is and the more time in systole the better. But diastole—the relaxation phase—is where the coronary blood vessels fill and supply life sustaining oxygen to the heart muscle itself. Pausing, it turns out, is what sustains the heart.

This is why solitary reflection and self-awareness play such a critical role in preparing us for relationships with others. As we become attuned to our own inner signals and frequencies, we naturally gain an empathic (and largely unconscious) ability to recognize and relate to these signals in others. This internal attunement helps us feel centered, confident, and calm, securing the foundation of self-knowledge from which we can build strong connections outward, not only with other people but also with the wider world. We might notice patterns in nature, like an iridescent dragonfly or a majestic cloud formation, or marvel at a clear night sky filled with the Milky Way. We might also discover wonders in the humanity around us—the love with which a parent reads to his child, the generosity of a commuter who gives up her seat for a stranger, the gentle way a young boy takes his little sister's hand. What we are experiencing is connection *within* our solitude.

Art is another means of accessing this sense of solitary connection. As Susan Cain reminded me, the connection between a reader and writer or between a composer and person hearing the music is "like a feeling of joining of souls when you read something that is articulating exactly what you have experienced." Through characters on the page we exercise our empathy and compassion for struggles beyond our own.

I love the way Cain likened reading to belonging to a "community of kindred spirits. Sometimes you need them in real life and sometimes on the page." Music is even more visceral. When we listen to music it's akin to sharing chords of pure emotion with the musicians and composer—and, if listening to a live concert, with other members of the audience, as well. Who hasn't felt goose bumps in response to profoundly beautiful music? Similarly, through visual art we can share the pure joy of beauty, as well as the creative vision of the painter or sculptor.

These experiences are vital to our sense of connection and security because they remind us we are never truly alone. It's as if they compel us to zoom out from our self-focused concerns to feel a more peaceful, even spiritual, sense of belonging, both among our fellow humans and in the larger sense.

This relationship with others and with a larger universe is a connection that we all instinctively crave, because belonging involves more than being accepted, known, and loved; it also means sharing in the concern and responsibility for others. This fundamental need dates back to our evolutionary roots as tribal members. It's baked into our DNA.

And so is our sense of awe. Dr. Dacher Keltner, a professor of psychology at the University of California, Berkeley, has spent much of his career understanding the origins and power of such "goose bump" moments. (While other mammals get goose bumps when frightened, he points out that only humans get them when awed.) Keltner defines awe as an emotion we feel in response to vast things that are mysterious, that challenge our current way of understanding the world. In a *New York Times* article, Keltner noted that such moments have the capacity to "shift our focus from our narrow self-interest to the interests of the group."[13] They expand our sense of purpose and significance, reminding us of the true scale of the home to which we all belong. They inspire a sense of oneness, which in turn results in greater empathy and altruism.

To test this effect, Keltner and his colleagues conducted an experiment with two groups of individuals on the Berkeley campus.[14] The first group was asked to stand in front of a grove of breathtaking two-hundred-foot-tall Tasmanian blue gum eucalyptus trees and gaze up at them for one minute. The other group was asked to stand in the same spot but instead to gaze up at an adjacent tall building for one minute. After the minute elapsed, it had been arranged that someone would walk by the group and "accidentally" drop a set of pens. What they found was the group that stared at the trees helped pick up more pens for the person who dropped them than the group that looked at the building. The awe-inspiring experience of staring at the Tasmanian trees lasted only one minute, but it had a positive impact on the behavior of the participants, opening them up to the world around them and making them more responsive and generous toward that world.

When I spoke to Keltner, he lamented the fact that our culture allows too little time for these experiences, particularly in nature. Many of us sink blindly into work and technology without even realizing what we're missing. "In a time where we feel less connected, the world could use more awe," he said.

All of these experiences deepen our connection with ourselves even as they remind us that we're part of something more *inter*-connected than we can fathom. This is both humbling and consoling. Each of us has a lot to feel grateful for. We each have a lot to offer. And when we reach out to one another from a place of self-knowledge and compassion, we have the power to transform our lives and heal the world.

CHAPTER 7

Circles of Connection

The only way to have a friend is to be one.

—Ralph Waldo Emerson, "Of Friendship"

The friend who can be silent with us in a moment of despair
or confusion, who can stay with us in an hour of grief and
bereavement, who can tolerate not knowing, not curing, not
healing, and face with us the reality of our powerlessness, that
is a friend who cares.

—Henri Nouwen, *Out of Solitude*

If we imagine human connections forming through a process
that starts within each of us then reaches out to others and
loops us closer together, what would we call that process? The
best term may be *friendship*.

Everyone, at virtually every stage and station of life, needs
friends. Friendship, in essence, is the social glue that keeps
couples, families, kindred spirits, and communities together.
It's fundamental to successful professional, as well as personal,
relationships. Yet some people have more difficulty than others
when it comes to making and keeping friends, and this obstacle
can raise the risk of loneliness. On the other hand, those who

are skilled at friendship may have a natural defense against prolonged or severe loneliness. Fortunately, these skills can be developed.

But what does it mean to be skilled at friendship? I remember being somewhat bewildered by this process when I was a child. I wish I'd had a role model like Sarah Harmeyer back then.

Even when she was a kid, Sarah told me, her life revolved around two great loves. One was food, and the other was people. And early on, she realized just how naturally these two passions go together. Sharing meals is a global practice that dates from the beginning of our species. Not only is this practical, since humans need to eat several times a day, and it's more efficient to cook in quantity than one serving at a time, but it's also enjoyable to gather around the tastes, smells, and energy that good food creates. And all this shared enjoyment has a bonding effect. It's only natural, then, that food often plays a central role in the establishment of friendships, whether around the family dinner table, in the school cafeteria, or in the neighborhood diner or coffee shop.

Gathering people together around food became one of young Sarah's greatest pleasures. She even hosted a regular lunchtime "cafe" back in her dorm room at college. But in her late twenties she moved from her hometown of Houston to Dallas and got so wrapped up in her work as an event planner that she lost track of that pleasure. Single, she lived alone and knew no one in her new neighborhood.

"I didn't have kids to get me outside my house," Sarah said, looking back eight years later. "I didn't even have a dog to walk to help me get to know people." But that began to change after a pastor friend identified her as "a people gatherer."

"He said, 'Sarah, you just love creating experiences for people and you love sharing love and connecting in a really real way with people.'" He suggested she try to think of ways to develop and share this passion with her community.

"So I thought of the very best moments of my life," she told me, "and they've always been around the table. That's how I wanted to gather people."

But Sarah's house was small, and the table she envisioned was big enough to seat at least twenty people. It would only work in the backyard. And the only way she could afford such a table would be if her father built it for her. And he'd never built a table, though he did like to whittle wood.

None of these obstacles proved to be barriers. Sarah's dad built her an eighteen-foot table, which they placed in the yard, with chandeliers strung overhead. With "community" as her intention, Sarah set a goal of serving five hundred people that year around her table.

Because she didn't even know her neighbors' names, she turned to the social networking app Nextdoor for assistance. Nextdoor allowed her to reach three hundred households nearby. She invited all of them to a potluck.

"I was so honest on the invitation," she recalled. "I said, 'If you've never stepped outside of your house to meet neighbors, would you consider coming this night? I don't know anyone, and I'd love to meet you. Bring a beverage and bring a dish to share and I'll have live music.' I had ninety people show up that night, and my heart just grew so big knowing that people wanted to be invited."

Sarah understood that people crave connection. Still, she was surprised by the eagerness of her neighbors to meet and the ease with which they overcame differences in professions, status, and cultural backgrounds. The big table seemed to function like a big tent of safety—a shared space, as John Paul Lederach might say, where all sorts of people could find common ground.

"The table belongs to each person," Sarah said. "People can come as themselves and feel like we all have something to learn from each other. I've seen my plumber sit next to an executive. I've seen eighth graders next to their teachers. All races, all religions, all sexual orientations, you name it, they've sat around my table."

But a big reason why this happened that first night—and at the hundreds of gatherings she's hosted since then—is Sarah's intuitive understanding of the elements of friendship and her generous willingness to nurture them. The first element is a sense of familiarity and ease, which Sarah found can be cultivated even among total strangers with a little gentle nudging.

"Before we sit down around my table," she told me, "I will go around and introduce people by name. Like, if I just met you, and I remember your name as George, then I tell everyone, 'Hey, this is George, and he is an incredible dad, and I can tell because you should have seen the way he lit up talking about his boy's baseball game this morning. He's also an attorney. So, if you have any questions he'll be at this end of the table.' To see the smiles creep out of people's hearts on their faces when you acknowledge their name! It gives people confidence then to sit down at the table and engage with people around them."

That sounded so simple, but I had to agree. Names and personal anecdotes can be powerful connectors, especially when the names are properly pronounced (as someone whose name is usually mispronounced, I always notice and appreciate when someone makes the extra effort to say it properly). Sarah also uses tried-and-true hosting tools like place cards and seating charts to help people remember one another's names and to connect individuals who are likely to have good conversations.

At the same time, she explicitly relinquishes enough control to give everyone a stake in the space and in serving one another, to cultivate another important element of friendship, which is mutuality. "I say, 'I know I'm hosting. But truly, it's up to us what we want out of this experience. So if you see water glasses low, jump up and fill them. If you want to, grab another bottle of wine and serve the people around you. If you want to help, bring dishes in and if you want to, load the dishwasher."

What Sarah said next about loading the dishwasher gave me an insight into the genuine depth of her care for the people she gathers. She told me she always invites guests to help with the dishes because "a lot of the introverts, they want a job so they don't have to talk as much."

Sarah understands that people relate in all different kinds of ways. While some become friends trading jokes in a group, others are much more likely to bond if they're able to chat quietly with just one other person while, say, loading the dishwasher.

She also understands that healthy friendships are based on two-way communication. "I even suggest, 'I hope we will do more listening than talking tonight at the table,' which is a funny thing. You can see people whisper to each other, 'What does she mean by that?' But truly, what if we're just with each other, coming from a place of learning and wanting to connect?"

Toward the end of each potluck, Sarah will call everyone together again and toss out a single idea, question, or word to prompt a group discussion that's more thoughtful and personal than her guests might dare to start up on their own—more like the conversations at Serena Bian's Space Gatherings. This is when the "table" Sarah has set yields the rewards that we all crave in friendship. "I just see people sharing really beautifully. I see more of a depth to them. And there's a real respect, and there's a little love at the table."

Love is not just an idea for Sarah. It's a way of life that's also core to her approach to friendship. One year, she told me, her neighbor asked if he could come to her house on Christmas because he didn't have friends or family nearby. Sarah decided to expand his circle. She sent out an invitation to the neighborhood. She invited whoever "wanted to have lunch with a stranger on Christmas." The response expanded her own circle, as well. "People came out I had never met." All of them would have spent Christmas alone. The emotions were palpable. One of her guests pointed to the four large block letters on her lawn and said, "That's what this place feels like." Those letters spelled L-O-V-E.

Today Sarah knows virtually all her neighbors. She's forty-three, never married and has no kids, but she has an enormous family of friends. She knows who to call for any kind of help she might need, whether it's a spare flashlight or a shoulder to cry on. She's also met neighbors who've never shown up at her table but still feel connected to her, just because she reached out to invite them.

Sarah's story reminds us that we're all people gatherers. Maybe we're not as fearless or as practiced as Sarah at bringing new people into our lives. Maybe we prefer to gather friends one at a time, rather than throwing parties. But whether we're planning the future with our partners, dining with neighbors, or chatting with strangers on a train, the lessons in friendship that Sarah shares around her table offer keys that each and every one of us can use to widen, strengthen, and deepen our own connections.

Friendship Circles

When John and Stephanie Cacioppo were studying solutions for loneliness, they found that the most beneficial relationships for our social and emotional health are reciprocal in nature. In other words, people who support each other tend to build the healthiest friendships. These mutually beneficial relationships, in turn, help to secure people individually and protect against loneliness. This is the cycle of high-quality social connection at work.

The Cacioppos weren't talking just about close friendships. As Sarah Harmeyer demonstrates at each of her gatherings, the principle of reciprocity can apply even to brand-new acquaintances. That's why she encourages her guests to listen as much as they talk, and to pitch in and serve each other, instead of waiting to be served. Friends who share and sincerely listen to each other have a stronger sense of connection than do those for whom the interactions focus only in one direction. This is one reason why therapy, however valuable, cannot replace truly mutual friendships. Looking back, this was the experience of Serena, whose yoga group and Space Gathering friendships provided the deepest cure for her sense of isolation. It was also the experience of Phillip Lester and Richard Lopez when they joined the brotherhood of ARC.

What makes a relationship "mutual"? Listening and helping each other is important, but the most fundamental element may be what lies beneath those interactions: reciprocal feeling. Friends want to spend time together and will make the effort to do so. They put each other at ease and strive to understand each other. They share common interests and respect each other. In the most basic terms, friends show that they care about each other, and in so doing, they mirror each other's human value.

When our friends support us, they remind us that we are worthy of love, which makes us feel better about ourselves. Caring for others may also strengthen our sense of purpose and meaning, as it shows us that we have the ability to make others' lives better. In these and many other ways, friendship creates a positive feedback loop, teaching us to relate to ourselves with love even as we relate to our friends.

Unfortunately, many people confuse friendship with transactional relationships, viewing friends as sources of social or professional status or material favors. Dr. Ronald Sharp, who teaches a course on the literature of friendship at Vassar College, lamented this confusion in an interview in 2016. Friendship, he said, is "not about what someone can do for you, it's who and what the two of you become in each other's presence." He added, "The notion of doing nothing but spending time in each other's company has, in a way, become a lost art."[1]

Loneliness, too, can impede mutuality, because when we're lonely, the urgency of our own social need can make it difficult to honor and respond to the concerns of others—even if they are our friends. In a 2017 interview with *The Atlantic*, John Cacioppo explained that loneliness can make us overeager, excessively focused on ourselves, and preoccupied with our own emotional state.[2] Thus, even when meeting close friends, if we're lonely and have been by ourselves too long, we may unwittingly come on strong, talking a little faster and longer than we otherwise would, because we're craving the feeling of connection. Being mindful of the distortions that loneliness can cause, as well as remembering to pause and really try to listen, can help.

Friendship needs to be tended with kindness. This kindness requires openhearted care and trust, empathy and honesty, and a generous dose of understanding so that the connection can flourish and endure. "No one treats other individuals perfectly all the time," Cacioppo told an interviewer in 2008.[3] "We don't treat ourselves perfectly all the time, so we don't treat our friends ideally all the time." That's why forgiveness is such a crucial part of friendship.

Because of all this, a profound side effect of friendship is gratitude. Gratitude for the opportunity to show vulnerability and still be loved. For the forgiveness of our flawed lives. For the shared trust and time together and the feeling of belonging, which is the ultimate glue that holds friends together.

Of course, not all friendships are equally close. Even high-quality social connections naturally vary in intimacy, intensity, and depth.

British evolutionary psychologist Dr. Robin Dunbar has found that human beings are remarkably consistent in their need for different types of friendships. If you imagine yourself as the center of your social world, you can visualize inner, middle, and outer circles of friendship as a series of rings around a bull's-eye. Humans have formed these different levels of friendship, Dunbar told me, ever since we were hunter-gatherers.

These three circles of connection roughly correspond to the three dimensions of loneliness: *Intimate*, *Relational*, and *Collective*. We all need close friends and intimate confidantes with whom we share deep bonds of mutual affection and trust. We need casual friends and social relationships that offer shared support and connection. And we need to belong to communities of people—

neighbors, colleagues, classmates, and acquaintances—with whom we experience a sense of collective purpose and identity.

In the simplest evolutionary terms, within our inner circle, we rely on a small set of people for protection, support, and sustenance. These are our romantic partners, the close friends and family that we depend on in a crisis, the people we want to spend time with on a frequent basis. These inner-circle relationships are our strongest mutual bonds. They also require the most time and energy—which limits the number of such relationships that we can sustain to about fifteen at any given time. According to Dunbar, we're wired to devote a whopping 60 percent of our time and energy to our inner-circle friends and confidantes, and most of this is spent with our closest intimates, who rarely number more than five.

Most of the remaining 40 percent of our time is devoted to the people who make up our middle and outer friendship circles. These friends are not the first ones we turn to for support, but they are likely to lend a helping hand if we asked and vice versa. They're buddies we spend time with a few times a year, the old school friends and relatives we reach out to during the holidays, the well-wishers we inform about our marriage or the birth of a child, and neighbors we meet over dinners such as those Sarah Harmeyer hosts.

Naturally, middle and outer circle ties are weaker than close friendships. Those with whom we spend the least time and attention tend to be our least secure friendships. However, these circles are not fixed. Many of our friendships naturally migrate over time, as when a close school pal becomes a more distant acquaintance after graduation, or when a work colleague turns into a close confidante. Sarah Harmeyer has found, for example, that some of the guests who arrived at her table as strangers have since become close friends, while close friends who move away may shift into her middle or outer circles.

The simple fact is that the less time we physically spend with friends, the more likely they are to slip into our outer circles.

Dunbar believes that's because core friendships will wither without the direct face-to-face communication that allows us to be fully present and available to one another. We need to make the effort to see the friends we want to keep close, to work through conflict with them and exchange help in times of need.

In some respects, technology can facilitate quality relationship by allowing us to virtually spend time with friends and loved ones even when we can't be in the same location. It can enable us to keep some people from drifting entirely out of our lives when they move away. It can also help us locate and communicate with friends to arrange in-person meetings. However, technology can also weaken friendship by draining the available time for meaningful connection. It's so easy to flip that sixty-forty ratio and spend more hours digitally chatting with people we barely know than connecting meaningfully with those we love the most. When I began using digital media to stay connected with people, I found that it slowly but insidiously moved the balance of my social time away from the center and toward my middle and outer circles. It was often easier to wish one hundred distant acquaintances happy birthday on Facebook than it was to make time and space for a difficult but important conversation with a close friend. If we are not careful, technology can make lower-quality social interactions the path of least resistance.

As our options for communicating have grown, we have also become less comfortable with the uncertainties of direct interaction. We hesitate to pick up the phone, because we don't know how long the call might take. We avoid spoken questions that would be easier to handle via text. We discourage spontaneous visits, because we might get sucked into a long conversation or be inconvenienced. But the richness of relationships is in their texture—in the sound of someone's voice, in their smile and their body language, in the unexpected moments of honesty that tend to occur during unplanned conversation. The irony is that we're almost always left feeling better when we take those risks with friends.

Inner Circle: Close Friends and Confidantes

In 1938, during the Great Depression, Harvard University initiated a long-term study of 268 men from the Harvard classes of 1939 to 1944 with the hope of learning what helped people lead healthy and fulfilled lives. Longitudinal studies are common, but this study has exceeded nearly all of them, still ongoing after eighty years. The original subjects included men who went on to become successful politicians, entrepreneurs, and doctors, and others who got into trouble with the law and had financial problems. Since its inception, the study has expanded to the children and wives of the original study participants. It also merged with a study that started around the same time with 456 young men from Boston's poorest neighborhoods.[4]

Dr. Robert Waldinger, the current director of the study, is kind, patient, whip smart, and humble enough to consider new ideas. By his own account, he had certain expectations when he came in as director. He anticipated finding that good nutrition, exercise, and genetics are critical factors in health and happiness. As a Zen priest, he also understood the importance of meditation and other spiritual practices. But he did not expect one result that has emerged as a central health factor in the study's rich treasure trove of data: close relationships.

According to Waldinger, the Harvard data showed that inner-circle relationships were better predictors of health and happiness throughout life than IQ, wealth, or social class. Having someone you can call for help at three a.m. can be a buffer against mental and physical decline. "The people who were the most satisfied in their relationships at age fifty," Waldinger said in his TED talk about the study, "were the healthiest at age eighty."[5] These close relationships also are our primary defense against *intimate* loneliness.

As comforting and healing as these relationships are, they are rarely conflict-free. In fact, we challenge our closest friends and intimate partners more than any others. We often get angry or become disappointed in them, and vice versa—because close confidantes are so emotionally invested in each other. But we choose to be more honest and engaged in these relationships precisely because they create a safe place where we can more fully be ourselves.

Intimacy also is physical, even when it's not sexual. Touch releases a host of brain chemicals, including the hormone oxytocin, which enhance our focus on social information and strengthen ties between friends and family, helping to reassure us that we're cared for and protected. Touch also releases endorphins, the opioid-like neuropeptides that are nature's built-in pain relievers and sources of euphoria.

When I asked Robin Dunbar to explain this, he brought up our primate cousins' habit of social grooming, which is a potent trigger for the brain's release of chemicals that strengthen intimacy. These chemicals make apes feel so good, Dunbar told me, that they can spend three hours a day grooming one another. Both the groomer and the groomed feel the rush, which secures the bonds between them and mutually reduces their stress. Humans feel a similar rush when we touch in love and friendship. Just as they do in primates, all these chemicals function as a kind of emotional binder.

Given the powerful effects of physical affection, it makes sense that most people's closest friends are their spouses or romantic partners. We call this person a "significant other" for good reason, since this is the person we expect to always be there for us— ideally, the person we confide in at midnight and turn to at dawn.

However, it's important to remember that intimate relationships are not always romantic in nature. In fact, an enthralling romance can involve less desirable inner-circle trade-offs. The release of molecules like endorphins and oxytocin that accompanies intense romance, especially when love is new and physical affection is peaking, means that couples are biologically incentivized to focus on each other. As a result, as Dunbar told me, there's diminished social energy or inclination to connect with anyone else. While romance may feel exciting in the short term, if a relationship is so all-encompassing that it excludes other important friendships too completely or for too long, a love affair actually can lead to *relational* and *collective* loneliness. That can pose a social hazard when the relationship matures, and the rush of social hormones and neurotransmitters inevitably fades. It can compound emotional distress if the romance ends badly and *intimate* loneliness also sets in.

Older cultures seem to have understood how risky it is to prize romantic love above all other friendships. Historian Stephanie Coontz, in a *New York Times* op-ed, wrote that until a hundred years ago, "most societies agreed that it was dangerously antisocial, even pathologically self-absorbed, to elevate marital affection and nuclear-family ties above commitments to neighbors, extended kin, civic duty and religion."[6]

While isolated romantic relationships tend to be fragile and subject to break under pressure, healthy intimate relationships—whether we're talking about a spouse or a best friend—actually benefit from the social cushion that surrounding circles provide. That's because the comfort, calm, and emotional energy we gain from all supportive friendships strengthen our emotional core. And the stronger we are at the center, the more we have to offer everyone else in our lives.

But today we face a different challenge. While many still embrace the "one and only" idealization of romantic love, fewer and fewer people in America are getting married.[7] The number of adults age twenty-five or older who have never married is at an all-time high of one in five, up from one in ten in 1960.[8]

Such societal changes prompt us to stop, look around, and recognize that we may need to intentionally redesign our social lives to protect the vital resource of intimacy. Our closest confidantes might be our lovers, husbands, or wives. They might be our best friends, housemates, cousins or siblings. Inner circles, like intimacy, can take many forms. Many single people devote time to their families and social networks in ways that make them less lonely than couples who isolate themselves. The point is that all of us—whether we are married or not—need to love and be loved by people who know us well.

Middle Circle: Occasional Companions

As essential as our inner-circle relationships are, the middle circle, which may expand our friendships to 150 or so, is just as vital. In this social region, we may not necessarily know one another's deepest secrets, but we enjoy having our lives intersect. Middle-circle friends provide a vital buffer against *relational* loneliness.

When we were growing up, many of us may have taken our casual friendships for granted. Our classes, sports, camps, and clubs gave us plenty of opportunities to cultivate our middle circle. We saw most of our friends every day in school or around the neighborhood. Such casual connections are harder to establish in adulthood, especially when we've left our hometowns and plunged into career and family demands. Not only is there less time for social activities, but competition and status can complicate the bonds of friendship. Differences in achievement and wealth can cause distrust and jealousy, which make it difficult to gauge the mutuality of new relationships. This is why celebrities and people in top levels of leadership often feel lonely, why many still rely as adults on the communities of their youth and take pains to maintain their original and most trusted friendships, rather than risking new ones.

But most of us can form new middle-circle friendships just as we did when we were kids: by joining groups. Whatever our age, humans tend to meet one another by gathering, and we tend to gather around shared interests and activities like sports, the arts, or a neighborhood potluck. Belonging to a group can help reduce stress, repair emotional damage, and promote meaning and purpose. This is why groups also form around common struggles and why so many forms of therapy today include support groups.

Much of this therapeutic effect stems from the ways we interact when we gather. We tell stories. We laugh. We sing and dance and play music. We move and walk and work together. We give and take, call and respond, and synchronize with one another. This behavior comes naturally in every culture on earth. As Robin Dunbar explains, it's all part of a long line of biochemical substitutes for social grooming.

These substitutes became necessary as humans evolved to expand their social circles. Because grooming requires direct one-to-one physical contact, it was an inefficient way to connect large communities. So evolution came up with other feel-good strategies to create a sense of belonging among many people at once.

Laughter is one of the most contagious, universal, and instinctive connectors, Dunbar told me. Like touch, it's a trigger for endorphin release, so when we share laughter, we feel happier, more familiar with those around us, and more at ease. The Dalai Lama employs his infectious laugh to connect with crowds and world leaders alike. Laughter reduces stress and feels good both because it induces a positive biochemical response and because it brings people together—we rarely laugh alone. In a comedy club, when one audience member laughs, others almost always follow. At a party, when someone laughs out loud, others instinctively smile and turn to find out what's so funny. In movie theaters, jokes onscreen often produce a wave of laughter that starts with one or two people, then builds as others latch on. Humor creates a powerful bond among people who all find the same thing funny. It's a form of common ground.

So, too, is rhythmic, synchronized sound and movement. If we're lonely, Dunbar says, one of the best ways we can develop a middle circle of friends is to join a singing group, be it a barbershop quartet, a church choral group, or a local blues or rock band. His research has found that singing produces far more satisfying social bonds than group activities such as creative writing and crafts. He calls the bonding power released by group singing the "icebreaker effect."

The cooperation and close attention that are exchanged through synchronized activity turbocharge the benefits of group activity. Dunbar points out that any form of physical exercise will produce an endorphin kick, but having a partner and working out in sync will dramatically escalate the reward. This is true of jogging, biking, dancing—virtually any form of exercise. When our movements are orchestrated to coordinate with those of others, that interaction increases the natural high. Dunbar told me about a study he conducted on college teams rowing crew, which found that rowing in synchrony increased the endorphin release by 100 percent as compared to rowing alone. The shared movement, the shared experience, and the shared endorphin high all enhanced the team's performance at the same time that they bonded the team socially.

The endorphin effect is just one of many biochemical phenomena that explain why people all over the world have traditional folk songs and dances; why children recite the Pledge of Allegiance together in school; why most religions involve congregational singing or chanting as a regular part of services; and why millions around the globe engage in sports. These chemical responses reward us for bringing friends together, secure our sense of belonging, and make social activities *good* for us, both physically and emotionally.

Outer Circle: Colleagues and Acquaintances

Of course, there are plenty of people in our lives who connect to us more peripherally but still contribute to our sense of belonging.

These outer-circle relationships are the amicable acquaintances we build through occasional interactions on the job, in our neighborhoods, through civic and social organizations, places of worship, or online. This circle, which can expand our social network up to five hundred people or more, comes to us through common experiences and helps us feel more secure in our communal identity. A sense of shared purpose and interests with this set of people helps stave off *collective* loneliness.

These distant relationships don't have the degree of openness and vulnerability that characterize closer friendships, but just the flicker of recognition and a welcoming smile help us feel known in a subtle but meaningful way. Familiar people make us feel welcome. They help us feel rooted in place. Over time, they can evolve into friends.

Connecting at Work

One of our most important sources of connection is the workplace. Given that most of us today spend more of our waking hours on the job than at home, and many of us interact more with our colleagues than with our non-work friends, we need meaningful connections at work to sustain us. But often these friendships require an encouraging nudge.

While I was at the surgeon general's office, our staff grew so quickly and was so busy dealing with pressing public health issues that many of our team members didn't have a chance to get to know one another. The team included a decorated Army nurse; a woman who had spent years providing dental care to incarcerated individuals; an accomplished pianist and preacher; an Olympic-level runner; and several team members who had struggled with addiction in their families. People generally got along well, but we didn't fully recognize one another's rich life experiences. So to bring us closer, we developed "Inside Scoop," a practice at our all-hands meetings designed to strengthen connection.

At each weekly staff meeting, one team member was asked to share something about themselves through pictures for five minutes. Presenting was an opportunity to share more of our lives, and listening was an opportunity to recognize our colleagues in the way they wished to be seen.

I remember one Inside Scoop from a team member who had proudly served in the US Marine Corps. I expected him to talk about his experiences in the military. Instead, he spoke about the complex relationship he'd had with his father and how he could see his father's spirit living on in the musical talent of his own children. He described his mother as his hero and shared how remembering her in the face of a challenge would transform his doubts into strength. As he spoke, his eyes glistened. I felt a deep connection to him in that moment. I was inspired by his honesty and felt compelled to reflect on my own relationships. These few moments of honest sharing helped to solidify a bond between us.

Inside Scoop quickly became the team's favorite time of the week. Everyone felt more valued after seeing their colleagues' genuine reactions to their stories. Team members who had traditionally been quiet during discussions began speaking up. They appeared less stressed at work. And most of them told me how much more connected they felt to their colleagues and to the mission they served.

In many companies, however, individualism dominates despite the fact that most work enterprise requires collective effort. The gig economy has doubled down on that individualistic thrust, as a growing number of people work alone as ride-share drivers, freelance consultants, and on-demand assistants. Meanwhile, the growing trend toward automation further threatens to undermine the human relationships that make work socially as well as economically rewarding. All of this is contributing to workplace alienation and loneliness.

Gallup's 2017 "State of the American Workplace"[9] report revealed that just four in ten US employees strongly agree that their supervisor or someone at work seems to care about them as a person. That may be, in part, because many workplace cultures often overtly or implicitly discourage friendship, especially across hierarchical lines. So do certain professions. One survey of 1,624 full-time employees, published in 2018,[10] found that the loneliest by far were those with degrees in law and medicine.

Apart from the emotional toll this takes on individuals, it's also bad for business, as Dr. Sigal Barsade, a professor of organizational behavior at the Wharton School of the University of Pennsylvania, found with her 2018 study of loneliness in the workplace. Her data showed that lonelier employees feel less committed to their employers and also to their coworkers. In moments of stress or conflict, lonely employees are more likely to decide that certain relationships are not worth the effort.[11] This attitude then fans out to ever-widening circles of potential connections within the organization. When social ties begin to fray among colleagues, distrust infects communication and collaboration. Entire teams and even departments can suffer.

Gallup's report found that having positive personal relationships was among the most important factors in employee engagement, alongside personal development opportunities and a sense of purpose. Gallup further found that when workers are respected and relationship is valued by the culture, friendships can generate innovative discussions that benefit the team and organization, as well as individuals. In other words, the social health of workers is closely intertwined with the overall health of the workplace.

Still, resistance to the idea of friendship at work is stubborn. When Gallup created a survey[12] asking if employees had "a best friend at work," one *Washington Post* columnist puzzled, "What is this? High school?"

Gallup wasn't asking about *close* friends, however. The question was meant to help respondents distinguish genuinely supportive and durable relationships from surface, weak, and negative interactions. It was the general quality of connection that mattered to the researchers, even in passing acquaintances.

Gallup found that when coworkers have a friend at work, they're inspired to act on behalf of their company in ways that employees without connected relationships are not. These actions extend to the sharing of useful information, voicing constructive opinions, and giving feedback without feeling threatened. But the more important effects benefit workers themselves. Having a friend at work makes us feel safer, more resilient and calmer when disagreements arise and more likely to support one another emotionally and physically. Gallup found that when two-thirds of a team strongly agreed that they had a best friend at work, they averaged 20 percent fewer accidents than teams in which only one-third of the members had a best friend.[13] When asked why, the workers said simply that they look out for their friends. Because they care and are paying more attention, friends will remind one another to wear their hard hat. They'll announce hazards and pitch in to stop injuries in the making.

Gallup found that having friends at work is particularly important to women. Friendships enhance their enjoyment of work and their performance and make them less likely to quit or search for other employment. Having friends at work led to women feeling less stressed and more connected to and trusting of coworkers.[14] Researchers call this the power of "relational energy."

"Relational energy" refers to the emotional energy generated (or depleted) in every social interaction. According to Dr. Wayne Baker, faculty director of the University of Michigan's Center for Positive Organizations, relational energy often sparks a chain of reactions. The first reaction is emotional, when we feel good making a strong positive connection with another person. The second is cognitive, clarifying our thoughts and improving our memory and cognitive performance. In short, connection often makes us feel better emotionally, which fires up our engagement with the tasks in front of us. And when we're energized and engaged at work, it leads to the third reaction—productivity.

Baker and Dr. Rob Cross conducted the first study of relational energy and its effects on individual performance in 2003.[15]

This study of social networks, Baker told me, included one key question in an organizational survey: "When you typically interact with this person, how does it affect your energy level?"[16]

Baker and Cross's team wasn't necessarily looking at friendships here, but at "high-quality connections," a term coined in 2003 by Dr. Jane Dutton and Emily Heaphy to describe work relationships that allowed people to flourish and organizations to achieve their goals.[17] Whether these connections are fleeting or enduring, they are marked by warmth, generosity, and sense of engagement. We know we're experiencing a high-quality connection if we feel a sense of uplift when encountering someone who expresses genuine concern and interest in our well-being. Think of how you feel when a friend shows concern for you after you've had a grueling meeting or work shift. Or how much more clearly you can think and function if a colleague gives you a genuinely encouraging or reassuring comment before you enter an important meeting.

In my work building nonprofit and business organizations, I found that the relationships between my colleagues were strengthened through what Barsade calls "micro-moments," or small, spontaneous interactions. When you look at someone and ask how they're doing—and you actually care. When you bring a cup of coffee to someone who is working late. When you're patient after someone falls short. Though small and brief, these exchanges can be powerful.

High-quality connections produce feelings of vitality that influence not just mood but also performance. Baker and his colleagues tested this with supervisors and their direct reports at a large health care company.[18] [19] First, they measured relational energy between supervisors and their team members. Four weeks later, they surveyed each employee about their energy on the job using standard engagement measures. Then, for about a month after that, they measured employee performance.

The results of this study showed that employees who had more relational energy with their supervisors also had higher engagement and better job performance. And, Wayne told me, "We know that high-quality connection practices increase relational energy."

One important key to high-quality connection, Wayne has found, is the exchange of help. And this includes *asking* for help.

"The secret to giving is asking. That was a big breakthrough," he explained one day when I was observing him lead a training for a group of corporate leaders. "Ninety percent of helping in the workplace is in response to requests for help. But most people won't ask for what they need."

As someone who has a hard time asking for help, I could certainly relate to what he was saying. People fear that if they ask for help, they're going to be perceived as needy, incompetent, weak, or ignorant. They think that admitting they have a problem is going to harm their reputation. But Wayne has found that none of that is true. "There's research that shows, as long as you make a thoughtful request, people will think you are *more* competent, rather than less."

The fact is, Wayne said, most people do want to help. But that's not always intuitive. "We've shown that engaging in the process of both asking for and receiving help, and building the network actually elevates people's emotional energy and decreases their negative energy."

When the active exchange of help is incorporated into an organization's culture and used over time, Wayne said, people start to build positive relationships that change their behavior at work and also their beliefs. "They see the importance of asking for what they need while they generously help other people. And they start to practice it more in their daily interactions."

High-quality connections also create what Dutton and her colleagues at the Center for Positive Organizations call positive regard, or "a sense of feeling known and loved, or of being respected and cared for in the connection."[20] This effect is created by the exchange of vulnerability and responsiveness in the moment. Far from simply being pleasant, high-quality human connections are life-affirming and energizing. This is why they add so much meaning to our lives.

Few employers have embraced the power and value of high-quality work connections as wholeheartedly as Ari Weinzweig and Paul Saginaw, the founders of Zingerman's in Ann Arbor, Michigan. This family of local food-related companies is famous for their Reuben sandwiches, sour cream coffee cake, and carefully packed gift boxes, but the company is beloved by employees and customers alike because Ari and Paul have created a culture where every person feels personally valued and connected.

This happened instinctively, Ari told me over a meal at one of Zingerman's dine-in establishments, The Roadhouse. "It's not like we sat down to create a culture of connection. It was more we said, this is a way that it makes sense to live and work. In nature's ecosystem, everything is connected. When we don't honor our connection to the community, to each other, and to ourselves, we don't do well. In the workplace when we violate human nature, we create a crisis that causes disengagement, depression, and loneliness. This comes in part from not honoring people's humanity and not honoring their unique contribution as human beings."

Great care is taken to prevent that disengagement and loneliness at Zingerman's.

To that end, every new employee takes an orientation course taught by Ari and Paul. This gives them an occasion to get to know each person as they join the Zingerman's team. As Ari and Paul see it, every person in the company is valuable not only because of the role they play but because they are diverse and multidimensional human beings.

"We are teaching everyone to be a leader from the moment they arrive and involving them in the organization," Ari told me. "Even if you're bussing tables, you're interacting with more customers than I am, so from the beginning you're being a leader."

I asked Ari how the employees get to know one another. He explained that they're not explicitly told to ask each other questions, but the environment encourages this. "If you have a culture where people are engaged with each other and learn about each other, then people will naturally do that."

As if to illustrate the culture of trust and inclusion that he and Paul have created, he turned to Mara Ferguson, an employee who happened to be nearby, and asked her what she thought. Mara told me that her first job at Zingerman's was in the bakeshop working behind the counter. After two years, she moved to ZingTrain, their training company, to do in-house events. There she wrote a vision for new roles within the organization, including one for a keynote liaison. She now holds that role, which she describes as a "one-woman speakers bureau for the organization."

Mara credits Ari and Paul with holding and sustaining Zingerman's workplace culture. "Leaders model it." She remembers Ari listening closely during her welcome class and reacting genuinely to her personal backstory. After that, whenever she saw him, he would always ask her questions about her story—about her family, her past jobs, her future aspirations. She could tell he remembered her story. Not many employers respond to individual staff members this way, but Ari and Paul do with *every* employee, and they don't make a big fuss about it. "It didn't strike me at the time," Mara said. "It just felt comfortable and normal."

To Ari, it feels normal because it's natural to be interested in the different dimensions of people. "Nothing in nature does only one thing. Assigning them a single task isn't consistent with nature."

Nor is it good for business. So Zingerman's offers employees a variety of classes that help build their skill sets while enriching the company's social and emotional culture. The classes are mixed, so everyone is learning together. "You're building a healthier care map . . . a web of inclusion so relationships are built across lines. A manager is having a conversation with a dishwasher, which is a perfectly normal human behavior, but would not happen in other organizations."

The structure of operations also encourages connection. Any employee can attend meetings of any department, including Zingerman's board meeting. A truck driver can help plan a menu, and a chef can help strategize on the online marketing strategy. To Ari, part of the benefit of this is disabusing people of the notion that leadership always knows what they are doing. It's okay to acknowledge that everyone is fallible even as they strive to make the company stronger.

The commitment to people both on their best days and their worst allows people to bring their whole selves to work. And workers don't have to pretend to be perfect to get a job. Ari introduced me to a young woman named Amanda, who applied for work as a line cook after falling ill while on tour as a rock musician. "When I came to Zingerman's, I felt defeated by the world," she told me. The years of sleeping on tour buses, being told she wasn't good enough because she was a woman, and having one-dimensional transactional relationships had taken a toll on her. She felt like no one saw her for who she was as a person, and she felt alone. At Zingerman's, she was hired and welcomed.

The reception astonished her. "I was the only woman in an all-male kitchen, everyone's older than me, and I never worked as a line cook," she recalled. "But never once did I feel like it was me against other people. At Zingerman's, they told me there are so many things you can do and achieve, and they put me through so much training and encouragement. And that's why I stayed. I was immediately accepted just for being who I was."

One day, Amanda overheard her boss tell her supervisor how unhappy he was with one of their graphic designs. She'd studied graphic design in college, so she piped up and offered to give it a try. They gave her the assignment, which led to her being promoted to a marketing role. Also, her paintings have been hung in the restaurant, and she started a music club with Ari's blessing to create a space where musicians from within the company can play together with and for the local community. Not everyone Amanda knows through her work at Zingerman's has become a *close* friend, but what matters is that all who work there are *indeed* friends.

The Kindness of Strangers

Many of these lessons from the microcosm of the workplace are transferable to society and our daily social behavior in general. Do we encourage high-quality connection and service to others in our interactions while shopping or taking our kids to the park or even just standing on the corner with others waiting for the light to change? Do we approach one another as multifaceted people who are more than their function in our lives? Do we ourselves feel seen within our communities in ways that encourage engagement? Models such as Zingerman's can help us all build more of a sense of belonging even when we're among strangers.

When Wayne Baker was testing the power of relational energy among employees, he was struck by the finding that even momentary high-quality interactions can make people more likely to share information and resources and to help one another. On the other hand, workers whose brief encounters are socially aloof, demanding, hostile, or disdainful drain one another of energy and result in less cooperation.[21] Relational energy, in other words, can surge in both positive and negative directions. And the positive charge that's ignited by high-quality connections can have a powerful impact on us even when we don't know one another at all.

This means that our circles of friends are not the only people who matter in our lives. Our social universe is filled with strangers, and our interactions with them can also help stave off loneliness and make us feel more connected.

Another team of researchers put this specific notion to the test during the summer of 2011, when the city of Chicago announced that it would have quiet cars on its Metra commuter rail system. In a survey conducted by the city, 84 percent of respondents supported having a quiet car. But University of Chicago psychologist Dr. Nicholas Epley and his associate Dr. Juliana Schroeder suspected this number didn't tell the whole story, so they designed a study in which one group of commuters was asked to initiate a conversation with fellow travelers. A second group was asked to keep to themselves. A final group received no instructions. All three groups predicted that their commute would be less pleasant and productive if they spent time talking with strangers, but their experience proved just the opposite.[22]

Compared to the silent group and the one that got no instructions, the conversation group enjoyed their commute *more*. What's more, extroverts and introverts alike enjoyed their conversations with strangers.

These results flew in the face of a culture conditioned to fear "stranger danger." While common sense is necessary and caution warranted in certain instances, the truth is that most people we encounter are no more dangerous than we are. Most of the impromptu interactions that we're avoiding are chock-full of richness. Almost all of us stand to gain from acts of kindness, even gestures as simple as a smile or a word of encouragement. Such acts actually reduce the threat level by helping everyone relax around one another.

Many of us misguidedly assume that strangers don't want to be approached. It's one of the reasons we refrain from chatting with people in line at the grocery store. We tell ourselves we don't want to impose or intrude. We worry they will think we're weird for initiating a conversation. The truth, however, is that even those who do want to be left alone will welcome friendly interaction. The data also suggests that we're happier when we take the initiative to connect with them.

As a person who tends toward introversion, I've been conducting an informal study of my own lately whenever working at a coffee shop or cafe. I'll push myself to smile and strike up conversations with the people working alongside me. Then, rather than pack up all my belongings each time I want to get some water or use the restroom, I ask a stranger to watch my bag and my papers. No one has ever let me down.

The first time I did this, I was struck by how good it felt to place my trust in someone and ask for help. This surprised me. But the response of the people I've asked has surprised me even more. One young man said to me when I came back, "Thank you for asking me to watch your things and for trusting me. Most people wouldn't do that. But it felt good." The whole interaction took next to no time, but the positive effect resonated with me for hours. It made the cafe feel more familiar and less impersonal, a place I looked forward to going each day. That's what the kindness of strangers can do for us.

These experiences have confirmed what Epley and Schroeder found on those commuter trains. Kindness, appreciation, and generosity are as essential in brief interactions with strangers as they are in closer friendships. A smile for the neighborhood barista, holding the elevator for a neighbor, yielding right of way to allow a family to cross the street. These exchanges take only seconds, but they can create a meaningful sense of connection, and they subtly reaffirm our self-worth by reminding us that we have purpose and value for others.

This is particularly important to remember given the prevalence of loneliness. Most of us are interacting with lonely people all the time, even if we don't realize it. And due to the state of hypervigilance that loneliness creates, many of these people will be anxious and on edge. For someone in such a state, kindness can be a disarming force. One never knows when a moment of appreciation or generosity can open the door to connection for someone who is struggling alone. As New York University sociologist Dr. Eric Klinenberg found when he began studying the social infrastructure of urban neighborhoods, connecting with strangers can have life-and-death consequences.

Klinenberg was a graduate student when the record-breaking Chicago heat wave of 1995 led to a perplexing tragedy: hundreds of people died alone, and most of them were African American. At the same time, only 2 percent of the heat-related deaths were Latinos, even though they accounted for 25 percent of the city's population and were disproportionately poor and sick.

Why was the death rate in the Latino Little Village neighborhood so much lower than in African American North Lawndale? Klinenberg's investigation, chronicled in his book *Heat Wave*,[23] pointed to the social and spatial context of these communities.

"Chicago's Latinos tend to live in neighborhoods with high population density," Klinenberg told me. "Busy commercial life in the streets, and vibrant public spaces. Most of the African American neighborhoods with high heat wave death rates had been abandoned—by employers, stores, and residents—in recent decades." In the abandoned communities, residents had no sense of shared space, no investment in common ground. As a result, they became estranged from one another and from the rest of the world. No one knew they were there, let alone that they needed help.

Even though the natural circumstance of the heat wave played a major role, Klinenberg said, "these deaths were not an act of God." The weather could not explain why hundreds of Chicago residents died alone, behind locked doors and sealed windows, out of contact with friends, family, and neighbors, unassisted by public agencies or community groups. "There's nothing natural about that."

This observation reminded me of the community contagion of loneliness that John Cacioppo talked about in his 2016 interview with the *Guardian*. "Let's say that you and I are neighbors,"

Cacioppo said. "I have become lonely for some reason and . . . as a suddenly lonely person I am now more likely to deal with you cautiously, defensively, as a potential threat to me, and you recognize that, so we are going to have more negative social reactions." Over three or four years, Cacioppo continued, "because you interact less well with me as a neighbor, when you go to work we can see you are more likely to interact negatively with someone else."[24]

This spiral reduces our collective capacity for connection, a phenomenon that communities and governments around the world are increasingly recognizing as a problem. In response, many cities, states, and countries are ramping up more intentional efforts to create common spaces where strangers can come together around shared interests, needs, or purposes. Such spaces include traditional parks, schools, greenspaces, and libraries, which Andrew Carnegie called "palaces for the people." Bogotá, Colombia, has set an example by closing seventy-six miles of city streets to cars from seven a.m. to two p.m. on Sundays and holidays so people can share the space for biking, walking, and other recreational activities. One-quarter of the city's population shows up each week for it. Other cities and towns are employing friendship and chat benches to counteract loneliness. In a couple of towns in the UK, the police department designated "Happy to Chat" benches with signs reading: THE "HAPPY TO CHAT" BENCH: SIT HERE IF YOU DON'T MIND SOMEONE STOPPING TO SAY HELLO. The idea is to invite connection by giving people permission to admit they would welcome engagement with strangers.[25]

Government has an important role to play in combating loneliness by understanding and optimizing the impact of policies on human connection, by funding research into the causes of loneliness, and by creating a public vision, strategy, and coalitions to address it. But while government is uniquely positioned to direct and mobilize society, the ultimate solution lies with all of us recognizing that we share the risk of loneliness as well as the power to prevent it. As I witnessed firsthand in the aftermath of

Hurricane Andrew, we exercise this power by coming together in service, friendship, and concern for one another.

That August morning in 1992, I huddled with my family in our living room as two-hundred-mile-per-hour wind gusts and torrential rain pounded Miami. Through a small opening in the wooden barricades on our windows, we could see debris whipping past as palm trees bent, as if bowing to the storm. After the winds died down, we ventured out into a virtual war zone. Telephone poles had snapped like toothpicks. Roofs were shredded, fish were blown into the trees and crabs were scattered on the ground, even though we were over a mile from the ocean. Like countless South Florida residents, we found ourselves without power, water, or telephone lines for weeks, but we were fortunate that our home was still standing. Andrew left more than 160,000 Florida residents homeless. It was a bleak and lonely experience to look out over that scene.

In the face of tragedy, however, something wonderful happened. Those who had been affected by the storm suddenly came together. Neighbors who'd lived side by side for years but hardly spoke began helping to clear one another's property. One of ours helped us find a backhoe to move one of our big trees that had fallen. And people whose homes had been spared drove nearly an hour from Broward County to bring us food and water. Hurricane Andrew created a powerful sense of connection in South Florida. A community formed in our formerly disconnected region, and with service as the binder, friendship flourished, and loneliness subsided.

Hurricane Andrew catalyzed the process of connection that comes naturally to us all—when we give it a chance. Family, friends, and strangers alike spent meaningful time in each other's company. We learned one another's names and shared our stories. We offered and asked each other for assistance and support. We shared both the burden of our losses and the relief of recovery.

We dared to get to know each other and to extend genuine kindness to strangers, as they did for us. We didn't all become close friends, but through the sharing of attention, service, and time, we made meaningful connections. We gained courage and confidence in ourselves, as well as in the resilience of the human spirit. We grew stronger together.

But it shouldn't take a tragedy for strangers to meet and help one another. As neighbors and communities, we need to learn how to hold on to that spirit of mutual concern and service even when the crisis is not so obvious. We must resist the tendency to slip back into our separate preoccupations after neighborhood dramas subside. Community can be a vital resource not just in moments of public anxiety but in quiet, private times of need, too. It can also enhance our quality of life and our human experience.

CHAPTER 8

A Family of Families

Peace is the beauty of life . . . It is the smile of a child, the love of a mother, the joy of a father, the togetherness of a family.

—Menachem Begin, Nobel lecture

There is something you must always remember. You are braver than you believe, stronger than you seem, and smarter than you think. But the most important thing is, even if we're apart, I'll always be with you.

—Christopher Robin, *Pooh's Grand Adventure:*
The Search for Christopher Robin

As hard as we may work to strengthen our connections within our communities and countries today, the future will depend on our children. It's up to all of us to teach them how to build a more connected and compassionate world.

Spending time with small children reveals how central human contact is to their existence. Beyond their physical dependence on the adults who care for them, babies and young children thrive on emotional connection with parents, siblings, and close family and friends. They demand to be held, to sit in a lap to read

a book, to have you share in their latest triumphs and disappointments. From infancy through adolescence, kids face a host of
social hurdles that can be both complex and rewarding, painful
and instructive. They need helping hands and thoughtful guidance every step of the way. Just our being adults doesn't guarantee
that we always have the answers for them.

Dramatic changes are shaping the lives of children today. Our
youngest generations are growing up amid a barrage of cultural
messages that prioritize fame, wealth, and status at the expense
of kindness, honesty, and character. While counting "friends"
and "likes" are priorities for kids in this age of social technology,
adolescents and young adults have some of the highest rates of
loneliness today.

One mother who knows all too well the price that these counter-
productive and often harmful messages can exact is Laura Talmus, executive director of Beyond Differences, an organization
dedicated to ending adolescent social isolation. Laura and her
husband, Ace Smith, founded Beyond Differences in memory of
their daughter, Lili, who died in 2009, when she was just fifteen
years old.

The story of Lili is as uplifting as it is tragic, because this child's
spirit was so extraordinary. Though born with Apert syndrome,
a rare genetic disorder, Lili also seemed to have been born happy.
Laura helped me to see the breadth of Lili's early life through her
contrasting recollections.

On the day of her daughter's birth, Laura remembers, the faces
of hospital staff in the delivery room dropped as they realized
something was wrong with the shape of Lili's head. Later the
family would learn that Apert syndrome causes the skull bones
to fuse prematurely. Lili's early years were filled with medical
procedures. "Every time she had a craniofacial surgery," Laura
recalled, "she had seizures."

On the other hand, "Lili was the happiest little child I could imagine. After four years in Montessori, she was in public school K–4, and she did great. The other students didn't seem to notice how physically different she was."

Lili's early childhood was a reflection of the natural compassion of very young children. As I've observed with my own pre-schoolers, small children who are treated kindly generally reflect that treatment. They may squabble over sharing, but they don't judge unless they're treated unfairly. Lili treated her friends with kindness, and she was loved in return.

But that began to change as she approached middle school. Looks suddenly mattered more, as did social status. Lili's class-mates began to shun her. No matter what she did, she couldn't find a way into the social circles around her. Instead, she found herself alone, and her distress grew. Then her grades began slipping, and she had trouble keeping up academically.

"I started getting calls from Lili from school, where she would be hiding in the bathroom," Laura told me. "She would tell me that the girls in her class were turning their backs on her during lunchtime. I tried to construct activities for her after school and on the weekend, but the lack of acceptance from the people at school really hurt her."

Laura emphasized that Lili was never directly teased or bullied. What she endured—social isolation—was much more common-place and insidious. In fact, Laura has come to realize that almost every child experiences a version of this shunning at some point during their school years. But for Lili, the pain became intolerable. "She was so miserable that by the beginning of seventh grade, she was pleading with us to have her homeschooled. Something told me that she might have a better sense of her needs at that point than us. So we mustered up all the finances we could, and we hired private teachers for seventh and eighth grade."

The two tutors they hired to work with Lili helped her regain her confidence and equilibrium. She became active in a variety of service projects and, through the Children's Craniofacial Association, she connected with other kids who had conditions like Apert syndrome. Those connections had a profound impact on Lili's life. In 2008, she wrote this reflection for the association:

> My years in our local middle school were some of the hardest and worst I can remember. My peers really didn't accept me for who I was, and my teachers didn't believe I could learn. I never thought it would be possible to do the work that I am doing today in my home school. I now know that I am equal to my peers . . . Do not ever let someone tell you that you can't do something—not even yourself!

"There was something so prescient about her that told her to live life to the fullest," Laura reflected.

Lili wanted to go to boarding school for her high school years, and after a great deal of thought and discussion, Laura and Ace consented. In 2009 they flew to Iowa to get Lili set up and bought their tickets to come see her again at parents' weekend later that fall. But before that weekend arrived, they got the call no parent ever wants to receive. Lili had passed away in her sleep, her death most likely a result of the episodic seizures she had been having since birth.

The loss for Laura, Ace, and Lili's older brother was almost unendurable. Laura recalled, "For a year, I couldn't breathe. I don't know how I got through it. During the second year, I felt the sidewalk wasn't flat. I felt tilted to one side." She managed to go back to work and kept herself occupied with her job. But sometimes when she reached the parking lot, she would just break down and start sobbing.

The seeds for survival were sown at Lili's memorial service, when Laura described her daughter's experience in middle school, including her loss of friends and the isolation that had driven her to leave that school. One of the mothers who was there asked her son that night, "Matt, were you still friends with Lili?" He said, "Of course. Everyone was friends with Lili."

When Matt's mother relayed his comment to Laura, it revealed an uncomfortable truth about social isolation. "Matt was never mean to her," Laura told me. But almost no one invited her to join them when they went to the movies. And when Lili was alone and hurting, no one noticed, or if they did, they didn't try to reach out.

This was the flash that kept going off in Laura's mind as those first grief-stricken months went by. "No one thought they were doing anything mean. They just left her out and turned their backs on her."

Laura decided to meet with Matt and a few of Lili's other former classmates and childhood family friends. They talked about the loneliness that Lili had felt and the reasons why she'd been left out. They decided together to share Lili's story with the rest of their former middle school, and the principal arranged an assembly for them.

"We were so scared," Laura recalled. "The auditorium was full. We each spoke, we showed a video about Lili. I asked the audience if they'd ever felt anything like Lili felt. And hands went up. Everyone wanted to tell their story."

Kendra Loo was one of the students sitting in the auditorium that day. Confident, extroverted, and easygoing, Kendra was anything but lonely. Yet as she listened to Laura speak, she was struck by the sadness of people who felt left out. "I just wasn't aware people were feeling this way," Kendra told me years later. "I didn't know that people ate their lunch in the bathroom because they had no one to sit with. I was shocked. And I wasn't doing anything to make their lives easier."

In that assembly, some students shared their experience of feeling lonely. Others acknowledged the role they had played (often inadvertently) in isolating others. Then they broke into small groups to talk about steps they could take to create a more connected, less lonely school. If everyone took a little responsibility for making sure people around them weren't lonely, it would go a long way, they were told. Throughout the school year, the small groups would meet weekly to keep addressing loneliness in the school.

"They gave us simple things to commit to," Kendra recalled. "Like I'm going to commit to going up to someone sitting alone once a week. Or just, I'm going to smile when I pass someone in the hallway. These little things mean a lot."

That was the beginning of Beyond Differences, a nonprofit organization that Laura and Ace launched with the aim of raising awareness about social isolation and loneliness in youth. At first people discouraged them because they assumed the focus was on bullying, and there were already many antibullying programs and initiatives. But Laura knew that the mission of Beyond Differences was different—and equally important.

"I ask kids," Laura said, "'Tell me what social isolation looks like and what it feels like.' They say, 'It's feeling not accepted for who you are, feeling invisible, feeling left out.'" It's a quiet and potentially lethal experience, Laura realized. "So much self-harm and violence is traced back to being lonely and isolated as a child. And so many adults are triggered by the trauma that happened during their adolescence."

Yet adults can be the most difficult customers for Beyond Differences' message and the need for it. "I don't think parents model inclusive behavior as much as they think they do," Laura told me.

Research bears this out. While 96 percent of parents in one survey viewed the development of strong moral character as being very important and most of them highly valued being honest, loving, and dependable,[1] a survey of ten thousand American middle and high school students by the Harvard Graduate School of Education showed that "60 [percent] of students ranked achievement above caring for others." Furthermore, "nearly two-thirds reported that both their parents and peers would rank achievement above caring for others." The vast majority of teachers, administrators, and school staff agreed that parents treat their kids' achievement as the top priority.

"How can we close the gap between what adults say and what they actually seem to prioritize?" the authors of the study asked in their 2014 report, *The Children We Mean to Raise*. "The big challenge is not to convince parents and teachers that caring is important—it appears they already believe it is. The challenge is for adults to 'walk the talk,' inspiring, motivating, and expecting caring and fairness in young people day to day, even at times when these values collide with children's moment to moment happiness or achievement."[2]

Laura saw this challenge. Beyond Differences encourages parents to join in at home, talking with their kids about friendship and compassion, reminding them to invite classmates sitting by themselves to join them at lunch or recess, to get to know kids from different backgrounds and religions, to befriend the quiet kids and be kind to one another online.

But Laura wanted to be more than a parental role model. She wanted to help kids become their *own* caring role models. "People think of middle school as something you have to get through. We reject that. We are committed to raising a new generation of young people who are confident and grounded and don't feel like victims. This is about more than kindness. It's about acceptance and lifting everyone up together."

Today, Beyond Differences is active in more than six thousand schools around the country, offering a variety of programs to help kids bridge their social divides. The goal is to shift the culture of middle school away from the normalization of cliques and social exclusivity. "We're trying to make a new generation of kids feel included," Laura said.

By the time kids are in middle school, she emphasized, they're most likely to listen to messages delivered by their peers. So, the organization relies on a teen board of directors made up of 120 high school students who are trained to go into middle schools and talk to students—peer to peer—about what social isolation is and how to combat it.

Students learn to take responsibility for how they treat one another and to recognize the physical, emotional, and psychological impact of social isolation. Since they all know the pain of rejection, Beyond Differences helps middle schoolers see that they can *prevent* this pain for all, if they come together.

Kendra Loo soaked up these lessons when she joined the teen board as a leader for Beyond Differences. Through her training, for instance, she realized how much body language influences conversation. By slightly shifting her body toward someone, she could help them feel she was paying closer attention to them. Making sure to keep eye contact while others were speaking, sharing brief comments in response to what people say to let them know you hear them, and making it a point to acknowledge all the people who were part of the conversation—these were some of the many skills she honed as a youth facilitator.

Kendra had graduated from high school and enrolled in college by the time we spoke, but the lessons she learned through Beyond Differences still affected her. "Learning how to connect with other people involved a lot of self-reflection. Everything I learned in Beyond Differences helped me find my people in college. And it gave me skills I will use for the rest of my life. I'm now known as someone who can talk to anyone. And I've learned how to show that I'm approachable."

What particularly impressed me about Kendra's story is that she herself wasn't experiencing loneliness when she attended Laura's general assembly, and yet she welcomed this wake-up call. She told me that the people who powered the program came from all backgrounds—some never experienced loneliness, and others constantly felt lonely. All came together to create a more connected community at school. And they all realized there was more they could do to create stronger connections in their own lives.

Teaching Relationship

For better or worse, it's a fact of life that social acceptance matters. We all want to be accepted. We all want to belong to a supportive circle of friends. Our kids are no different, and yet, too often, the importance of healthy social relationships can get lost amid the other priorities of school, sports, grades, chores, and family pressures. As parents, we need to remind ourselves that our kids' social educations are as important as their academic education and that the two are deeply intertwined.

In 2002, psychologists Drs. Roy Baumeister and Jean Twenge published the results of three small-scale but fascinating studies[3] that looked at the relationship between social belonging and academic performance.[4] The subjects were college students who were randomly assigned to three groups, divided according to a preliminary (but fake) personality test that purportedly predicted their future. Members of the "future alone" group were told that the results of their personality test predicted with high likelihood that they would end up alone in life. The second group, labeled "future belonging," were told that they would likely have a lifelong support network, including a long, stable marriage and lasting friendships. The third group's "test" predicted that they would become increasingly accident-prone over time, leading to broken bones and multiple visits to hospital emergency rooms, but no mention was made of their social life. This "misfortune control" group was included to differentiate the distress of expected physical pain from the distress of predicted social isolation. Immediately after learning their supposed fates, all the students were given a set of standardized IQ, reading, and memory tests.

The results of these studies were remarkable for several reasons. Faced with the prospect of a life without friends, both male and female students performed equally poorly on IQ and complex academic exams. Compared to *both* of the other groups, all the "future alone" students attempted to answer far fewer questions and took longer to puzzle out the answers they did get right. Their performance was unaffected on simple reading and memory quizzes, but the researchers "found significant and large declines in performance on an intelligence test . . . on challenging questions that involved recalling a complex passage . . . and on a test of logic and reasoning."

The other compelling finding was that the prospect of physical pain didn't affect the students' scores at all. The "misfortune control" group scored just as consistently high as the "future belonging" group. Only when faced with *social isolation* did students experience enough distress to disrupt their intellectual reasoning and logic. What's more, this drop in performance happened even among the "future alone" students who appeared cheerful and confident in spite of the prediction.

These studies suggest that the impact of social exclusion could be damaging in far more insidious ways than parents and educators traditionally have recognized. It would appear that when students feel shunned, they become preoccupied with the problem of their social fate, thus diverting brainpower from learning.

The researchers speculated that the effort to hide social distress—including fear and shame over the threat of future isolation—might also impair the mental functioning required for intellectual processes. And given that these tests measured the response to possible *future* isolation, it's alarming to think of the impact that social exclusion might have on kids like Lili Smith while it's actually happening. Perhaps that is why Lili had no difficulty keeping up academically *until* she felt shunned socially.

Before writing their book *Peer Power*,[5] sociologists Drs. Patricia and Peter Adler spent eight years intensively observing the lives of American preadolescent children in a dozen neighborhood schools. Their research described the complicated and ever-changing peer culture that normally takes place out of view of adults. Friendships and cliques form and dissolve. Leaders of groups try various techniques to retain power and popularity. Children find themselves accepted one day and rejected the next, often with little fanfare but much angst on the part of the child who does not know why they are suddenly out. A pecking order develops from most popular to least, affecting what children think of themselves and how they interact with one another.

The damaging behavior that affects kids during this phase can include hurtful rumors and insults, threats to break off friendships, exclusion from games or conversations, or public confrontations. Often the digs and attacks are unprovoked and may feel to the target as if they come out of nowhere. In this confusing competition, friendship can get warped into a status wedge, causing genuine connection to suffer and loneliness to proliferate.

Other research[6] has shown that the importance of popularity in kids' lives fluctuates with the years. While individual friendships matter much more in the early school years, around fifth grade popularity, or social status, starts to become more important. The power of popularity typically rises during the middle school years, between ages twelve and fifteen, and levels off toward the end of high school.

Meanwhile, of course, kids are also dealing with puberty, their first romantic desires (both requited and unrequited), and growing independence. With so much change happening at once, it shouldn't surprise us that many kids have a hard time figuring out who they are and where they belong at this age.

The question is, how can adults help?

We know the stakes are high. Like adults, when young people feel socially isolated, their risk[7] increases for depression, anxiety, and poor sleep. All this can take a serious toll on their health and performance at school. Fortunately, when these kids have adult support and positive role models, the picture improves dramatically.

In 2007, a survey[8] of more than forty-two thousand children aged eleven to seventeen found that kids with close families and supportive parents tended to feel more socially adept and have higher self-esteem and fewer academic problems than kids with disengaged or aggressive parents. Describing their findings in *Pediatrics*, the study's authors wrote, "'Mundane' aspects of family life such as talking to one another, having dinner together, and knowing about the adolescents' friends seem to matter."

So, too, do the neighbors. In neighborhoods where people watch out for and are trusted to help with each other's children, adolescents had greater social competence as measured by the respect they show teachers and neighbors, how they got along with other kids, and their efforts to empathize and resolve conflicts. Our social villages, which extend to teachers, youth leaders, and extended relatives, really do help raise our children.

Guy Winch, who often counsels parents whose kids have been bullied or socially isolated, says the first step for all adults is to respect and acknowledge the importance of children's concerns.

The most common thing adults say when trying to reassure kids, Guy said, is, "It doesn't matter what other people think."

Guy's response? "No! You may wish it didn't hurt, but it does."

Recalling the *Cyberball* studies by Naomi Eisenberger and others, Guy said that most people who experience this rejection react with distress, including anger and sadness. It doesn't matter if the people rejecting you are identified as members of a hate group. It also doesn't make a difference if they are revealed to be part of the setup. In other words, even if we know the rejection is fake, we still feel the same emotional pain.

Humans, Guy said, "are so hardwired to experience rejection as painful that finding out that people who have rejected us are people we despise, or that it never even happened, still doesn't take the sting away. So yeah, kids are going to be hurting when they get rejected, and telling them they shouldn't be is actually the wrong thing to do."

This well-intentioned response can make lonely kids feel even worse, Guy said, "because now they're thinking, 'I shouldn't be hurting but now I am hurting, so what does that mean?'" Instead, he believes, kids need to be reminded in that moment of the people who do value and accept them, whether they be a different group of friends, a club or community group, or their favorite family members.

"Invite one of those friends over that day, that afternoon, to do some microengineering, wiring, or whatever they do. That will remind them, 'Wait, I have a group. I belong somewhere.'"

Also, Guy said, don't forget to remind them that *you* care about them. "Listen and be there and remind them that they're loved."

Connecting Kids in the Digital Age

The influence of technology adds a particularly daunting dimension to parenting today. Teenagers are spending on average more than six and a half hours a day on screen-based media entertainment, including watching videos and participating in social media.[9] That's apart from the eight hours they spend sleeping and the six to eight hours they spend at school, and it leaves little to no time available for nondistracted, screen-free, face-to-face interaction. It would seem that something needs to change. However, it's not easy to know what to change, much less how to effect this change. It feels particularly high stakes, though, as childhood and early adulthood are when we develop the foundation for our social skills and awareness.

To help me make sense of how we should approach children's technology use, I spoke with Dr. David Anderson, senior director of National Programs and Outreach for the Child Mind Institute. Anderson has worked with kids his entire adult life, from running summer camps to counseling children in foster and adoptive care. He's trained health care practitioners and developed school-based services and a whole suite of resources for families, all on a national basis. At Child Mind, he develops resources for children and families struggling with a variety of mental health challenges.

While some experts warn that the internet and video games pose a clear and present danger to our kids' social development, Anderson's take is more nuanced. It would be wrong to assume all children are harmed by social media and technology, he said. Many kids say social media actually increases their opportunities for connection and allows them to find communities of belonging. At the same time, he believes technology can be harmful for children who are at higher risk for behavioral and mental health problems, as well as for those who are having problems meeting developmental benchmarks.

The bottom line is, not all screens have the same effects on all children. Each child is different in their needs and underlying susceptibility to social media's harms, and parents need to take those differences into account when setting limits around their screen time.

Most kids, Anderson said, use their smartphones and computers for stress reduction, relaxation, amusement, and social connection. For some, text messaging has simply replaced the phone call as the channel through which kids chat, arrange to meet, and catch up on homework. Moreover, technology is now so thoroughly woven into modern life that kids actually need a certain familiarity with digital culture in order to be conversant with their peers. It's become their common ground.

But children have no owner's manual for technology, and they are also apt to be exposed through technology to a broader world beyond the gaze of their parents and teachers. "Kids may not be able to handle what they encounter online," Anderson said to me. That's why parents do need to set reasonable boundaries around their use of technology. "You have to take a look at both what they're doing when they're online, and the amount of time they're spending. And there's no one-size-fits-all solution to this."

He reminded me of Przybylski and Weinstein's "Goldilocks hypothesis" that not only do adolescents with high digital screen time (more than two hours a day on weekdays) report lower levels of well-being than those with moderate use, but those who have minimal to no digital screen time *also* report lower levels of well-being than kids with moderate screen usage. "The hard part," Anderson said, "is that sometimes teens really want to be off it but the ways they communicate with friends are so limited to these platforms, they feel trapped."

The key is to help kids find the right level of moderation, so they can connect with their friends both online and off, without becoming overly tethered to their devices. That moderation starts at home, with parents' own use of *their* devices.

Small children especially need their parents' attention. They need eye contact, conversation, emotional engagement. I recalled Robin Dunbar stressing the complexity of the human skills that underpin our ability to build social relationships. To develop them fully, kids need lots of human contact and direct interaction. These engagements teach them how to read faces, gestures, moods, and emotions in themselves and others, how to build empathy and hone their emotional intelligence.

Parental interaction also helps kids learn how to behave, how to get along with others, how to give and take. This is the learning that tells us not to grab the piece of cake before anyone else, not to smack someone on the head when they upset you. When parents spend all their time on their phones instead of engaging with their kids, they're skipping these lessons. Then, as they get older, what will they do? Just like their parents, they'll ignore their own friends in favor of their devices. This is a recipe for loneliness.

For kids who have preexisting mental health disorders, like depression or anxiety, Anderson said, "Social media also can exacerbate those symptoms or lead these kids to retreat into an online world." Online communities such as those that actively promote eating-disordered behavior can make sick kids sicker and less equipped to engage in healthy relationships or take good care of themselves.

However, technology also can provide marginalized kids, such as LGBTQ+ youth, with a sense of peer connection that helps them feel less alone, anxious, or depressed. If no one in your school community is like you, Anderson said, it can be vitally reassuring to find kindred spirits through an online community.

But all parents need to monitor their children's relationship with the virtual world. Problems show up, Anderson told me, when kids start to confuse their own self-worth with the number of likes they get online, and especially when their personal relationships are *replaced* by virtual connections.

The key, he said, is to "check the developmental boxes" periodically, to make sure kids are getting enough of the social nourishment they need for their physical and mental health. If they're falling short, it may be advisable to reevaluate their use of screen-based technology. These "boxes" include:

1. High-quality and age-appropriate face-to-face friendships. When they're young, do they have playdates with one or two peers outside of school? As they get older and into middle school, are they hanging out in groups, either right after school hours or sometimes on the weekend? As teenagers, do they have one or two very close friends?

2. Extracurricular activities. Do they have strong personal interests? Have they found a sport or an instrument? Have they joined a school club or youth group related to art, nature, service, culture, or spiritual affiliation?

3. Family time. Has the family set regular screen-free periods? Does the family get together for meals? Do you spend time talking and engaging in offline activities together on weekends and holidays?

4. Shared screen time. Do you help your child learn how to navigate the digital world by going online together? Do you have certain shows or movies that you watch and discuss together? Talking about the relationships in a video can be a great learning experience that doesn't involve lecturing about social skills.

5. Free time. When your child has downtime, is there a healthy balance between online and offline play? Do they have adequate time to rest and reflect? Consider your child's particular needs and temperament before determining the boundaries you set around this time.

6. School performance. Are your children engaged in school? Do they have adequate time and space to do their homework and study for exams?

7. Basic wellness practices. Is your child getting enough of the daily habits that contribute to mental health and wellness? Are they getting enough exercise? Are they sleeping near the recommended number of hours for their age? Are they eating a healthy diet, including breakfast before school and a variety of fruits and vegetables? Are screens turned off an hour before bedtime?

Dr. Delaney Ruston is a physician and documentary film-maker, whose film *Screenagers* focuses directly on the challenge of raising healthy children in the digital age. She launched this project around 2011 after starting to notice the level of argument and tension in her own family rising because of technology. Her teenage son wanted to play more video games, and her daughter was always on social media. "I saw the tsunami writing on the wall that was going to be digital devices 24/7 in younger hands and the homework on computers. I knew we were setting ourselves up for major conflict."

Ruston's experience interviewing teens for her film has left her with some simple yet effective suggestions for reducing this conflict. First and foremost, she told me, it requires a collaborative rather than a heavy-handed disciplinary approach. "The best parenting thing we can do is listen, because teens love to talk, and they love to teach, so we need to come to them with curiosity and have them explain what is happening on Instagram and their video games and so on."

A big part of this conversation needs to revolve around online behavior. What's okay to say online, and what's not? What does it mean when someone says things on Facebook that they'd never say to your face, and what's the right response? "These conversations about smart online conversation and being savvy and kind and how you talk about conflict afterwards are crucial," Ruston told me, and they need to begin in middle school or earlier.

It helps for parents also to be transparent in admitting their own struggles managing technology. "Then we are modeling the work that it takes." For example, she said, "I might tell them I try not to be on screens after dinner, but I'm struggling because I haven't gotten all my emails done. I might ask them to help me by reminding me earlier to finish up my work." This lesson by example and inclusion teaches kids about the process of behavior change through mutual understanding.

Like Anderson, Ruston has found that many kids don't really want to spend most of their time online, and when they're empowered to come up with their own solutions, these can be much more effective than parental time limits. For instance, some teens have a rule when eating with their friends that everyone puts their phones in a pile on the table; the first person who checks their phone during the meal has to pay a penalty, like buying everybody dessert.

These conversations made it clear to me that teaching our kids to be present doesn't require sweeping changes. Small gestures can have big effects if we're conscientious about implementing them.

One of our models for parents looking to rebalance their children's lives, Dr. Catherine Steiner-Adair suggests, is summer camp. In her book *The Big Disconnect*,[10] Steiner-Adair describes herself as a lifelong camper. She started going to summer camp at five years old, later became a camp counselor, and now serves as a consulting psychologist to summer camps. Like Yalda Uhls, who found that outdoor camp can increase empathy among kids, Steiner-Adair describes camp as an important setting for youth.

"There's no better place that I can think of to learn social emotional intelligence," she told me when we spoke recently. Not all camps are equal, of course. Nor is camp the only place where kids develop social intelligence. However, the summer-camp model is worth examining because, as Steiner-Adair said, "The canons at a good camp are empathy, authenticity, and social and emotional intelligence."

At camp, kids are released from what Steiner-Adair calls the digital pacifier. "Everybody is present to each other. There's no digital distraction and everybody has to be included. We are connected through camp—whether you like that girl or not, you are in the same boat."

Campers also can reconnect with their inner selves. Instead of checking their phone every minute, they check in with themselves as they walk through the woods, or paddle their canoe, or practice archery. "It's like a complete reboot for your soul."

The counselors also play an important role, Steiner-Adair said. They're like supportive siblings who "are here to help you connect and stay present in a way that is true to who you are and also create space for being true to who they are. The power of the 'we' is so strong that we can hold all our individuals."

In this sense, camp culture is the opposite of our wider status-driven culture where kids learn there's only room for one at the top, whoever has the best toys wins, whoever has the best body wins, whoever went to an Ivy League school wins. "Young people have always gotten their identity by comparing themselves to other people, but what's so hard for kids today is that comparison goes on 24/7."

All this comparison and competition breeds anxiety and fear of missing out (FOMO), says Steiner-Adair. Camp, then, can be a FOMO-free zone where kids can be themselves and connect as themselves. And that kind of connectedness grounds kids and helps them feel present in their own lives.

This doesn't mean it's easy. Working through conflicts in person when you're used to the distance of text messaging can be uncomfortable. For young adults, having to figure out how to tell someone to their face that you're romantically interested in them without the aid of technology and emojis can be harrowing as well. But the more time kids and their young adult counselors spend together and the more present they are with each other, the more they are able to be themselves and successfully navigate their other relationships.

The lesson is not that everyone should send their children to camp. Not every family can afford to do so, of course, and face-to-face time is important all year round, so it's a good thing the lessons of camp are transferable. Just imagine if we all made sure our children had time on a regular basis that was free from screens. If all meals were tech-free, we'd have more and better dinner table conversations with them. If their slumber parties were free of screens, the kids would be more present with each other. If their phones were turned off during school trips, they'd be more likely to discuss their discoveries about the places they were visiting together. They'd be more available *to* one another.

Teaching Emotional Fitness

When Delaney Ruston trained her camera on adolescents to make *Screenagers*, she noticed something about their emotional responses to being online that she hadn't expected. "All day long," she said, "there are moments where they feel great, and moments of likes, and moments of despair and disgust and sadness." Each kid seemed to experience a wide spectrum of fleeting emotions online, sometimes without any provocation or obvious explanation, throughout the day. Ruston also noticed that many kids didn't know how to manage or even identify these "micro-emotions."

Educators, who've noticed the same phenomenon, recognize that these wild fluctuations can wreak havoc on students' academic performance as well as their social interactions. So schools around the world have begun to welcome programs focused on social and emotional learning. By equipping kids with the tools they need to manage emotions and foster strong connections—including self-esteem, empathy, and strong interpersonal communication skills—and by giving them opportunities to use these tools to develop healthy relationships, they hope to help the next generation build a more connected future.

One of these programs, launched in 2005 by the Yale Center for Emotional Intelligence, is called RULER—an acronym that stands for five key skills:

- ✤ Recognizing emotions (by interpreting other people's facial expressions, body language, and vocal tones and one's own physiology and cognition)

- ✤ Understanding emotions (including the causes, consequences, and influence of different emotions on thinking, learning, decisions, and behavior)

- ✤ Labeling emotions (with a vocabulary to describe the full range of emotions)

- ❖ Expressing emotions (aptly with different people and in multiple contexts)

- ❖ Regulating emotions (with helpful strategies to promote personal growth, build relationships, achieve greater well-being, and attain goals)

Dr. Marc Brackett, who leads the team that created the program, is personally familiar with the need for social and emotional learning. As a shy kid growing up in suburban New Jersey in the 1980s, Marc was bullied often and felt alienated and forgotten. His trauma was compounded by early sexual abuse, which he wrote about in his 2019 book *Permission to Feel*. After he became a psychologist, he realized that part of what had been missing for him and his peers (and his teachers and parents) throughout childhood were tools for recognizing and managing emotions. In his studies and research, Marc found that kids who have trouble socially tend to have lower emotional intelligence scores, which also are associated with aggressive, risky, and disruptive behavior. When he became director of the Yale Center for Emotional Intelligence, Marc and his colleagues decided to try to improve the social climate by cultivating emotional awareness and skills throughout the school community. The result was RULER.

Marc refers to RULER as an approach rather than a "program" because it is not just a discrete class that students take during the school day. Instead, it consists of materials and practices that are integrated into the academic experience as a whole, involving parents, teachers, administrators, coaches, and staff, as well as students. In this way, it takes what Marc calls a "systemic approach" to healthy social and emotional development for everyone involved.

"All the therapy in the world doesn't do enough good when you return to a toxic environment. If the adults aren't modeling healthy emotional behavior, the kids won't do it," he told me. So, to change the environment for kids, RULER helps *all* the people in the environment better identify and manage their emotions.

The reported results of RULER—measurable improvements in empathy, social skills, classroom behavior, and school performance—almost seemed too good to be true when I first read about them. So, one crisp autumn morning, I visited Marc at Yale to see RULER in action.

We went to a public elementary school in the nearby town of Hamden, where I was immediately struck by the tenor of the hallways between classes. Kids were laughing and talking. There was a noticeable lack of tension. In fact, it felt peaceful.

Marc took me first to a third-grade class where the teacher was starting a short film clip on the television at the front of the room.

After it concluded, she asked the students, "Can you tell me what the characters might have been feeling?"

One boy said he thought the high school student in the film felt stressed and anxious when she was confronted by a bully in the bathroom. A girl lifted her hand confidently in the air. "I think the bully might be scared, too," she said.

As the other children volunteered their observations, the teacher gently nudged for more, asking what clued them in to the feelings they saw. Was it the tone of voice? Body language? A person's clothes? What did they think they might do if they encountered someone like this in real life? How would they help?

Later, I had a chance to speak with three fourth-grade students about their experiences with RULER. A girl named Tanya told me she'd transferred into this school from New Haven where she was bullied and not doing well academically. "I didn't even want to go to class before this school," she said. "But people here, they're different. They're nice, and we're all nice to each other."

Her classmates nodded. Carlos, a short, slender boy with black glasses that seemed in perpetual danger of sliding down his nose, piped up next. One of his classmates had come to school that morning in a terrible mood. "When she came into class," he said, "she was being mean to us. But we figured she was frustrated. Maybe she had an argument with her mom and dad. So we just asked her how she was doing and tried to be kind to her. By the end of class she was nice again. We felt good, too."

I was amazed. When I was in fourth grade, I wouldn't have had the vocabulary to describe my feelings the way these children did, much less the skills to think through someone else's emotions and mine with such maturity. But at their school, these kids were the norm, not the exception.

Tanya told me her parents had noticed a difference in her as well. "They see that I'm happier at home now because I'm happier at school."

The teachers at this school confirmed the positive effects of RULER. Their students were more empathic and less aggressive, they told me. They built stronger friendships. Fights still happened, but they were more likely to be dealt with calmly and with words, as opposed to anger and physical violence.

RULER is based on the simple but powerful idea that emotions matter. When we acknowledge the power of our emotions and when we have the skills to calmly consider and shape our reaction to people and circumstances, we feel and do better in our relationships, in school, and in the workplace. To date, more than two thousand public, private, independent, and parochial schools have implemented RULER worldwide, and data from many of the schools show that the program meaningfully shifts the emotional climate of the classroom.[11 12 13 14 15 16 17] This, in turn, improves social confidence and emotional intelligence scores while reducing aggression and emotional distress, Marc shared with me, and there is preliminary data that the program improves academic performance. The benefits have extended to teachers as well. One study has shown that teachers who participate in RULER are less stressed and burned out and report higher levels of engagement.

Marc pointed to another benefit of RULER that I hadn't anticipated: it levels the playing field between parents of different educational backgrounds. "Say my mom and dad were not highly educated, so they couldn't do much of my homework with me.

But with RULER, I could come home and say, 'We learned this new feeling word today in school. Can we talk about it?' Parents can participate. And the student becomes the teacher."

Marc recalled one sixth-grade student who went home with the word "alienation," one of the words in the RULER curriculum. She was telling her mom about what makes her feel alienated. Then she asked what makes her mom feel this way. The mother happened to be a police officer in New York City and the only woman in her precinct. This led to a serious conversation between mother and daughter that helped the mother realize she was lonely and that she needed to address it.

"One feeling word can open up an entire discussion," Marc said.

As important as it is for kids to cultivate social and emotional skills, there's a next step in developing social connectedness that involves active compassion, or service. It's not enough just to tell our kids to care for others. To grow up feeling that they truly matter to one another and to society, they need to learn to give and receive help, which in turn teaches them that they can make a meaningful difference in the world. This idea was driven home for Justin Parmenter in 2018 after a high school shooting took place in Charlotte, North Carolina, where Parmenter has been a teacher for over twenty years.

I learned about Justin when listening to a radio interview about the compassion project he launched with his seventh-grade students after the shooting. "For personal conflict to turn into one of these children dying and the other going to prison," he said, "it seems to me the antidote to that kind of situation is empathy and kindness." When I heard that his project was called Undercover Agents of Kindness, I had to learn more.

When we spoke, Justin told me the inspiration for his project was a 2013 study by Drs. Richard Davidson and Helen Weng of the Center for Healthy Minds, which showed how the brain can be trained toward more compassionate behavior simply by practicing kindness. Even before the shooting, Justin had been frustrated by online conflicts and bullying behavior that bled over into the classroom. But he understood that these conflicts had complex roots, especially given the age of his kids, and as much as the children fought or ignored one another at other times, he didn't think they were fundamentally mean. "I think it's more self-preservation and kind of being hardened so that they are not vulnerable to being hurt by other people." This fear of being hurt seemed to be erasing the kids' capacity for compassion. And that left many of them feeling lonely and excluded.

Maybe, he thought, if he could help them see that just being nice to someone was normal and not weird, they'd let go of the meanness. "It's such an important time of life for them to be reflecting about their interactions with other people and the way that they treat each other. Lessons about this stuff can actually make a long-term difference."

Here's how Undercover Agents of Kindness works: Parmenter puts the names of all his students in a bowl, and each student then draws a single name. The assignment is to perform an act of kindness for the person they selected, then write a "mission report" summarizing the experience.

The immediate response of most kids was gratifying. In the weeks that followed his class's first few drawings, Parmenter began to see notes of encouragement posted on lockers before an exam, homemade cupcakes and bags of candy delivered to students, inspirational quotes and origami placed on desks in the classroom by students looking to make a classmate smile and feel a bit better.

He told me about Maya, a young girl who was assigned to do something kind for her classmate Sonia, who'd experienced a concussion while playing soccer and was restricted from playing outside. Maya had never spoken to Sonia before, but instead of going out to play with her friends, she bought Sonia ice cream and stayed inside with her to talk so she wouldn't feel lonely.

Another student, Jeff, drew the name of a classmate who had a low threshold for frustration—so much so that if there was an assignment he didn't understand, he would throw his folders on the floor. Having observed the boy enough to recognize this, Jeff brought him a stress ball from home so he could squeeze something when he felt the frustration welling up. "I've seen that child bring that stress ball to class now, and I've seen him really improve at how he deals with frustration," Justin told me. "I think a lot of it has to do with just making a human connection with another person and realizing there are other people in my life who understand what I'm going through and want to help me."

Justin acknowledges that not all of the kids embraced the assignment right away. For the very shy and socially anxious students, the prospect of approaching someone they didn't know was agonizing, and he had to come up with ways to protect their anonymity while also making sure that kids didn't get left out on the receiving end. But after several rounds, most of the students clamored for the next drawings. They became more creative and more sensitive in their acts of kindness. They began to make an effort to get to know their recipients, asking other people about their interests and what they could do for that person that would be meaningful to them.

A number of Justin's students observed that it shouldn't take an assignment for them to be kind to one another. Justin agreed, but he told them, "That's exactly the point. It really shouldn't but seems like it does. Sometimes when you make just the smallest move in the right direction in an individual interaction, you have no idea what it's going to do in the other person's life."

Since he started Undercover Agents of Kindness in 2017, teachers from cities around the United States to Colombia and Micronesia have been contacting Parmenter for tips on starting their own initiatives to give students a chance to practice being kind and caring. As for his own classes, he just hopes the messages the kids are receiving will stay with them. "The long-term goal is that they apply what they're learning from that practice in new situations, when they're at the grocery store and when they're dealing with strangers."

The gold standard for childhood compassion lies in acts of kindness that kids initiate on their own. This simple truth was imprinted on me after the Newtown, Connecticut, school shooting in 2012, during a heartbreaking conversation I had with the father of one of the victims, a seven-year-old named Daniel Barden.

Daniel's special gift was compassion. Whenever there was someone who was left out or sad on the playground or in the cafeteria, Daniel would notice. But a lot of kids noticed. What made Daniel different was that he also tried to help. He would walk over to the child to talk or just quietly sit with them. Though only in first grade, Daniel realized that the values of kindness and inclusion were not always reflected in the world around him. No one taught him to do this. He naturally empathized with others who were lonely. And he responded with compassion.

When children like Daniel are bold enough to be of service to one another, their parents and teachers need to acknowledge and applaud this kindness—and build on it so that the wave of compassion continues. That's exactly what happened at Boca Raton High School in South Florida in response to a program started by a student, Denis Estimon, and his classmates.

Denis is the son of Haitian immigrants who moved to South Florida when he was in elementary school. As a new arrival, unfamiliar with American customs and accents, he often felt lonely at school, and he could see that he wasn't the only one. Many other kids seemed to be lonely as well, and the loneliest time for all of them was lunchtime.

To change this, Denis and three other classmates started a program called We Dine Together. Like Daniel, he and his fellow organizers would walk the school grounds at lunchtime and find people who were alone. They'd sit and talk with them.

And then they took the next step. If they sensed the students were open to it, they'd invite them to join the We Dine Together group at lunchtime. If students preferred solitude, that was okay, too.

When I first spoke with Denis, he was one year into the program. Already, they had a community of over fifty students who ate lunch together. Students told him it felt good to belong to a group of peers. They also realized that by joining the group, they were providing company to other students who didn't want to be alone. The feeling of gratitude was mutual, and some of the relationships built through the program developed into friendships beyond the lunch hour. For other students, this supportive interaction simply helped them feel better about themselves—and less lonely.

We Dine Together was so successful that it spread to fifteen schools the following year. Denis has since graduated from high school, but he was so inspired by the success of the program that he's stepped up to become director of Be Strong, a student-led movement for inclusion that is now promoting We Dine Together around the world.

When I spoke with him in the fall of 2019, he was brimming with pride at the nearly 250 schools that had started We Dine Together clubs. He told me about a recent visit back to Boca Raton High School. "At one point, a lady I've never met before runs up to me, and she gives me a big hug. She starts crying and says, 'I want to thank you because last week my son who has Asperger's came up to me and said, "Mommy, Mommy, I have friends, I have friends!"—all because the club members welcomed him in with open arms.'"

Then Denis grew more thoughtful. "We have a generation that is starving for company," he said, "when they should be looking for community. 'Company' just means that someone is around you. Many of us have company but not true community. Everyone needs community, whether you're the popular kid or the loner."

Parents in Community

The more I learned about all these programs, the more I kept thinking about the dual challenge that parents—including me—face as they strive to show their children better ways to connect. The American Academy of Pediatrics and countless experts agree that parents are critical role models when it comes to building social and emotional skills and developing healthy relationships. But many parents are struggling with loneliness themselves.

Some of these parents are dealing with stressors like poverty, violence, their own history of trauma, and other hardships that will make parenting especially challenging and isolating. These are the very parents who most need to come together. Having a group of peers with whom to learn better skills and build mutual support can radically ease the burden on their whole families. Yet these also are the parents least likely to have the time or resources to initiate such groups.

Recognizing this, Dr. David Satcher, one of my predecessors as US surgeon general, launched the Smart and Secure Children (SSC) parent leadership program about eight years ago. Now in communities from Atlanta to Houston, the fifteen-week program brings groups of six to ten parents together for two-hour weekly discussions, which take place over a meal in neighborhood locations such as barbershops, churches, Salvation Army centers, and United Way locations. During these sessions, trained facilitators guide parents through conversations about child development, social and emotional health, positive disciplinary choices, family use of media, and practices to strengthen their own social and emotional well-being.

The project director, Dr. LeRoy Reese, told me that SSC not only raises parents' child-rearing knowledge and skills but also measurably reduces their social isolation and improves their mental health. People end up helping one another with everything from parenting to job searches. And the connections continue beyond the program with the help of parent liaisons, graduates of SSC who live locally. One such liaison started a chess club for participants. Another began working specifically with black fathers to support them after they completed the program.

"We create a web of continuity," LeRoy told me.

Strong social connections, of course, are important for parents regardless of circumstance, but many new parents don't realize that and are stunned to find themselves lonelier after their baby is born than before. We rarely talk about this, not only because of the stigma around loneliness, but also because it seems ungrateful to feel lonely after being blessed with a child.

However, the blessing of a child historically came with lots of help. In more collective cultures, and in extended families that live close together, this still is true. Those parents have built-in local support and companionship. When grandparents and other family members are nearby and integrated into the children's care and upbringing, everyone can benefit.

Today, unfortunately, many new parents have neither family nor close friends nearby, and this particular form of isolation can be especially stressful during times of family crisis. This was the situation that Alice and I found ourselves in on Presidents' Day weekend just after our daughter, Shanthi, turned one, when we realized something was alarmingly wrong.

That morning began like any typical Saturday in our household. Alice and I changed diapers, brushed teeth, and tried to cajole our two-year-old, Teyjas, to eat a little breakfast while Shanthi laughed, played with her brother, and ate like a champ. She'd been a little more irritable than usual the night before, but we chalked that up to teething, and by morning she seemed fine.

Which is why we were caught off guard when we noticed later in the day that she wasn't putting any weight on her right leg. When we tried to straighten the leg, she whimpered and pushed us away.

Our hearts sank. Had she injured herself while roughhousing with her brother? Or was there something more ominous going on, like an infection?

We put Teyjas in the care of our weekend babysitter, packed Shanthi into the car, and headed to the children's hospital emergency room. Minutes dragged into hours as we waited. Blood tests confirmed that she had an infection, but the doctors couldn't tell what exactly was going on without an MRI. At Shanthi's age, that meant she needed to be completely sedated. And since it was the Saturday of a holiday weekend and the hospital was short staffed, we learned it might be impossible to arrange an MRI before Tuesday. Three days? This was a potentially fatal eternity. If there was an infection, it could spread throughout her body in three days' time.

As doctors who'd cared for thousands of patients, worked on shaping national health policy, and led public health efforts for the nation, Alice and I had witnessed and helped plenty of patients through medical emergencies. In this moment, though, none of that mattered. We were just two scared parents worried about our baby. We'd been in the emergency room, holding our sick, hungry, frightened daughter for more than eight hours.

We'd called our families right away, but they were thousands of miles away. Most of our closest friends lived in other states, and the friends who did live in the area had small children of their own. We sent text messages to a few of them to tell them what was happening. But we were reluctant to impose on them so late at night as we pictured them busily putting their own kids to bed. We didn't usually ask our friends for help, and I felt in those terrible hours more alone than ever before.

We were surrounded by people, from hospital staff to other worried parents and children, and in time we'd come to appreciate the presence of all of them, but in those early moments our anxiety isolated us. When you feel your ability to protect your child is compromised, it strikes at your core in a way that few other challenges do. The stakes and your fears feel highest when your child's well-being is at risk.

A friend once told me, becoming a parent is signing up for a lifetime of love and worry. Both were roaring that night. Our hearts were aching with love for Shanthi and terror for her future. We felt 100 percent responsible for everything that was happening and yet we were also helpless to change it. We felt guilty and, on some level, I think I felt ashamed to have allowed this to happen to one of the two most precious beings in our lives. And there is nothing more isolating than shame. So even though every other parent in the emergency room was dealing with a sick child, we couldn't bring ourselves to reach out to one another. There is great power in parents in such situations being able to connect with one another, but it's not easy to do this when that power is most needed. In truth, it didn't even occur to me. My loneliness in that moment blinded me.

But for me, this emergency also revealed a gap that had been widening for some time between the work-driven life I'd created for myself and the connected life that I deeply desired. The loneliness I felt was not the result of true isolation. I'm very close to my family and I have a fairly large social network. But when we moved to DC, I'd neglected to build a community and I'd let work consume me to such an extent that I neglected many of my strongest friendships from earlier chapters of my life. The truth is that I could have called any of those friends. They would have responded in a heartbeat. But they were in different cities across the country. And the energy it would have taken to reach out again after letting them go was just too fraught. I didn't think I had the right.

How had I drifted so far from my "village"? Geographic distance was only partly to blame. I recalled the words of a friend from residency during an earlier period in my life when I was feeling lonely. She'd said, "Vivek, you have friends. You're just not experiencing friendships."

This wasn't how I'd grown up. Although they didn't have extended family around, either, my parents had built a strong network of friends that became like family to me and my sister. These honorary uncles and aunties would babysit us, sometimes even overnight when our parents went out of town. And when the four of us were in a car accident that caused my sister to be hospitalized, those friends stepped up and helped us with everything from meals, to rides, to babysitting me. Sitting with Shanthi in the hospital, remembering that long-ago trauma and the ease that our circles of friends had brought to my family back then made the absence of equivalent circles in my life now achingly clear.

We spent the night in the emergency room. The next morning, Sunday, we received some unexpected news. Shanthi's MRI had been scheduled for noon. We owed this to a group effort.

A team of doctors, administrators, and nurses had pulled together staffing and logistics so that the test could happen quickly. We didn't know these people but they recognized that a hidden infection in such a young child could be serious, and they'd moved mountains to get our daughter the care she needed to save her life.

At the appointed hour, we took Shanthi down to the radiology suite, where the team was waiting for us. As we held her close, they injected her with the anesthetic. Within seconds, she closed her eyes and went completely limp. For the next hour, we paced the halls, wishing we could be with our daughter inside that MRI machine.

Suddenly, the doors to the waiting area burst open and a group of surgeons swept in. Behind them, we saw Shanthi lying on the gurney, still sedated.

They told us there was likely an infection deep in the tissue just above the knee. I asked if it had spread to the bone, which could threaten the growth of her leg or, worse, her life. "We don't know," said the attending surgeon. "We need to take her immediately to the operating room before it spreads further."

The doctor uttered the words as gently as she could, but it was one of those moments when time slowed, and reality became hazy. I couldn't speak over the lump in my throat. I just couldn't get any words out. Eventually, I put my hand on the surgeon's shoulder and managed, "Please, just take care of our baby."

With that, they whisked Shanthi away. And the hole her absence made in that instant was like a bottomless well. Watching our child disappear like that, I'd have given anything to be able to take her place.

For ninety agonizing minutes, we waited. We called our parents and sisters. We held each other. We cried. Those were the longest minutes of my life.

As the seconds ticked past, I thought how often we'd felt lost as parents. Trying to figure out how to get the babies to eat. How to get them to sleep. How to teach them to talk and crawl and walk—any of the routine miracles that were within our job description as parents but which we felt utterly ill equipped to do. All of this lostness resurfaced and felt especially acute during Shanthi's crisis because our need for support, guidance, and wisdom was so intense—and the absence of that support so stark.

I couldn't pretend that this way of living—apart from family and close networks of friends and not really knowing our neighbors—was how we were meant to live and raise children. If we ever emerged from this nightmare, I thought, something had to change.

Finally, the attending surgeon appeared. "We caught it just in time," she said. "We don't think it spread to the bone."

Those words were like a gift from on high. I gave the doctor a bear hug as if she were one of my dearest friends, and in that moment, she was. We were strangers to her and her team, yet they had brought our baby back to health.

We breathed an enormous sigh of thanks and relief and rushed to the recovery room to see Shanthi.

Over the next few days, all my reflections on the power of community for families were confirmed. First, my mother and

Alice's mother dropped everything to come to us. When they arrived, Teyjas lit up and jumped into their arms as soon as they appeared at the door. The whole ordeal had been stressful for him, too, and there was something vital for both children in the presence of these trusted sources of kindness and love.

The reunion brought relief to our mothers, as well. We weren't the only ones who belonged to Shanthi, and vice versa. They were happy to be there. They *needed* to be there not only for us, but for themselves. They wanted to be needed. Everyone does.

When I finally did reach out to my close friends, they, too, responded with concern and offers of help. And so did the doctors, nurses, and administrators who came to visit our hospital room every day. There was a moment where our moms were at the hospital, having brought food and extra clothes. A kind woman from the hospital had stopped by with a puzzle and some stuffed animals for the kids. She had spread a blanket on the floor and was entertaining them, and they were laughing and playing together the way they had before this whole ordeal began. The administrator who'd helped coordinate Shanthi's MRI in the middle of the night swung by at the same time. Meanwhile, our phones were filling up with calls and texts from friends who were checking on us and asking how they could help.

As lonely as I had felt in the emergency room, when I took in the scene in Shanthi's room I was reminded that more often than not, the people who love us will step up if we just have the courage to invite them into our lives.

My father used to say that timing matters when it comes to reaching out to people during times of need. He was usually referring to our stepping up to help others as soon as we saw their need, rather than waiting until it was convenient for us. But I now think his advice applies conversely, as well: it's important to reach out as soon as we need help and not wait until the worst is over. We should never be afraid of inconveniencing the people who love us. Especially when our families are at stake.

The experience with Shanthi was like taking my dark glasses off and seeing the brilliance of human connection in its full force. It was why I found myself in tears so often when speaking to the many people who helped us. There is much more love and connection in the world than I had allowed myself to see. And much of it during those days and since, I've found right in front of my eyes.

Had I but realized it, some of my clearest examples were my own children. As Shanthi recovered, I gained a new appreciation for the unabashed affection that bonds our children and the natural ease with which they give and receive it. Teyjas freely hugs Shanthi when she's sad, feeds her when she's hungry, looks for her when she's been out of sight for too long, and consoles her when she is crying. He is only three, but these gestures of kindness come instinctively and without inhibition. He and Shanthi, like all young children, are a tender reminder that all of us were meant to be in relationship with one another.

What is humanity, really, but a family of families? We all share this planet. And all our children together shall inherit this earth.

I don't know if it is presumptuous to speak for other parents, but when I think of the message I want my children to carry within them as they grow, I can't limit the words to my children alone. These are really my hopes and dreams for generations to come.

Dear Ones,

May you inhabit a world that puts people at the center, where everyone feels they belong. Where compassion is universal and kindness exchanged with whole-hearted generosity for all.

The most important thing we wish for you is a life filled with love—love that is given and received with a full heart. Love is at the heart of living a connected life. Choose love, we tell you. Always.

Yet we worry about the world you are inheriting. When you reach out with kindness, will your compassion be reciprocated? When you are in need of support, will others reach out to you?

Right now, the world you are inheriting is locked in a struggle between love and fear. Fear manifests as anger, insecurity, and loneliness. Fear eats away at our society, leaving all of us less whole. So we teach you that every healthy relationship inspires love, not fear. Love shows up as kindness, generosity, and compassion. It is healing. It makes us more whole.

The greatest gifts you'll ever receive will come through these relationships. The most meaningful connections may last for a few moments or for a lifetime. But each will be a reminder that we were meant to be part of one another's lives, to lift one another up, to reach heights together greater than any of us could reach on our own.

Our hope is that you will always have friends in your lives who love and remind you of your innate beauty, strength, and compassion. Equally as important, we hope you will do the same for others.

You are precious precisely because you have the ability to give and receive love. That is your magic. And it is our mission as parents to make sure you know that no one can ever take that away from you.

It pains us that we won't always be there for you when you feel lonely and sad. But we offer this simple prescription to remind you, you are loved:

When those moments of loneliness and suffering arise, take both hands and place them on your heart. And close your eyes. Think about the friends and family who have been there for you throughout your life, in moments of joy and also in the depths of disappointment. The people who have listened to you when you were sad. The people who believed in you even when you lost faith in yourself. The people who have held you, lifted you up, and seen you for who you really are. Feel their warmth and their kindness washing over you, filling you with happiness.

Now. Open your eyes.

Conclusion

In 1978, my parents, Hallegere and Myetraie Murthy, left the United Kingdom for a small town in Newfoundland, the easternmost province of Canada, with my two-year-old sister, Rashmi, and one-year-old me in tow. As the new district medical officer, my father was to be responsible for the health of this community, but he and my mother knew no one in the area—or, for that matter, in the entire country. To make matters worse, they landed in the middle of a winter storm, which greeted them with whiteout conditions and bitter, howling winds.

As I grew up, I often wondered how two people raised in the warmth of South India could have sustained themselves in such harsh circumstances.

"It was the connections we formed with people," my father told me.

In the blistering cold of Newfoundland, my parents found themselves warmed by the kindness and friendship of people who were their patients but also their community. "They made us part of their family when we had no family," my parents responded when I asked if they ever got homesick.

My father made house calls in subzero weather, bundled up in multiple coats. He trudged overland in his snowshoes until every patient was seen. Throughout the year, he would suture wounds in his clinic when fishermen sustained lacerations. He delivered babies in the hospital. He would minister to people at the end of life, too, guiding them and their families during the delicate journey from dying to death.

In return, the people of the community took it on themselves to be responsible for this darker-skinned family with strange accents from half a world away. They babysat my sister and me, brought our family fish and fresh lobsters, baked us pies, and even dug us out of the snow when we were buried by a blizzard.

Later, my parents carried this lesson to Miami, where they set up a medical practice. It was there that I had my early exposure to medicine, watching them build beautiful, mutually therapeutic relationships with patients who once again became part of their community.

I tell this story here and now because I realize, looking back, that it has served all along as my guiding light. My parents and my sister have modeled the healing power of human connection throughout my life. Their example has always given me courage and hope. And yet witnessing connection is no guarantee that we will live a connected life. Even though I was blessed with these amazing role models, that didn't stave off my loneliness.

There was a journey I had to make on my own to learn about myself and the compassion I needed to extend to myself and others. This journey required me to move through the pain of my own disconnection, and it took a long time before I could appreciate the true meaning of my father's simple reply to my question about their migration. I needed to get more perspective on my own life before I could see what a miracle and what a gift it was that the people of Newfoundland "made us part of their family when we had no family." Why don't we all treat one another as family? Why can't we? In fact, we can, and we must.

The people I've met while writing this book have reminded me that even those, like Phillip Lester or Richard Lopez, who grow up in the harshest of circumstances and endure decades in prison can build lives filled with love, service, and connection.

Their examples compel me to believe that we are indeed wired for connection. It is our evolutionary birthright.

Our greatest moments of joy involve other people—the birth of a child, finding love, reunions with dear friends. And our moments of greatest sorrow often involve separation and loss of those connections—the death of a loved one, a romantic breakup, an irreconcilable dispute with a close friend.

The great challenge facing us today is how to build a people-centered life and a people-centered world. So many of the front-page issues we face are made worse by—and in some cases originate from—disconnection. Many of these challenges are the manifestation of a deeper individual and collective loneliness that has brewed for too long in too many. In the face of such pain, few healing forces are as powerful as genuine, loving relationships.

People like Anthony Doran, Serena Bian, and Laura Talmus found themselves pushed by their suffering to face a fundamental question: What really matters in life? Through each of their journeys, the answer became clear. Strong relationships are what matter most. They improve our health, enhance our performance, and enable us to rise above differences of opinion and ideology to come together and take on big challenges as a society. Human connection is the foundation on which we build everything else.

Creating a connected life begins with the decisions we make in our day-to-day lives. Do we choose to make time for people? Do we show up as our true selves? Do we seek out others with kindness, recognizing the power of service to bring us together?

This work isn't always easy. It requires courage. The courage to be vulnerable, to take a chance on others, to believe in ourselves. But as we build connected lives, we make it possible to build a connected world. In such a world, we design our schools, workplaces, and technology to support human connection. We shape our laws to be forces for strengthening community. We treat kindness and compassion as sacred values that are reflected in our culture and our politics.

When I think back on the patients I cared for in their dying days, the size of their bank accounts and their status in the eyes of society were never the yardsticks by which they measured a meaningful life. What they talked about were relationships. The ones that brought them great joy. The relationships they wish they'd been more present for. The ones that broke their hearts. In the final moments, when only the most meaningful strands of life remain, it's the human connections that rise to the top.

It is true that many people are struggling with loneliness. It is true that forces much bigger than us are affecting the fundamental nature of our interactions with one another—and often to our detriment. But I've also seen that the universal drive to connect is still alive and well. It may be buried at times in the throes of everyday life and strife, but it surfaces during times of crisis and in unexpected acts of kindness that remind us who we really are.

I first witnessed such an act in the middle of the night when I was seven years old. I woke up suddenly to find my mother shaking me to get up. "Hurry," she said, "we have to get in the car and leave right now."

Half-asleep, I piled into the back seat with my sister, and my father started to drive the four of us to a trailer park in Miami. On the way, my parents explained to us that one of their patients, Gordon, had just passed away after a long struggle with metastatic cancer. My parents were worried that his widow, Ruth, was grieving alone, so they wanted to go to her home and check on her.

I will never forget the image of my mother in her traditional Indian sari standing on the steps of the trailer and embracing Ruth as she cried and cried. Their life paths were so different, and yet in that moment they were family—not the kind of family that is chosen for you, but the kind that you choose for yourself. Sitting in the car that night, I was given a glimpse of the extraordinary potential of love to heal and to bring us together as one.

Acknowledgments

The process of writing this book was at once an extraordinary gift and one of the greatest challenges of my life. People invited me into their lives. Researchers gave me a window into knowledge acquired over decades. Children I met reminded me often that our true nature is to be kind, compassionate, and connected. I will always be grateful to the hundreds of people who shared their journeys with me in hopes that their stories could be of help to others. While not all of their stories are written in these pages, they have all shaped my thinking and the book in essential ways. Perhaps most of all, they have collectively given me reasons to be optimistic about the future. They remind me that our drive to connect is still alive and well.

The writing process wasn't easy, though. I learned a lot about myself, and not all of it was good. I had to grapple with the reality that I had fallen short in living the kind of connected life I knew was important. One of the great ironies of writing this book on loneliness and social connection is that there were times during the writing when I became quite lonely and disconnected. What helped me in the end more than anything was people. Family and friends who reminded me of who I was in those dark moments when things felt bleak. Their love kept me on the path.

This book wouldn't have made it past its most embryonic phase had it not been for my agent extraordinaire, Richard Pine, who convinced me that writing a book on this topic was the best way to have a conversation with the world about a subject I cared deeply about. He has been a friend, advisor, and compass during this confusing, confounding, and exhilarating journey. My publisher and editor, Karen Rinaldi, helped me shape this book and see more clearly at many points with her thoughtful feedback and tough love. I'm grateful to her for helping me bring this idea to life.

I had a merry band of old souls who helped meticulously assemble and stitch the threads of this book together for more than a year. The research needs for this book were enormous and without the help of Laurie Flynn, I would still be sitting in a pile of scientific papers and newspaper articles. Serena Bian helped me make my way through that pile as well with her extraordinary mix of brilliance, empathy, speed, and judgment (I wish I had a fraction of her talent when I was twenty-three). Stacey Kalish was instrumental in finding many of the stories that brought the ideas in this book to life. I will always remember the empathy and care with which she treated people's precious life experiences. Aimee Liu helped bring all the words on the page to life with her exquisite insight and skill. She was my writing guide in many ways these past few months, and my respect and admiration for her have only grown with time. Connecting all the dots in this process was the one and only Jessica Scruggs, my right hand since my days as surgeon general, and the chief of staff I am so blessed to have now. I will be forever thankful for her loyalty, her dedication, and her great big heart.

Akil Palanisamy, my closest friend since our days as college roommates, and my dear friends Michael Goldberg, Allen Kachalia, and Mark Berman were always there to listen and advise when I was at a difficult point in my writing journey, no matter how incoherent or glum I was. Sunny Kishore and Dave Chokshi were my *moai* brothers during these last couple of years.

The deep bonds we intentionally built with one another are the clearest illustration for me of what it means to cultivate a connected life. I can think of so many mentors and friends whose conversations and life lessons informed my thinking for this book and have shown the indispensable power of connection in my own life—Howie Forman, Ann Kim, Miriam Udel, Davang Shah, Raani Punglia, Shilpa Rao, Meredith Nierman, Nazleen Bharmal, Rab Razzak, Indu Chugani, Sarah Hurwitz, and the Shah and Sheth families to name a few. While I cannot include all of them here, I am indebted to them for their wisdom, patience, and love.

It takes a village to write a book. And my village grew in unexpected ways to include people like the staff at Abe's Café, where I wrote much of this book, who would often give me an extra serving of my favorite tapioca pearls with an encouraging smile when I was on my tenth hour straight of writing. It also included the babysitters, neighbors, and relatives who stepped in to help care for our children before critical deadlines and Uber and Lyft drivers who frequently offered their takes on the book and some of whose stories are included in these pages. In their own beautiful ways, they reminded me often of the healing power of human connection. We really do need one another.

My mother-in-law, Sylvia Chen; father-in-law, Yong-Ming Chen; and sister-in-law, Michelle, put up with many visits that involved me writing endlessly at the dining table or in coffee shops on our visits to see them in California. I'm so appreciative of their patience and support. And for nourishing me with delicious home-cooked Chinese food and pineapple mooncakes.

My mother, father, and sister, Rashmi, have been my inspirations and guides since the very beginning. They were my original teachers when it came to the power of social connection, and in their own humble way, they continue to teach me quietly about how to build a connected life. I am somewhat embarrassed to think back on how many conversations I had with them when I was snappy or grumpy during one of the inevitable lows of writing. They never snapped back. They never ran away. In their gentle way, they reminded me of what love does in good times and bad. It stands firm and remains kind. They have been and always will be my rocks and constant reminders of true connection. My brother-in-law, Amit; grandmother, Sarojini; and uncle Thammiah have been powerful reminders as well, blessing me with their unwavering support and faith throughout this undertaking.

Most of all, I want to thank my best friend, wise advisor, and life partner in all matters big and small: my dearest love and wife, Alice. She shouldered a greater share of so many responsibilities while I was in the throes of writing, handling weekend playdates and toddler tantrums without as much support as she deserved. But even beyond those sacrifices of time and energy, Alice helped me with every step of this book, from conceiving it, to summoning the courage to write it, to formulating questions, puzzling over interviews, analyzing scientific papers, and editing countless drafts. When I read the book now, I see words she added and ideas she sharpened. I see characters we met together and came to admire and love. Her spirit and her handiwork are on every page of this book. From the day I met Alice more than a decade ago, we have been cocreators—of organizations, movements, ideas, and idealistic dreams. This book was no different. It is our joint effort to help shape a more loving, more kind world for our children and future generations.

My dear children, Teyjas and Shanthi, are so small yet the role they played in sustaining my drive to write this book couldn't be bigger. When difficult questions arose about how to handle a topic in the book, Alice and I would often think about them. What would help them if they were to read the book later in life? What would help create the world they deserved? When I began writing, Teyjas could barely speak and Shanthi had just been born. The week I finished, Teyjas had learned enough to ask me one morning, "Papa, are you done with your book yet?" I can't describe how excited I was to tell him, "Yes!" Teyjas and Shanthi, Mama and I wrote this book for you. We love you always.

Vivek H. Murthy
Washington, DC

Notes

Preface

1   Tom Hanks, *Boatlift*, YouTube, Directed by Eddie Resenstein and Rick Velleu (USA: Eyepop Productions, 2011), https://www.youtube.com/watch?v=M-DOrzF7B2Kg.

Chapter 1: Under Our Noses

1   Bruce A. Austin, "Factorial Structure of the UCLA Loneliness Scale," *Psychological Reports* 53, no. 3 (December 1983): 883–89, https://doi.org/10.2466%2Fpr0.1983.53.3.883.

2   Louise C. Hawkley, Michael W. Browne, and John T. Cacioppo, "How Can I Connect With Thee? Let Me Count the Ways," *Psychological Science* 16, no. 10 (October 2005): 798–804, https://doi.org/10.1111%2Fj.1467-9280.2005.01617.x.

3   Stephanie Cacioppo, Angela J. Grippo, Sarah London, and John T. Cacioppo, "Loneliness: Clinical Import and Interventions," *Perspectives on Psychological Science* 10, no. 2 (2015): 238–49, https://doi.org/10.1177/1745691615570616.

4   Bianca DiJulio, Liz Hamel, Cailey Muñana, and Mollyann Brodie, "Loneliness and Social Isolation in the United States, the United Kingdom, and Japan: An International Survey," The Henry J. Kaiser Family Foundation, August 30, 2018, https://www.kff.org/other/report/loneliness-and-social-isolation-in-the-united-states-the-united-kingdom-and-japan-an-international-survey/.

5   G. Oscar Anderson and Colette E. Thayer, "Loneliness and Social Connections: A National Survey of Adults 45 and Older," AARP Foundation, 2018, http://doi.org/10.26419/res.00246.001.

6   "2018 Cigna U.S. Loneliness Index: Survey of 20,000 Americans Examining Behaviors Driving Loneliness in the United States," Cigna, May 2018, https://www.multivu.com/players/English/8294451-cigna-us-loneliness-survey/docs/IndexReport_1524069371598-173525450.pdf.

7   Parminder Raina, Christina Wolfson, Susan Kirkland, and Lauren Griffith, "The Canadian Longitudinal Study on Aging (CLSA) Report on Health and Aging in Canada: Findings from Baseline Data Collection 2010–2015,"

Canadian Longitudinal Study on Aging (CLSA), May 2018, https://www.ifa-fiv
.org/wp-content/uploads/2018/12/clsa_report_en_final_web.pdf.

8   "Australian Loneliness Report: A survey exploring the loneliness levels of
Australians and the impact on their health and wellbeing," Australian Psychological Society and Swinburne University, Psychweek.org.au, November
17, 2018, https://www.psychweek.org.au/wp/wp-content/uploads/2018/11
/Psychology-Week-2018-Australian-Loneliness-Report.pdf.

9   "All the Lonely People: Loneliness in Later Life," Age UK, September 25,
2018, https://www.ageuk.org.uk/latest-press/articles/2018/october/all-
the-lonely-people-report/.

10 "Do Europeans Feel Lonely?," Eurostat, June 28, 2017, https://ec.europa.eu
/eurostat/web/products-eurostat-news/-/DDN-20170628-1.

11 Nicolas Tajan, Hamasaki Yukiko, and Nancy Pionnié-Dax, "Hikikomori:
The Japanese Cabinet Office's 2016 Survey of Acute Social Withdrawal," *The
Asia-Pacific Journal* 15, issue 5, no. 1 (March 1, 2017): Article ID 5017, https://
apjjf.org/2017/05/Tajan.html.

12 "613,000 in Japan aged 40 to 64 are recluses, says first government survey of
hikikomori," *The Japan Times*, March 29, 2019, https://www.japantimes.co.jp
/news/2019/03/29/national/613000-japan-aged-40-64-recluses-says-first-
government-survey-hikikomori/#.XdW3QZNKgWo.

13 Jordan Muto, "'I didn't want to be alive'. . .": Michael Phelps talks about struggle with depression," Today, December 13, 2017, https://www.today.com
/health/michael-phelps-struggle-depression-mental-health-issues-t119969.

14 *Harper's BAZAAR* Staff, "Lady Gaga On Love and Lies," *Harper's BAZAAR*,
February 5, 2017, https://www.harpersbazaar.com/celebrity/latest/news
/a1542/lady-gaga-interview-0314/.

15 Elahe Izadi, "'You are not alone': Dwayne 'The Rock' Johnson opens up about
depression," *Washington Post*, April 2, 2018, https://www.washingtonpost.
com/news/arts-and-entertainment/wp/2018/04/02/you-are-not-alone-
dwayne-the-rock-johnson-opens-up-about-depression/.

16 J. K. Rowling, "Text of J.K. Rowling's Speech," *Harvard Gazette*, June 5, 2018,
https://news.harvard.edu/gazette/story/2008/06/text-of-j-k-rowling-speech/.

17 Julianne Holt-Lunstad, Timothy Smith, and J. Bradley Layton, "Social Relationships and Mortality Risk: A Meta-Analytic Review," *PLOS Medicine* 7, no.
7 (July 2010), https://doi.org/10.1371/journal.pmed.1000316.

18 Julianne Holt-Lunstad, Timothy B. Smith, Mark Baker, Tyler Harris, and
David Stephenson, "Loneliness and Social Isolation as Risk Factors for Mortality," *Perspectives on Psychological Science* 10, no. 2 (2015): 227–37, https://doi
.org/10.1177/1745691614568352.

19 Louise C. Hawkley and John T. Cacioppo, "Loneliness Matters: A Theoret-
ical and Empirical Review of Consequences and Mechanisms," *Annals of Behavioral Medicine* 40, no. 2 (October 2010): 218–27, https://doi.org/10.1007
/s12160-010-9210-8.

20 Campaign to End Loneliness, "Family Doctors Ill-Equipped for Loneliness
Epidemic," *British Journal of Family Medicine*, November 15, 2013, https://
www.bjfm.co.uk/family-doctors-ill-equipped-for-loneliness-epidemic.

Chapter 2: The Evolution of Loneliness

1   Tim Adams, "John Cacioppo: 'Loneliness Is like an Iceberg—It Goes Deeper than We Can See,'" *Guardian*, February 28, 2016, https://www.theguardian .com/science/2016/feb/28/loneliness-is-like-an-iceberg-john-cacioppo-social-neuroscience-interview.

2   Emily Singer, "New Evidence for the Necessity of Loneliness," *Quanta Magazine*, May 10, 2016, accessed September 5, 2019, https://www.quantamagazine.org/new-evidence-for-the-necessity-of-loneliness-20160510/.

3   Susanne Shultz, Christopher Opie, and Quentin D. Atkinson, "Stepwise evolution of stable sociality in primates," *Nature* 479, no. 7372 (2011): 219–22, https://doi.org/10.1038/nature10601.

4   William von Hippel, *The Social Leap: The New Evolutionary Science of Who We Are, Where We Come From, and What Makes Us Happy* (New York: Harper Wave, 2018).

5   Christopher Weber, "Division of the Social Sciences," Psychology's John and Stephanie Cacioppo: Love on the Brain," Division of the Social Sciences, University of Chicago, accessed September 22, 2019, https://socialsciences.uchicago.edu/story/psychologys-john-and-stephanie-cacioppo-love-brain.

6   Tiffany M. Love, "Oxytocin, motivation and the role of dopamine," *Pharmacology Biochemistry and Behavior* 119 (2014): 49–60, https://doi.org/10.1016 /j.pbb.2013.06.011.

7   Oscar Arias-Carrión and Ernst Pöppel, "Dopamine, learning, and reward-seeking behavior," *Acta Neurobiologiae Experimentalis*, US National Library of Medicine, 2007, https://www.ncbi.nlm.nih.gov/pubmed/18320725.

8   Gareth Cook, "Why We Are Wired to Connect," *Scientific American*, October 22, 2013, https://www.scientificamerican.com/article/why-we-are-wired-to-connect/.

9   Ibid.

10 Olga Khazan, "How Loneliness Begets Loneliness," *The Atlantic*, April 6, 2017, https://www.theatlantic.com/health/archive/2017/04/how-loneliness-begets-loneliness/521841/.

11 CC Goren, M. Satry, and PY Wu, "Visual Following and Pattern Discrimination of Face-like Stimuli by Newborn Infants," *Pediatrics* 56, no. 4 (October 1975): 544–49, https://www.ncbi.nlm.nih.gov/pubmed/1165958.

12 Olivier Pascalis, Michelle de Haan, and Charles A. Nelson, "Is Face Processing Species-Specific During the First Year of Life?," *Science* 296 (May 2002): 1321–23, https://doi.org/10.1126/science.1070223.

13 David J. Kelly, Paul C. Quinn, Alan M. Slater, Kang Lee, Alan Gibson, Michael Smith, Liezhong Ge, and Olivier Pascalis, "Three-month-olds, but not newborns, prefer own-race faces," *Developmental Science* 8, no. 6 (2005), https://doi.org/10.1111/j.1467-7687.2005.0434a.x.

14 David J. Kelly, Paul C. Quinn, Alan M. Slater, Kang Lee, Liezhong Ge, and Olivier Pascalis, "The Other-Race Effect Develops During Infancy Evidence of Perceptual Narrowing," *Psychological Science* 18, no. 12 (December 2007): 1084–89, https://dx.doi.org/10.1111%2Fj.1467-9280.2007.02029.x.

15 Liu Shaoying, Naiqi G. Xiao, Paul C. Quinn, Dandan Zhu, Liezhong Ge, Olivier Pascalis, and Kang Lee, "Asian infants show preference for own-race but not other-race female faces: the role of infant caregiving arrangements," *Frontiers in Psychology* 6 (2015): 593, https://dx.doi.org/10.3389%2Ffpsyg.2015.00593.

16 Steven W. Cole, John P. Capitanio, Katie Chun, Jesusa M. G. Arevalo, Jeffrey Ma, and John T. Cacioppo, "Myeloid Differentiation Architecture of Leukocyte Transcriptome Dynamics in Perceived Social Isolation," *Proceedings of the National Academy of Sciences* 112, no. 49 (2015): 15142–47, https://doi.org/10.1073/pnas.1514249112.

17 John T. Cacioppo, Louise C. Hawkley, Gary G. Berntson, John M. Ernst, Amber C. Gibbs, Robert Stickgold, and J. Allan Hobson, "Do Lonely Days Invade the Nights? Potential Social Modulation of Sleep Efficiency," *Psychological Science* 13, no. 4 (2002): 384–87, https://journals.sagepub.com/doi/10.1111/1467-9280.00469.

18 S. Cacioppo, M. Bangee, S. Balogh, C. Cardenas-Iniguez, P. Qualter, J. T. Cacioppo, "Loneliness and implicit attention to social threat: A high-performance electrical neuroimaging study," *Cognitive Neuroscience* 7, no. 1–4 (January–October 2016): 138–59, https://doi.org/10.1080/17588928.2015.1070136.

19 Emily Singer, "New Evidence for the Necessity of Loneliness," *Quanta Magazine*, May 10, 2016, accessed September 5, 2019, https://www.quantamagazine.org/new-evidence-for-the-necessity-of-loneliness-20160510/.

20 Jianjun Gao, Lea K. Davis, Amy B. Hart, Sandra Sanchez-Roige, Lide Han, John T. Cacioppo, and Abraham A. Palmer, "Genome-Wide Association Study of Loneliness Demonstrates a Role for Common Variation," *Neuropsychopharmacology* 42, no. 4 (2016): 811–21, https://doi.org/10.1038/npp.2016.197.

21 Heather Buschman, "Do These Genes Make Me Lonely? Study Finds Loneliness is a Heritable Trait," UC San Diego News Center, September 20, 2016, https://ucsdnews.ucsd.edu/index.php/pressrelease/do_these_genes_make_me_lonely_study_finds_loneliness_is_a_heritable_trait.

22 Emily Singer, "New Evidence for the Necessity of Loneliness," *Quanta Magazine*, May 10, 2016, accessed September 5, 2019, https://www.quantamagazine.org/new-evidence-for-the-necessity-of-loneliness-20160510/.

23 Olga Khazan, "How Loneliness Begets Loneliness," *The Atlantic*, April 7, 2017, https://www.theatlantic.com/health/archive/2017/04/how-loneliness-begets-loneliness/521841/.

24 Naomi I. Eisenberger, "The Neural Bases of Social Pain," *Psychosomatic Medicine* 74, no. 2 (2012): 126–35, https://doi.org/10.1097/psy.0b013e3182464dd1.

25 N. I. Eisenberger and M. D. Lieberman, "Why rejection hurts: The neurocognitive over-lap between physical and social pain," *Trends in Cognitive Sciences* 8 (2004): 294–300, https://doi.org/10.1016/j.tics.2004.05.010.

26 C. Nathan DeWall, Geoff MacDonald, Gregory D. Webster, Carrie L. Masten, Roy F. Baumeister, Caitlin Powell, David Combs, et al., "Acetaminophen Reduces Social Pain," *Psychological Science* 21, no. 7 (2010): 931–37, https://doi.org/10.1177/0956797610374741.

27 Naomi I. Eisenberger, Matthew D. Lieberman, and Kipling D. Williams, "Does Rejection Hurt? An FMRI Study of Social Exclusion," *PsycEXTRA Dataset*, October 10, 2003, 290–92, https://doi.org/10.1126/science.1089134.

Chapter 3: Cultures of Connection

1 Amanda Mabillard, "Words Shakespeare Invented," Shakespeare-online.com, August 20, 2000, accessed September 5, 2019, http://www.shakespeare-online.com/biography/wordsinvented.html.

2 John Donne, *The Best of John Donne*, CreateSpace Independent Publishing Platform, 2012.

3 John Milton, *Paradise Lost*, 1667, reprint Sirius Entertainment, 2017.

4 Fay Bound Alberti, "The history of loneliness," *The Week*, October 13, 2018, https://theweek.com/articles/798959/history-loneliness.

5 Ami Rokach, "The Effect of Gender and Culture on Loneliness: A Mini Review," *Emerging Science Journal* 2, no. 2 (April 2018), https://doi.org/10.28991/esj-2018-01128.

6 Bastian Mönkediek and Hilde Bras, "Strong and weak family ties revisited: reconsidering European family structures from a network perspective," *History of the Family* 19, no. 2 (March 2014): 235–59, https://doi.org/10.1080/1081602x.2014.897246.

7 Ami Rokach, *Loneliness Updated: Recent Research on Loneliness and How It Affects Our Lives* (New York: Routledge, 2015).

8 D. Paul Johnson and Larry C. Mullis, "Growing old and lonely in different societies: Toward a comparative perspective," *Journal of Cross-Cultural Gerontology* 2, no. 3 (1987): 257–75, https://doi.org/10.1007/BF00160684.

9 *Holy Bible: Containing the Old and New Testaments: King James Version* (New York: American Bible Society, 2010).

10 Kevin MacDonald, *A People That Shall Dwell Alone: Judaism as a Group Evolutionary Strategy* (Westport, CT: Praeger, 1994), https://pdfs.semanticscholar.org/0379/ec6cce2c8b6054547e0acf4dc417ce0b950c.pdf.

11 Amanda Duberman, "Here's What One Of America's Most Isolated Communities Can Teach Us About Getting Along," HuffPost, April 13, 2018, https://www.huffpost.com/entry/hutterites-rural-religious-photos_n_5accee42e4b0152082fe4005.

12 Yossi Katz and John Lehr, *Inside the Ark: The Hutterites of Canada and The United States* (Regina: Canadian Plains Researcher Center Press, 2012), https://books.google.com/books?id=-00f6NEsLUQC&pg=PA160&lpg=PA160&dq=sorgalahutterite&source=bl&ots=6_JRNGy-6Wa&sig=ACfU3U2CbJzKyGSB6AtMqN6q204jrwydAQ&hl=en&sa=X-&ved=2ahUKEwjLl7aNwrHkAhVLFjQIHXD2D6IQ6AEwCnoECAIQA-Q#v=onepage&q=sorgalahutterite&f=false.

13 Mary-Ann Kirby, *I Am Hutterite: The Fascinating True Story of a Young Woman's Journey to Reclaim Her Heritage* (Nashville: Thomas Nelson, 2011).

14 John T. Cacioppo, Louise C. Hawkley, Gary Berntson, John M. Ernst, Amber C. Gibbs, Robert Stickgold, and J. Allan Hobson, "Do Lonely Days Invade

the Nights? Potential Social Modulation of Sleep Efficiency," *Psychological Science* 13, no. 4 (July 1, 2002): 384–87.

15 Lianne M. Kurina, Kristen L. Knutson, Louise C. Hawkley, John T. Cacioppo, Diane S. Lauderdale, and Carole Ober, "Loneliness Is Associated with Sleep Fragmentation in a Communal Society," *Sleep* 34, no. 11 (2011): 1519–26, https://doi.org/10.5665/sleep.1390.

16 Hlumelo Siphe Williams, "What Is the Spirit of Ubuntu – and How Can We Have It in Our Lives?," Global Citizen, October 19, 2018, https://www.globalcitizen.org/en/content/ubuntu-south-africa-together-nelson-mandela/.

17 Luzia C. Heu, Martijn Van Zomeren, and Nina Hansen, "Lonely Alone or Lonely Together? A Cultural-Psychological Examination of Individualism–Collectivism and Loneliness in Five European Countries," *Personality and Social Psychology Bulletin* 45, no. 5 (2018): 780–93, https://doi.org/10.1177/0146167218796793.

18 Dan Buettner, *The Blue Zones: Lessons for Living Longer from the People Who've Lived the Longest* (Washington, DC: National Geographic Society, 2010).

19 Ami Rokach, "The Effect of Gender and Culture on Loneliness: A Mini Review," *Emerging Science Journal* 2, no. 2 (April 2018), https://doi.org/10.28991/esj-2018-01128.

20 Barry Golding, *The Men's Shed Movement: The Company of Men* (Champaign, IL: Common Ground Publishing, 2015).

21 Lucia Carragher, "Men's Sheds in Ireland: Learning through community contexts," The Netwell Centre School of Health & Science, Dundalk Institute of Technology, February 2013, http://menssheds.ie/wp-content/uploads/2013/10/Men%E2%80%99s-Sheds-in-Ireland-National-Survey.pdf.

22 Ami Rokach, "The Effect of Gender and Culture on Loneliness: A Mini Review," *Emerging Science Journal* 2, no. 2 (April 2018), https://doi.org/10.28991/esj-2018-01128.

23 M. Katherine Weinberg, Edward Z. Tronick, Jeffrey F. Cohn, and Karen L. Olson, "Gender differences in emotional expressivity and self-regulation during early infancy," *Developmental Psychology* 35, no. 1 (1999): 175–88, https://doi.org/10.1037//0012-1649.35.1.175.

24 Helene Schumacher, "Why more men than women die by suicide," BBC, March 18, 2019, http://www.bbc.com/future/story/20190313-why-more-men-kill-themselves-than-women.

25 "Statistics on Suicide in Australia," Lifeline, accessed September 14, 2019, https://www.lifeline.org.au/about-lifeline/media-centre/lifeline-fast-facts.

26 "Suicide Statistics," American Foundation for Suicide Prevention, accessed September 14, 2019, https://afsp.org/about-suicide/suicide-statistics/.

27 "Male:Female Ratio of Age-Standardized Suicide Rates, 2016," World Health Organization, accessed September 14, 2019, http://gamapserver.who.int/mapLibrary/Files/Maps/Global_AS_suicide_rates_male_female_ratio_2016.png.

28 Paul R. Albert, "Why Is Depression More Prevalent in Women?," *Journal of Psychiatry and Neuroscience*, July 2015, https://dx.doiorg/10.1503%2Fjpn.150205.

29 Centre for Suicide Prevention, accessed September 6, 2019, https://www.suicideinfo.ca/.

30 Helene Schumacher, "Why more men than women die by suicide," BBC, March 18, 2019, http://www.bbc.com/future/story/20190313-why-more-men-kill-themselves-than-women.

31 Carol Gillian, Annie G. Rogers, and Normi Noel, "Cartography of a Lost Time: Mapping the Crisis of Connection," in *The Crisis of Connection: Roots, Consequences, and Solutions*, ed. Niobe Way, Alisha Ali, Carol Gilligan, and Pedro A. Noguera (New York: New York University Press, 2018).

32 Brené Brown, PhD, *I Thought It Was Just Me (but It Isnt): Telling the Truth about Perfectionism, Inadequacy, and Power* (New York: Gotham Books, 2008).

33 Brené Brown, PhD, *Women & Shame: Reaching Out, Speaking Truths & Building Connection* (Austin, TX: 3C Press, 2004).

34 Rosalind Wiseman, *Queen Bees and Wannabes: Helping Your Daughter Survive Cliques, Gossip, Boyfriends, and the New Realities of Girl World*, 3rd ed. (New York: Harmony Books, 2016).

Chapter 4: Why Now?

1 Robert Putnam, *Bowling Alone: The Collapse and Revival of American Community* (New York: Simon & Schuster, 2000).

2 Robert Putnam. Interview by author, October 22, 2019.

3 Rita Gunther McGrath, "The Pace of Technology Adoption Is Speeding Up," *Harvard Business Review*, August 7, 2014, https://hbr.org/2013/11/the-pace-of-technology-adoption-is-speeding-up.

4 Amy Orben and Andrew K. Przybylski, "The association between adolescent well-being and digital technology use," *Nature Human Behaviour* 3, no. 2 (2019): 173–82, https://doi.org/10.1038/s41562-018-0506-1.

5 Andrew K. Przybylski and Netta Weinstein, "A Large-Scale Test of the Goldilocks Hypothesis: Quantifying the Relations Between Digital-Screen Use and the Mental Well-Being of Adolescents," *Psychological Science* 28, no. 2 (2017): 204–15, https://doi.org/10.1177%2F0956797616678438.

6 Brian A. Primack, Ariel Shensa, Jaime E. Sidani, Erin O. Whaite, Liu Yi Lin, Daniel Rosen, Jason B. Colditz, Ana Radovic, and Elizabeth Miller, "Social Media Use and Perceived Social Isolation Among Young Adults in the U.S.," *American Journal of Preventive Medicine* 53, no. 1 (2017): 1–8, https://doi.org/10.1016/j.amepre.2017.01.010.

7 Ibid.

8 Liu Yi Lin, Jaime E. Sidani, Ariel Shensa, Ana Radovic, Elizabeth Miller, Jason B. Colditz, Beth L. Hoffman, Leila M. Giles, and Brian A. Primack, "Association Between Social Media Use and Depression Among U.S. Young Adults," *Depression and Anxiety* 33, no. 4 (April 1, 2017): 323–31, https://www.ncbi.nlm.nih.gov/pmc/articles/PMC4853817/.

9 Jon Hamilton, "Think You're Multitasking? Think Again," NPR, October 2, 2008, https://www.npr.org/templates/story/story.php?storyId=95256794.

10 Gloria Mark, Daniela Gudith, and Ulrich Klocke, "The Cost of Interrupted

Work," *Proceeding of the Twenty-Sixth Annual CHI Conference on Human Factors in Computing Systems - CHI 08*, 2008, https://doi.org/10.1145/1357054.1357072.

11 Clay Skipper, "Why the Sharing Economy Is Making All of Us More Lonely," GQ.com, August 10, 2018, https://www.gq.com/story/sharing-is-not-caring.

12 Ibid.

13 Ibid.

14 Catherine de Lange, "Sherry Turkle: 'We're losing the raw, human part of being with each other,'" *Guardian*, May 4, 2013, https://www.theguardian.com/science/2013/may/05/rational-heroes-sherry-turkle-mit.

15 Andrew K. Przybylski and Netta Weinstein, "Can you connect with me now? How the presence of mobile communication technology influences face-to-face conversation quality," *Journal of Social and Personal Relationships* 30, no. 3 (2012): 237–46, https://doi.org/10.1177/0265407512453827.

16 James A. Roberts and Meredith E. David, "My life has become a major distraction from my cell phone: Partner phubbing and relationship satisfaction among romantic partners," *Computers in Human Behavior* 54 (2016): 134–41, https://doi.org/10.1016/j.chb.2015.07.058.

17 Sara H. Konrath, Edward H. Obrien, and Courtney Hsing, "Changes in Dispositional Empathy in American College Students Over Time: A Meta-Analysis," *Personality and Social Psychology Review* 15, no. 2 (August 2010): 180–98, https://doi.org/10.1177/1088868310377395.

18 Victoria J. Rideout, Ulla G. Foehr, and Donald F. Roberts, "Generation M²: Media in the Lives of 8- to 18-Year-Olds," The Henry J. Kaiser Family Foundation, January 2010, https://www.kff.org/wp-content/uploads/2013/01/8010.pdf.

19 Yalda T. Uhls, Minas Michikyan, Jordan Morris, Debra Garcia, Gary W. Small, Eleni Zgourou, and Patricia M. Greenfield, "Five Days at Outdoor Education Camp without Screens Improves Preteen Skills with Nonverbal Emotion Cues," *Computers in Human Behavior* 39 (2014): 387–92, https://doi.org/10.1016/j.chb.2014.05.036.

20 Peter Dizikes, "3 Questions: Sherry Turkle on 'Reclaiming Conversation,'" MIT News, November 17, 2015, http://news.mit.edu/2015/3-questions-sherry-turkle-reclaiming-conversation-1117.

21 Jamie Ducharme, "Most Young Americans Are Lonely, Cigna Study Says," *TIME*, May 1, 2018, https://time.com/5261181/young-americans-are-lonely/.

22 "Are You Feeling Lonely?" Cigna, May 1, 2018, https://www.cigna.com/about-us/newsroom/studies-and-reports/loneliness-questionnaire.

23 Ellen E. Lee, Colin Depp, Barton W. Palmer, Danielle Glorioso, Rebecca Daly, Jinyuan Liu, Xin M. Tu, Ho-Cheoi Kim, Peri Tarr, Yasunori Yamada, and Dilip V. Jeste, "High prevalence and adverse health effects of loneliness in community-dwelling adults across the life span: role of wisdom as a protective factor," *International Psychogeriatrics* (December 2018): 1–16, https://doi.org/10.1017/S1041610218002120.

24 Catherine Steiner-Adair and Teresa Barker, *The Big Disconnect: Protecting Childhood and Family Relationships in the Digital Age* (New York: Harper, 2014).

25 "Suicide Rates (per 100,000 Population)," World Health Organization, December 27, 2018, https://www.who.int/gho/mental_health/suicide_rates /en/.

26 Holly Hedegaard, Sally C. Curtin, and Margaret Warner, Suicide Mortality in the United States, 1999–2017, National Center for Health Statistics, https://www .cdc.gov/nchs/products/databriefs/db330.htm.

27 Erika Beras, "Bhutanese Refugees Face a High Suicide Rate," Center for Health Journalism, January 29, 2014, accessed September 6, 2019, https://www .centerforhealthjournalism.org/bhutanese-refugees-face-high-suicide-rate.

28 Panos Christodoulou, "This is how it feels to be lonely," The Forum, March 11, 2015, http://migrantsorganise.org/wp-content/uploads/2014/09/Lone-liness-report_The-Forum_UPDATED.pdf.

29 Ibid.

30 Population Division of the UN Department of Economic and Social Affairs (DESA), "International Migrant Stock 2019," UN, accessed September 25, 2019, https://www.un.org/development/desa/en/news/population/inter-national-migrant-stock-2019.html.

31 "Global Migration Indicators 2018," Global Migration Data Analysis Centre (GMDAC) International Organization for Migration, accessed September 25, 2019, https://publications.iom.int/system/files/pdf/global_migration_ indicators_2018.pdf.

32 "Statistical Communiqué of the People's Republic of China on the 2018 National Economic and Social Development," National Bureau of Sta-tistics of China, February 28, 2019, http://www.stats.gov.cn/english/ PressRelease/201902/t20190228_1651335.html.

33 Haining Wang, Fei Guo, and Zhiming Cheng, "A distributional analysis of wage discrimination against migrant workers in China's urban labour market," *Urban Studies* 52, no. 13 (October 2015): 2383–2403, https://www.jstor.org /stable/26146146.

34 "Brakes on China's floating population," *South China Morning Post*, Septem-ber 19, 2019, https://www.scmp.com/article/980385/brakes-chinas-floating -population.

35 Hisao Endo, "National Institute of Population and Social Security Research," National Institute of Population and Social Security Research, 2017, http:// www.ipss.go.jp/pr-ad/e/ipss_english2017.pdf.

36 Yahoo! Travel, "From Rent-a-Friends to Chairs that Give Hugs: Japan's Wacky Anti-Loneliness Attractions," Yahoo! Lifestyle, November 7, 2014, accessed September 6, 2019, https://www.yahoo.com/lifestyle/attractions-to-beat -loneliness-in-japan-101965056519.html.

37 Elizabeth Shim, "South Korea's suicide rate declines, but not among elderly," UPI, June 11, 2019, https://www.upi.com/Top_News /World-News/2019/06/11/South-Koreas-suicide-rate-declines-but-not-among-elderly/8341560265246/.

38 "Why Are So Many Elderly Asians Killing Themselves?" NBC News, Feb-ruary 18, 2014, https://www.nbcnews.com/news/world/why-are-so-many-elderly-asians-killing-themselves-n32591.

39 "2017 National Population Projections Tables," United States Census Bureau, accessed September 25, 2019, https://www.census.gov/data/tables/2017/demo/popproj/2017-summary-tables.html.

40 D'Vera Cohn and Paul Taylor, "Baby Boomers Approach 65 – Glumly," Pew Research Center Social & Demographic Trends, December 20, 2010, https://www.pewsocialtrends.org/2010/12/20/baby-boomers-approach-65-glumly/.

41 Kim Parker, Juliana Menasce Horowitz, Anna Brown, Richard Fry, D'Vera Cohn, and Ruth Igielnik, "Demographic and economic trends in urban, suburban and rural communities," Pew Research Center Social & Demographic Trends, May 22, 2018, https://www.pewsocialtrends.org/2018/05/22/demographic-and-economic-trends-in-urban-suburban-and-rural-communities/.

42 Ruth Igielnik and Anna Brown, "5 Facts about U.S. suburbs," Pew Research Center, October 2, 2018, accessed August 29, 2019, https://www.pewresearch.org/fact-tank/2018/10/02/5-facts-about-u-s-suburbs.

43 Laura Santhanam, "Nearly 80 percent of Americans concerned lack of civility in politics will lead to violence, poll says," Public Broadcasting Service, November 1, 2018, https://www.pbs.org/newshour/politics/nearly-80-percent-of-americans-concerned-negative-tone-lack-of-civility-will-lead-to-violence-poll-says.

44 Adam Waytz, Liane L. Young, and Jeremy Ginges, "Motive attribution asymmetry for love vs. hate drives intractable conflict," *Proceedings of the National Academy of Sciences* 111, no. 44 (2014): 15687–92, https://doi.org/10.1073/pnas.1414146111.

45 "Welcome to the Center for Courage & Renewal," Center for Courage & Renewal, accessed September 6, 2019, http://couragerenewal.org.

Chapter 5: Unmasking Loneliness

1 Frieda Fromm Reichmann, "Loneliness," *Psychiatry* 22, no. 1 (1959): 1–15, https://doi.org/10.1080/00332747.1959.11023153.

2 Jean M. Twenge, Roy F. Baumeister, Dianne M. Tice, and Tanja S. Stucke, "If you can't join them, beat them: Effects of social exclusion on aggressive behavior," *Journal of Personality and Social Psychology* 81, no. 6 (2001): 1058–69, https://doi.org/10.1037/0022-3514.81.6.1058.

3 "California Criminal Justice Reform: Potential Lessons for the Nation," US House Committee on the Judiciary - Democrats, July 13, 2019, https://judiciary.house.gov/legislation/hearings/california-criminal-justice-reform-potential-lessons-nation.

4 John Cacioppo and Stephanie Cacioppo, "The Social Muscle," *Harvard Business Review*, October 2, 2017, https://hbr.org/2017/10/the-social-muscle.

5 A Vedanta Kesari Presentation, *Service: Ideal and Aspects* (Chennai, India: Lulu Press, Inc., May 2, 2014).

6 "Hinduism & Service," American World Hindu Service, accessed September 6, 2019, https://www.ahwsngo.org/hinduism-and-service.

7 Christian Smith and Hilary Davidson, *The Paradox of Generosity: Giving We Receive, Grasping We Lose* (New York: Oxford University Press, 2014).

8 Ashoka, "12 Great Quotes From Gandhi On His Birthday," *Forbes*, October 2, 2012, https://www.forbes.com/sites/ashoka/2012/10/02/12-great-quotes-from-gandhi-on-his-birthday/.

9 Valeria Motta, "Interview with Steve Cole on Loneliness," *Imperfect Cognitions* (blog), November 10, 2016, https://imperfectcognitions.blogspot.com/2016/11/interview-with-steve-cole-on-loneliness.html.

10 Tristen K. Inagaki, Kate E. Bryne Haltom, Shosuke Suzuki, Ivana Jevtic, Erica Hornstein, Julienne E. Bower, and Naomi I. Eisenberger, "The Neurobiology of Giving Versus Receiving Support," *Psychosomatic Medicine* 78, no. 4 (May 2016): 443–53, https://doi.org/10.1097/psy.0000000000000302.

11 Dawn C. Carr, Ben Lennox Kail, Christina Matz-Costa, and Yochai Z. Shavit, "Does Becoming A Volunteer Attenuate Loneliness Among Recently Widowed Older Adults?" *The Journals of Gerontology: Series B* 73, no. 3 (July 2017): 501–10, https://doi.org/10.1093/geronb/gbx092.

12 Bill Wilson, *Alcoholics Anonymous: The Story of How Many Thousands of Men and Women Have Recovered from Alcoholism* (New York: Alcoholics Anonymous World Services, [1939] 2001).

13 "Questions & Answers on Sponsorship," *Questions & Answers on Sponsorship* (New York: Alcoholics Anonymous World Services, Inc., 1976), https://www.aa.org/assets/en_US/p-15_Q&AonSpon.pdf.

14 Bryan E. Robinson, *#Chill: Turn off Your Job and Turn on Your Life* (New York: William Morrow, 2018).

15 "Trauma," SAMHSA-HRSA Center for Integrated Health Solutions, accessed September 30, 2019, https://www.integration.samhsa.gov/clinical-practice/trauma.

16 Melissa T. Merrick, Derek C. Ford, Katie A. Ports, and Angie S. Guinn, "Prevalence of Adverse Childhood Experiences From the 2011–2014 Behavioral Risk Factor Surveillance System in 23 States," *JAMA Pediatrics* 172, no. 11 (September 1, 2018): 1038–44, https://doi.org/10.1001/jamapediatrics.2018.2537.

17 Emmy E. Werner, "Risk, resilience, and recovery: Perspectives from the Kauai Longitudinal Study," *Development and Psychopathology* 5, no. 4 (1993): 503–15, https://doi.org/10.1017/s095457940000612x.

18 Emmy Werner, "Resilience and Recovery: Findings from the Kauai Longitudinal Study," FOCAL POiNT *Research, Policy, and Practice in Children's Mental Health* 19, no. 1 (Summer 2005): 11–14, https://www.pathwaysrtc.pdx.edu/pdf/fpS0504.pdf.

19 Emmy Werner and Ruth Smith, *Overcoming the Odds: High Risk Children from Birth to Adulthood* (Ithaca and London: Cornell University Press, 1992).

20 Emmy Werner, "Risk, Resilience, and Recovery," *Reclaiming Children and Youth* 21, no. 1 (2012): 18–23.

21 Mary Karapetian Alvord and Judy Johnson Grados, "Enhancing Resilience in Children: A Proactive Approach," *Professional Psychology: Research and Prac-*

tice 36, no. 3 (2005): 238–45, https://psycnet.apa.org/doi/10.1037/0735-7028.36.3.238.

22 Camelia E, Hostinar and Megan R. Gunnar, "Social Support Can Buffer against Stress and Shape Brain Activity," *AJOB Neuroscience*, US National Library of Medicine, July 1, 2015, https://www.ncbi.nlm.nih.gov/pmc/articles/PMC4607089/.

23 "Toxic Stress," Center on the Developing Child, Harvard University, accessed October 1, 2019, https://developingchild.harvard.edu/science/key-concepts/toxic-stress.

24 Jessica Mitchell, PhD, "2018 Big Brothers Big Sisters of America Annual Impact Report," Big Brothers Big Sisters of America, April 2019, accessed August 30, 2019, https://www.bbbs.org/wp-content/uploads/2018-BBBSA-Annual-Impact-Report.pdf.

25 "Research on Big Brothers Big Sisters," Big Brothers Big Sisters of America, accessed October 2, 2019, https://www.bbbs.org/research/.

26 René Veenstra, Siegwart Lindenberg, Anke Munniksma, and Jan Kornelis Dijkstra, "The Complex Relation Between Bullying, Victimization, Acceptance, and Rejection: Giving Special Attention to Status, Affection, and Sex Differences," *Child Development* 81, no. 2 (March 24, 2010): 480–86, https://doi.org/10.1111/j.1467-8624.2009.01411.x.

27 Shireen Pavri, "Loneliness: The Cause or Consequence of Peer Victimization in Children and Youth," *The Open Psychology Journal* 8, no. 1 (2015): 78–84, https://doi.org/10.2174/1874350101508010078.

28 Mechthild Schäfer, Stefan Korn, Peter K. Smith, Simon C. Hunter, Joaqún A. Mora-Merchán, Monika M. Singer, Kevin Van der Meulen, "Lonely in the crowd: Recollections of bullying," *British Journal of Developmental Psychology* 22, no. 3 (September 2004): 379–94, https://doi.org/10.1348/0261510041552756.

29 Deborah Lessne and Christina Yanez, "Student Reports of Bullying: Results From the 2015 School Crime Supplement to the National Crime Victimization Survey," National Center for Education Statistics (NCES) Home Page, a part of the US Department of Education, December 20, 2016. https://nces.ed.gov/pubsearch/pubsinfo.asp?pubid=2017015.

30 Pernille Due, Bjørn E. Holstein, John Lynch, Finn Diderichsen, Saoirse Nic Gabhain, Peter Scheidt, Candace Currie, and The Health Behaviour in School-Aged Children Bullying Working Group, "Bullying and Symptoms among School-Aged Children: International Comparative Cross Sectional Study in 28 Countries," *European Journal of Public Health* 15, no. 2 (April 2005): 128–32, https://doi.org/10.1093/eurpub/cki105.

Chapter 6: Relating Inside Out

1 "American College Health Association National Assessment, Fall 2018," American College Health Association (ACHA), October 2018, https://www.acha.org/documents/ncha/NCHA-II_Fall_2018_Reference_Group_Executive_Summary.pdf.

2 Kali H. Trzesniewski and Susan Ebeler, "First year college students' sense of belonging," Unpublished data, University of California, Davis, 2019.

3 Ibid.

4 Daniel Eisenberg, Ezra Golberstein, and Justin B. Hunt, "Mental Health and Academic Success in College," *The B.E. Journal of Economic Analysis & Policy* 9, no. 1 (September 14, 2009), https://doi.org/10.2202/1935-1682.2191.

5 Megan Foley Nicpon, Laura Huser, Elva Hull Blanks, Sonja Sollenberger, Christie Befort, and Sharon E. Robinson Kurpius, "The Relationship of Loneliness and Social Support with College Freshmen's Academic Performance and Persistence," *Journal of College Student Retention: Research, Theory & Practice* 8, no. 3 (2006): 345–58, https://doi.org/10.2190/a465-356m-7652-783r.

6 Catharine Beyes, Angela Davis-Unger, Nana Lowell, Debbie McGhee, and Jon Peterson, "UW Undergraduate Retention and Graduation Study," University of Washington Office of Educational Assessment, June 2014, accessed August 31, 2019, http://depts.washington.edu/assessmt/pdfs/reports/OEAReport1401.pdf.

7 Genevieve Glatsky, "A college junior wants you to have a deep conversation with 20 strangers in Center City," *Daily Pennsylvanian*, October 26, 2016, https://www.thedp.com/article/2016/10/space-conversation-with-strangers-serena-bian.

8 Thomas Merton, *The Wisdom of the Desert: Sayings from the Desert Fathers of the Fourth Century* (New York: New Directions Publishing Corp, 1970).

9 Susan Cain, *Quiet: The Power of Introverts in a World That Can't Stop Talking* (New York: Broadway Books, 2012).

10 Julieta Galante, Ignacio Galante, Marie-Jet Bekkers, and John Gallacher, "Effect of kindness-based meditation on health and well-being: A systematic review and meta-analysis," *Journal of Consulting and Clinical Psychology* 82, no. 6 (December 2014): 1101–1114, http://dx.doi.org/10.1037/a0037249.

11 Xianglong Zeng, Cleo P. K. Chiu, Rong Wang, Tian P. S. Oei, and Freedom Y. K. Leung, "The effect of loving-kindness meditation on positive emotions: a meta-analytic review," *Frontiers in Psychology* 6 (November 3, 2015): 1693, https://doi.org/10.3389/fpsyg.2015.01693.

12 Christopher R. Long and James R. Averill, "Solitude: An Exploration of Benefits of Being Alone," *Journal for the Theory of Social Behaviour* 33, no. 1 (2003): 21–44, https://doi.org/10.1111/1468-5914.00204.

13 Paul Piff and Dacher Keltner, "Why Do We Experience Awe?" *New York Times*, May 22, 2015, https://www.nytimes.com/2015/05/24/opinion/sunday/why-do-we-experience-awe.html.

14 Paul K. Piff, Pia Dietze, Matthew Feinberg, Daniel M. Stancato, and Dacher Keltner, "Awe, the Small Self, and Prosocial Behavior," *Journal of Personality and Social Psychology* 108, no. 6 (2015): 883–99, http://dx.doi.org/10.1037/pspi0000018.

Chapter 7: Circles of Connection

1 Kate Murphy, "Do Your Friends Actually Like You?," *New York Times*, August 6, 2016, https://www.nytimes.com/2016/08/07/opinion/sunday/do-your-friends-actually-like-you.html.

2 Olga Khazan, "How Loneliness Begets Loneliness," Atlantic Media Company, April 6, 2017, https://www.theatlantic.com/health/archive/2017/04/how-loneliness-begets-loneliness/521841/.

3 John T. Cacioppo, "John Cacioppo on How to Cope with Loneliness," Big Think, November 3, 2008, https://bigthink.com/videos/john-cacioppo-on-how-to-cope-with-loneliness.

4 Liz Mineo, "Good genes are nice, but joy is better," *Harvard Gazette*, April 11, 2017, https://news.harvard.edu/gazette/story/2017/04/over-nearly-80-years-harvard-study-has-been-showing-how-to-live-a-healthy-and-happy-life/.

5 Robert Waldinger, *What makes a good life? Lessons from the longest study on happiness*, November 2015, TED, 12:36, https://www.ted.com/talks/robert_waldinger_what_makes_a_good_life_lessons_from_the_longest_study_on_happiness..

6 Stephanie Coontz, "Too Close for Comfort," *New York Times*, November 6, 2006, https://www.nytimes.com/2006/11/07/opinion/07coontz.html.

7 Kim Parker and Renee Stepler, "As U.S. marriage rate hovers at 50%, educational gap in marital status widens," Pew Research Center, September 14, 2017, https://www.city-journal.org/decline-of-family-loneliness-epidemic.

8 Wendy Wang and Kim Parker, "Record Share of Americans Have Never Married," Pew Research Center Social & Demographic Trends, January 14, 2015, https://www.pewsocialtrends.org/2014/09/24/record-share-of-americans-have-never-married/.

9 Gallup, Inc. "State of the American Workplace," Gallup.com, 2017, accessed August 8, 2019, https://www.gallup.com/workplace/238085/state-american-workplace-report-2017.aspx.

10 Shawn Achor, Gabriella Rosen Kellerman, Andrew Reece, and Alexi Robichaux, "America's Loneliest Workers, According to Research," *Harvard Business Review*, April 11, 2018, https://hbr.org/2018/03/americas-loneliest-workers-according-to-research.

11 Hakan Ozcelik and Sigal G. Barsade, "No Employee an Island: Workplace Loneliness and Job Performance," *Academy of Management Journal* 61, no. 6 (2018): 2343–66, https://doi.org/10.5465/amj.2015.1066.

12 Annamarie Mann, "Why We Need Best Friends at Work," Gallup.com, January 15, 2018, https://www.gallup.com/workplace/236213/why-need-best-friends-work.aspx.

13 Rodd Wagner and Jim Harter, "The Tenth Element of Great Managing," *Gallup Business Journal*, February 14, 2008, https://news.gallup.com/businessjournal/104197/tenth-element-great-managing.aspx.

14 Annamarie Mann, "Why We Need Best Friends at Work," Gallup.com, August 7, 2019, https://www.gallup.com/workplace/236213/why-need-best-friends-work.aspx.

15 Wayne Baker, Rob Cross, and Melissa Wooten, "Positive Organizational Network Analysis and Energizing Relationships," in *Positive Organizational Scholarship Foundations of a New Discipline*, ed. Kim S. Cameron, Jane E. Dutton, and Robert E. Quinn (San Francisco, CA: Berrett-Koehler, 2003), http://webuser.bus.umich.edu/wayneb/pdfs/energy_networks/pona.pdf.

16 Ibid.

17 Jane E. Dutton and Emily D. Heaphy, "The Power of High-Quality Connections," in *Positive organizational scholarship: Foundations of a New Discipline*, ed. Kim S. Cameron, Jane E. Dutton, and Robert E. Quinn (San Francisco: Berrett-Koehler, 2003), http://webuser.bus.umich.edu/janedut/high%20quality%20connections/power%20high%20quality.pdf.

18 Wayne Baker, "The More You Energize Your Coworkers, the Better Everyone Performs," *Harvard Business Review*, September 15, 2016, https://hbr.org/2016/09/the-energy-you-give-off-at-work-matters.

19 Bradley P. Owens, Wayne E. Baker, Dana McDaniel Sumpter, and Kim S. Cameron, "Relational energy at work: Implications for job engagement and job performance," *Journal of Applied Psychology* 101, no. 1 (January 2016): 35–49, http://dx.doi.org/10.1037/apl0000032.

20 J. E. Dutton, *Energize Your Workplace: How to Create and Sustain High-Quality Connections at Work* (San Francisco: Jossey-Bass Publishers, 2003).

21 Wayne Baker, "The More You Energize Your Coworkers, the Better Everyone Performs," *Harvard Business Review*, September 15, 2016, https://hbr.org/2016/09/the-energy-you-give-off-at-work-matters.

22 Nicholas Epley, "Let's make some Metra noise," *Chicago Tribune*, June 3, 2011, https://www.chicagotribune.com/opinion/ct-xpm-2011-06-03-ct-perspec-0605-metra-20110603-story.html.

23 Eric Klinenberg, *Heat Wave: A Social Autopsy of Disaster in Chicago* (Chicago: University of Chicago Press, 2015).

24 Tim Adams, "John Cacioppo: 'Loneliness is like an iceberg – it goes deeper than we can see,'" *The Guardian*, February 28, 2016, https://www.theguardian.com/science/2016/feb/28/loneliness-is-like-an-iceberg-john-cacioppo-social-neuroscience-interview.

25 Michele Debczark, "English Towns Are Installing 'Chat Benches' to Combat Loneliness," Mental Floss, June 26, 2019, https://mentalfloss.com/article/586572/chat-benches-combat-loneliness-in-uk.

Chapter 8: A Family of Families

1 Carl Desportes Bowman, James Davidson Hunter, Jeffrey S. Dill, and Megan Juelfs-Swanson, "Culture of American Families: Executive Report," Institute for Advanced Studies in Culture, 2012, http://sociology.as.dev.artsci.virginia.edu/sites/sociology.as.virginia.edu/files/IASC_CAF_ExecReport.pdf.

2 "The Children We Mean to Raise: The Real Messages Adults Are Sending About Values," Making Caring Common, July 7, 2014, https://mcc.gse.harvard.edu/reports/children-mean-raise.

3 Roy F. Baumeister, Jean M. Twenge, and Christopher K. Nuss, "Effects of social exclusion on cognitive processes: Anticipated aloneness reduces intelligent thought," *Journal of Personality and Social Psychology* 83, no. 4 (November 2002): 817–27, https://doi.org/10.1037/0022-3514.83.4.817.

4 Helen Y. Weng, Andrew S. Fox, Alexander J. Shackman, Diane E. Stodola, Jessica Z. K. Caldwell, Matthew C. Olson, Gregory M. Rogers, and Richard

J. Davison, "Compassion Training Alters Altruism and Neural Responses to Suffering," *Psychological Science* 24, no. 7 (July 2013): 1171-1180, https://doi.org/10.1177/0956797612469537.

5 Patricia A. Adler and Peter Adler, *Peer Power: Preadolescent Culture and Identity* (New Brunswick, NJ: Rutgers University Press, 2003).

6 Kathryn M. LaFontana and Antonius H. N. Cillessen, "Developmental Changes in the Priority of Perceived Status in Childhood and Adolescence," *Social Development* 19, no. 1 (January 6, 2010): 130–47, https://doi.org/10.1111/j.1467-9507.2008.00522.x.

7 Nancy G. Guerra and Catherine P. Bradshaw, "Linking the prevention of problem behaviors and positive youth development: Core competencies for positive youth development and risk prevention," *New Directions for Child and Adolescent Development* 2008, no. 122 (2008): 1–17, https://doi.org/10.1002/cd.225.

8 Lise M. Youngblade, Christina Theokas, John Schulenberg, Laura Curry, I-Chan Huang, and Maureen Novak, "Risk and Promotive Factors in Families, Schools, and Communities: A Contextual Model of Positive Youth Development in Adolescence," *Pediatrics* 119, Supplement 1 (March 2007): S47–S53, https://doi.org/10.1542/peds.2006-2089h.

9 "The Common Sense Census: Media Use by Tweens and Teens," Common Sense, 2015, https://www.commonsensemedia.org/sites/default/files/uploads/research/census_researchreport.pdf.

10 Catherine Steiner-Adair and Teresa Barker, *The Big Disconnect: Protecting Childhood and Family Relationships in the Digital Age* (New York: Harper, 2014).

11 Lori Nathanson, Susan E. Rivers, Lisa M. Flynn, and Marc A. Brackett, "Creating Emotionally Intelligent Schools With RULER," *Emotion Review* 8, no. 4 (2016): 305–10, https://doi.org/10.1177/1754073916650495.

12 Marc A. Brackett and Susan E. Rivers, "Transforming Students' Lives with Social and Emotional Learning," in *International Handbook of Emotions in Education*, ed. Reinhard Pekrun and Lisa Linnenbrink-Garcia (New York: Routledge, 2014): 368, https://doi.org/10.4324/9780203148211.ch19.

13 Carolin Hagelskamp, Marc A. Brackett, Susan E. Rivers, and Peter Salovey, "Improving Classroom Quality with The RULER Approach to Social and Emotional Learning: Proximal and Distal Outcomes," *American Journal of Community Psychology* 51, no. 3–4 (2013): 530–43, https://doi.org/10.1007/s10464-013-9570-x.

14 Ruth Castillo, Pablo Fernández-Berrocal, and Marc A. Brackett, "Enhancing Teacher Effectiveness in Spain: A Pilot Study of The RULER Approach to Social and Emotional Learning," *Journal of Education and Training Studies* 1, no. 2 (2013), https://doi.org/10.11114/jets.v1i2.203.

15 Susan E. Rivers, Marc A. Brackett, Maria R. Reyes, Nicole A. Elbertson, and Peter Salovey, "Improving the Social and Emotional Climate of Classrooms: A Clustered Randomized Controlled Trial Testing the RULER Approach," *Prevention Science* 14, no. 1 (November 28, 2012): 77–87, https://doi.org/10.1007/s11121-012-0305-2.

16 Maria Regina Reyes, Marc A. Brackett, Susan E. Rivers, Nicole A. Elbertson, and Peter Salovey, "The Interaction Effects of Program Training, Dosage, and Implementation Quality on Targeted Student Outcomes for The RULER Approach to Social and Emotional Learning," *School Psychology Review* 41, no. 1 (2012): 82–99, http://ei.yale.edu/wp-content/uploads/2013/08/pub318_Reyesetal2012_SPR.pdf.

17 Marc A. Brackett, Susan E. Rivers, Maria R. Reyes, and Peter Salovey, "Enhancing academic performance and social and emotional competence with the RULER feeling words curriculum," *Learning and Individual Differences* 22, no. 2 (2012): 218–24, https://doi.org/10.1016/j.lindif.2010.10.002.

Index